John of Paris
On
Royal and Papal Power

Number XC of The
Records of Civilization
Sources and Studies

John of Paris
On
Royal and Papal Power

A Translation, with Introduction, of the De Potestate Regia
et Papali of John of Paris

Arthur P. Monahan

New York & London   1974
Columbia University Press

The Stanwood Cockey Lodge Foundation has generously provided funds
to assist in the publication of this work.

Library of Congress Cataloging in Publication Data

Jean de Paris, 1240?–1306.
   On royal and papal power.

   (Records of civilization: sources and studies,
no. 90)
   At head of title: John of Paris.
   Includes bibliographical references.
   1. Popes—Temporal power. 2. Church and state.
III. Series.
BX1810.J413 1973   262'.132   73-16302
ISBN 0-231-03690-6

Records of Civilization: Sources and Studies

Edited under the Auspices of the Department of History
Columbia University

To My Mother

Contents

General Introduction
Origins of the Church-State Problem

JOHN OF PARIS undertakes the investigation of a speculative problem which had existed for Christians for centuries, and which continues to exist today for adherents of any religion that claims to speak authoritatively for an omnipotent God directly to men, and that possesses an ecclesiastical structure embodying an endeavor to implement such claims for its members. Study of the history of church-state relations quickly uncovers the obvious but not unimportant point that the issue exhibits two distinct but related facets. The issue has its factual side, the historical data concerning the actual relationships between church and political authorities at different times and in different geographical and political circumstances. This makes for a fascinating and varied story and, like all historical relationships, will not cease to unfold and develop until either one or both of the elements in the relationship disappear from the stage of history. The factual history of church-state relations will cease only when church, state, or both cease to exist as concrete entities.

Church-state relations, however, have a theoretical, ideological side as well as a factual one. Theories or doctrines as to what should be the proper relationship between church and state have been formulated side by side with, and usually causally related to, the facts of church-state affairs; and such theories or doctrines also have a fascinating history. They are also in a real sense historical facts for a study of the problem of church-state relations. It is with this set of historical facts, or at least with a limited number of them, that the present introduction is concerned. It should be noted in passing too, that there is not always a close correlation between the facts of church-state relations at a given time and place and the facts of the theoretical doctrines on the subject formulated in that same time and place.

The formulation of theories of church-state relations began for the Christian church with the directive "to render to Caesar the things that are Caesar's, and to God the things that are God's," although obviously such a directive is almost purely hortatory, and requires interpretation to distinguish between the things which are Caesar's and those which are God's. The issue of formulating a theory of church-state relations did not arise in any significant way for the Christian church in the early centuries of its existence, although ingredients for the formulation of such a doctrine exist from the earliest Christian times (and, it goes almost without saying, the age and proximity to the actual time of church establishment of these early ingredients invariably compensated in the eyes of later Christian theorists for the frequent and normal incompleteness and ambiguity of the early "fragments").

It was not until after Constantine's formal establishment of Christianity as the state religion of the Roman Empire that serious and sustained efforts were made to work out the precise relationship between the Christian church and the state; and any substantial details of the history of this theoretical problem date from this period. These and most subsequent attempts to theorize on the proper structure of church-state relations exhibit a practical character in the impetus to develop a theory. Politics, after all, is a practical study even when it is a science; and the correlative existence of the two institutional realities of church and state led inevitably to the necessity and desirability of formulating a theory relating their proper spheres to one another.

It is important to get the history of these early efforts at formulation of doctrine "right," because so much of the later effort at doctrinal development employed the early work as authority for its own conclusions. Although this is not to say without qualification that later thinkers either simply repeated or simply accepted the positions of earlier thinkers, nevertheless the entire emphasis on authority so typical of medieval Christian speculation on any subject —vestiges of which are still all too evident in contemporary Chris-

General Introduction xiii

tian thinking and writing—required that due deference be paid to the ancient authorities. This attitude is not an exclusively Christian attitude, of course, but it is certainly a typical one.

One of the earliest Christians to formulate a theory of church-state relations, incomplete though it was, was Pope Leo I (440–461). Leo interpreted his succession to the Chair of Peter as pope of the Roman Church to mean that he was functionally qualified to rule the universal church according to a monarchic principle. He designated himself the "vicar of Christ," and while the idea behind this formula was not new, the formula itself was. It has been said that, "the formula chosen by Leo was the dress in which the idea of the *principatus* of the Roman Church was clothed." [1]

The notion of *principatus* had been used by Irenaeus to designate the position of the Church of Rome as early as the end of the second century, and this term was transformed by Leo into the concept of the *principatus apostolicae sedis.*[2] (The concept of Rome as an *apostolic seat* originated with Pope Damasus in 378; [3] but Leo was the first pontiff to popularize it, and gave it its peculiar ideological thrust in relation to *principatus.*) For Leo, the special status of the Church of Rome and correspondingly of its head, the pope, derived from the fact that Christ had made a personal commission to Peter alone of the "power of the keys," and the power to bind and loose on earth and in heaven. Peter had received this commission in his person; and he transmitted it to the other apostles.

According to this view, there is immediately seen to be a hierarchical order between Peter and the other apostles. While the other apostles do not differ from Peter in the power they share and enjoy, their possession of this power results from Peter's having transmitted it to them. Correspondingly, the pope, as Peter's successor, enjoys a comparable position with respect to other bishops. Insofar as the pope transmits their power to them, he has hierarchical jurisdiction over them. Therefore, as Peter's successor, the pope enjoys the plenitude of power that Christ personally committed to Peter; other bishops, while they share in the pope's governing authority insofar as he transmits it to them, do not share his plenitude of power. The pope as vicar of Christ is in a unique hierarchical position of authority. The sum total of his jurisdictional powers is conceived of by Leo as a *principatus,* from which ultimately all power, including temporal authority, derives. The Christian *corpus,* or totality of the Church, rested on Christ's commission to Peter; and all members of the Church, including political authorities, derive their function and jursidiction from this *principatus.* Leo was also the first to introduce the figure of Melchisedech as *rex et sacerdos* into the history of church-state theory. For Leo, this early patriarch was the symbolic forerunner of the pope insofar as he embodied in himself the fullness of spiritual and temporal authority.

The importance for medieval speculation on church-state relations of the Leonine theory of the Petrine commission is seen clearly in the amount of attention devoted to it in John of Paris's treatise. This point, along with the eighth-century forgery, the Donation of Constantine, constituted the foundation stones for the massive medieval edifice supporting papal claims for "plenitude of power" over both ecclesiastical and political affairs. Accordingly, John finds it necessary to devote careful attention also to interpretation of the Donation, and his considered response to these two major claims of his opponents takes up nearly the whole of his treatise.

The history of the medieval development of the argument in favor of the doctrine of full plenitude of papal power requires too lengthy a treatment for inclusion here, and has been recounted in detail elsewhere.[4] Some attention, however, should be given to the details of the precise historical context in which John's treatise is situated; and the more important of them are correlated with the following biographical data.[5]

The De Potestate: *Historical Context*

The treatise whose translation into English appears here was the work of John of Paris, master of theology at the University of Paris, a lesser and sometimes confusedly known late-thirteenth-century member of the Order of Preachers. Even though the title of the work *De potestate regia et papali* does not figure in the early catalogue lists of works attributed to this author, there can be no serious doubt that the work is his.[6]

What has been controverted, although the point is well settled by this date, is the set of biographical data concerning John. The fact of there having been in the late thirteenth and early fourteenth centuries several clerics and writers designated "John of Paris" was responsible for some confusion in earlier studies.[7] Our John of Paris, sometimes referred to as John Quidort,[8] was born about 1240 or 1241, and would therefore have been about 18 or 19 in 1259, when he began to study under Peter of Tarantasia (later Pope Innocent V). He died at Bordeaux in 1306, after having gone to the papal court at Avignon to defend himself against charges of heresy brought against his doctrine of the eucharist.

Although John's writings gave little or no evidence of his having been either particularly pugnacious or excessively radical in his opinions, he was embroiled in public controversy during much of his career. He was suspected of heresy in 1284 while, as a Dominican bachelor in the Faculty of Theology at the University of Paris, he commented on the *Sentences* of Peter Lombard; he was constrained to defend sixteen propositions extracted from his teachings and denounced to the Dominican master-general.[9] He also engaged in controversy over William de la Mare's attack on Thomas Aquinas in William's *correctorium,* and himself published a *correctorium corruptorii Thomae* to defend the views of his fellow Dominican.[10]

As can be seen from the Prologue to the *De potestate,* John was engaged in public controversy again in 1304, this time on the occasion of a dispute about the rights of mendicant friars to hear confessions. One of the qualities of Quidort's contribution to this dispute, a characteristic found again strikingly evident in the *De potestate,* is a relatively dispassionate and objective approach to the subject under examination, an approach which was in clear contrast to the contentious, even inflamed, atmosphere of the dispute itself.

As already noted, John's life ended on yet another note of controversy. His theory of "impanation," a doctrine which has led to him being considered by some as a forerunner of Martin Luther, caused him difficulties with Church authorities.[11] It has been pointed out that John's failure to achieve a master's status in theology until a few years before his death attests to the suspicion maintained towards him, although this can be qualified by the comment that "one should not forget that the reason why some writers get in trouble is that they write about controversial matters, not that they have a controversial mind." [12]

The issue of church-state relations—more specifically, the controversy between King Philip the Fair of France and Pope Boniface VIII—was the most far-reaching and explosive controversy in which John of Paris was involved. Yet even a careful reading of his treatise *De potestate regia et papali* provides only minimal evidence that its author was in any way associated with the most important politico-ecclesiastical confrontation of his period.[13] The *De potestate* cannot even be dated by reference to any external testimony; and internal evidence of any great substance on this point is lacking. The most authoritative efforts in this connection, however, locate the outside limits of the date of its composition between the end of 1302 and the spring of 1303; and it does not seem possible to become more precise than this.[14]

The year 1302 was itself a period in which the conflict between Boniface and Philip reached one of its high points. The French king had been at odds with Boniface for some time, and at the moment was engaged in an unpromising military campaign in Flanders, and in need of all the doctrinal, moral, and material support he could muster: Boniface had already attempted to intervene in French political affairs by prohibiting laymen from imposing taxes on the clergy without papal consent, by annulling all dispensations previously accorded in this connection, and by threatening all transgressors with excommunication (the bull *Clericos laicos*, 1296); [15] Philip had already responded by prohibiting all exports of money and letters of credit outside his kingdom, thus effectively threatening the papal treasury. Formal meetings had been held in both England and France—the January 1301 parliament of Edward I [16] and the first estates-general of France in April 1302—both of them decisively exhibiting the general popular consent for the temporal ruler's side of the dispute with the papacy. John's treatise, in fact, appeared between the two estates-general meetings called by Philip in this period, the first of which was held in April 1302, and the second in June 1303.

That John lent himself directly to the mobilization of French public opinion in Philip's campaign against Boniface is clear from the presence of his name on a petition from his Dominican convent in Paris calling for a Church council to examine the legitimacy of Boniface's papal election.[17] There is, however, no substantial evidence that in so doing John was acting more forcefully than any of his fellow Dominicans, all of whom had signed the same petition, or than any of the hundreds of other French clergy who had expressed themselves in similar ways at the same time. And any suggestion that John took a leading role in this campaign against Boniface [18] or that, as has been maintained, Quidort had a hand in the successful Nogaret plot to capture Boniface VIII at Anagni,[19] seems without foundation. Like the overwhelming number of his countrymen, clerics and laymen alike, John seems to have been a solid supporter of the French king's claims to the full integrity of political authority over his realm.

Professionally, John's support for this view was given expression in a manner proper to a member of the Faculty of Theology of the University of Paris. He published a calm, formidably objective, dispassionate treatise on the theoretical basis for an adequate doctrine of the relationship between temporal and papal power. Indeed, as has been said, even a careful reading of Quidort's *De potestate* could leave the historically uninformed reader completely unaware of the crisis conditions under which it was composed.

The treatise itself was of a genre that had found favor in the later decades of the thirteenth century, and was thus one of a number of more or less theoretical or polemical works on the subject. The stimulus for such works was twofold. First, the wide prominence given to Aristotle's *Politics* owing to its translation into Latin about 1250 in itself stimulated thinking on matters of political theory in academic and intellectual circles throughout Western Europe. Secondly, of course, the actual political circumstances of the period involving France, England, and the papacy led to a spate of polemical treatises defending or criticizing the opposing positions. John's treatise is somewhat unusual in this latter respect in that it exhibits a deliberate effort to respond to his opponents' views by dealing with both the canonical and the more "philosophical" arguments in favor of the papalist position. For the most part the papalist position traditionally had rested on canonical, legalistic arguments, and papalist treatises containing material of a noncanonical type were a late-thirteenth-century phenomenon. Such, for example, was the widely circulated *De ecclesiastica potestate* of Aegidius of Rome.[20]

The comprehensive approach taken by John to the subject of the *De potestate* makes it possible, as well as advisable, to examine the sources on which it rests, and to situate it with some precision vis-à-vis contemporary literature on the same subject. A first glance at John's treatise yields the general impression that it is a great mélange of views and counterviews taken from contemporary and earlier sources. Quidort's antagonists, for example, are provided in chapter 11 with more than forty arguments John claims to have found advanced in their behalf, and an analysis of his own position shows clear dependence in important areas on Aristotle[21] and Thomas Aquinas.[22] Withal, however, both in organization and vital points of doctrine, Quidort shows himself to be his own man.

Among contemporary papalist treatments of the basic problem, John's work shows explicit and extensive use of five sources: Aegidius of Rome, *De ecclesiastica potestate,* James of Viterbo, *De regimine christiano;* Henry of Cremona, *De potestate papae,* the treatise *Non ponant laici,* and the anonymous *Determinatio compendiosa de jurisdictione imperii.*[23] Other sources are used to a lesser degree. However only one of John's contemporaries, Henry of Cremona, is mentioned by name, and John directs almost every one of his infrequent lapses into sarcasm at this opponent. The main protagonist of the papalist position taken account of by John is Aegidius of Rome, whose treatise against Peter John Olivi, while never given explicit mention, is the source for much of the material John contests.

John also relies on Aegidius of Rome, again without explicit reference or acknowledgement, in the formulation of his own views on the subject of papal resignation.[24] Other contemporaries from whom John derives material supporting his views are Godfrey of Fontaines,[25] Moneta of Cremona (by way of Thomas Aquinas's *Contra impugnantes Dei cultum et religionem*),[26] and Vincent of

Beauvais.[27] Traces can also be seen in John's treatise of dependence on two contemporary anonymous works: *Quaestio in utramque partem* and *Rex pacificus*,[28] although the latter does not seem to have contributed any explicit formulations of position to John's work. The anonymous pamphlet in defense of Philip, *Disputatio inter clericum et militem*,[29] while supporting the same side of the controversy as John's treatise, proceeds in a different way to its conclusions; and the anonymous gloss on *Unam sanctam*,[30] while clearly showing a close conformity with the conclusions and arguments Quidort employs in the *De potestate*, cannot be dated with precision. Accordingly, it cannot be determined whether John was influenced by it or whether Quidort's work was the source for the gloss.

The De Potestate: *General Character and Outline*

A prominent feature of John's treatise is its clear and systematic structure, followed through in a logically coherent, objective, almost completely abstract way. While this is a common characteristic of the Scholastic literature of the late thirteenth and early fourteenth centuries, it is perhaps surprising to find it in John's work, given the fact that Quidort was deeply involved in the great contemporary controversy between Boniface VIII and Philip the Fair of France. The details of John's involvement in this classic collision between papal and monarchic power are not precisely known, but as already noted it seems probable that John was one of the major advocates of the royal position. And it is a fair assumption that his treatise was one of the principal literary weapons employed by Philip's supporters in their struggle with the papacy.

An examination of internal data in the *De potestate* shows clearly that its author's intention was more than merely polemical; in fact the work contains few explicit references to the contemporary scene. Twice it raises the issue of the "Donation of Constantine"; and several arguments attributed to John's opponents are designated as views advanced by "the Cremonan," the publicist Henry of Cremona. Given these exceptions, however, the work is ahistorical and abstract in its formulation and expression.

Another prominent and typically Scholastic feature of the treatise is John's use of authorities. The emphasis again is on comprehensiveness, and this adds much to the interest and value of the work insofar as John seems determined to present and deal with all facets of his problem. He employs textual authorities both for and against his own position from four basic types of source: Sacred Scripture, canonical writings, the Church Fathers and other ecclesiastical authorities, and contemporary positions, the last of which are all cited anonymously with the exception of the views already noted as attributed to the Cremonan. The references John offers display a truly magisterial grasp of his subject; they invoke comprehensively every type of authority. This is particularly significant in respect to Quidort's use of legal and canonical texts, which shows a familiarity with his opponents' home ground not reciprocated by these men, and not reflected elsewhere in any other advocates of what Ullmann has called "the lay thesis." [31] Not even John's more prominent successors in advocating the lay thesis—Dante, William of Ockham, and Marsilius of Padua [32]—show a comparable willingness to contest the canonists' position on their own ground. John, however, is willing to tackle his opposition on two fronts: (1) he rejects any rational basis for the doctrine of papal supremacy over temporal affairs; (2) he aims to show that the canonical literature is not univocal in its views on the subject.

The same thoroughness in dealing with his subject is illustrated in John's marshalling, in chapter 11, of some forty-two different arguments in support of the view he wishes to oppose. There is little reason to doubt Quidort's declaration in this connection that "these are all the arguments I have been able to hear and collect on this side of the issue"; and the comprehensiveness with which he deals with views opposing his own makes it possible to situate him rather carefully in respect of his contemporaries.

The systematic approach John takes to his subject is embodied also in the structure of the treatise itself. Initially, he makes an introductory declaration containing a brief statement of his own position regarding the nature of priestly and papal power over temporal affairs, and situating his position as a mean between two extremes. One extreme, a doctrine he attributes to the Waldensians, denies all temporal power or wealth by right to ecclesiastics; the other, which he terms the error of the Herodians, asserts that ecclesiastics, particularly the pope, enjoy temporal power by right. John then proceeds to offer the customary disclaimer about not wishing to teach or assert anything contrary to faith, good morals, sound doctrine, or against due reverence to the papacy, and goes on to provide an outline or table of contents for the remaining (25) chapters of his treatise, as shown in the accompanying diagram of this table of contents.

The De Potestate: *Systematic Analysis*

In chapter 1 John begins the formal presentation of his doctrine with an explanation of the term kingship (*regnum*), and proceeds in chapter 2 to compare and contrast temporal kingship with
its ecclesiastical correlative, priesthood (*sacerdotium*). This approach had had a lengthy history in the context of theoretical discussions of papal-monarchical relations, dating back to the Justinian
legal text which distinguished between *imperium* and *sacerdotium*,[33] although John has substituted *regnum* for *imperium* in
the dichotomy. Quidort defines kingship as "rule over a community
perfectly ordered by one person to the common good" (chapter 1),
and he properly and accurately attributes this conception of tem-

poral authority to Aristotle. In developing his concept of temporal authority as kingship he refers three times to Aristotle's *Politics,* and his explanation shows complete familiarity with this work, especially with Books 1 and 6.

Both the contents and the style of John's explanation of kingship are Aristotelian; the significance of his Aristotelianism on this and other points in his doctrine will receive separate consideration below (pp. xlii *ff.*). For John the basis and foundation of temporal or political authority derive from within the Aristotelian context of what is "natural" to man; and the consequences of this doctrine of nature are expressed in the Aristotelian meaning of the terms "natural law" and "common good." Human beings are naturally political or civil because, as the Philosopher says, a single human being is not self-sufficient, but must live in a community in order for all his needs to be met. In fact, he must live in a "perfect" community—one that provides him with all the necessities of life (food, clothing, defense)—the perfect community of a political society or state.

John takes care, too, to mention the character of human speech as a further indication of the natural tendency for man to live among and communicate with other humans. He accepts the Aristotelian view that speech is a sign of the naturally social character of man (chapter 1). A state or political community is necessary to man for his well-being, and is therefore natural to him.

The state, in turn, must have a leader, whose natural or necessary function is to supervise the state in order to assure promotion of the well-being of all its individual members: the *common good.* The common good is promoted best by a single leader or ruler, whose task it is to further this common good. The single leader should be "best," preeminent in virtue (chapter 1). In the emphasis on the single leader preeminent in virtue, John is borrowing from Aristotle once more. It is interesting to note, however, that he scants the Aristotelian qualification of this point in terms of the practical impossibility of finding such a paragon of virtue for political leadership; and hence John here ignores totally the ultimate preference Aristotle shows for a mixed-polity type of political society. John is willing to cite Aristotle when it is in his interest to do so, but he is no slavish follower of the Philosopher. As a Christian and a man of his time, Quidort is not unusual in this.

John's strong emphasis on a single kingly ruler is not so un-qualified, however, as to lead him to advocate a single world polity or empire, with a single ruler. Instead, he emphasizes the natural-ness of a plurality of states and a plurality of political forms corre-sponding to different conditions and circumstances of people in different parts of the world (chapter 3). This acceptance of political pluralism is one of the more important features of John's political philosophy. Certainly it has few parallels in his own day or earlier, although he invokes the support of St. Augustine for the view. The explicit contrast he introduces between the unity of spiritual society and the plurality of temporal political society marks an important divergence between John's position and that of his contemporaries (chapter 3).

The single ruler is the king or prince, however he may be termed; and his exercise of authority, directed to the common good of all those over whom he exercises authority, is termed *kingship*. This type of rule is natural to men insofar as it is natural and neces-sary for them to live in a political society. Kingship derives from the natural law (chapter 1).

The specific end or goal of the exercise of kingship, the com-mon good of all citizens in a political society, is that all men live according to virtue. The common good of any political society, then, is not physical well-being as such, although this is an essential condition of the state: it is primarily a moral value—virtue—inso-far as human beings are moral beings, not merely physical or ani-mate entities (chapter 2). Once again the position brought forward by John is that of Aristotle. Men are rational and therefore moral beings; their good is by nature a rational or moral good, and not merely a material good. The nature of man is to live morally or vir-tuously; the aim of any human political society is to have men live virtuously.

When John proceeds to a definition of priesthood (*sacer-dotium*), he introduces explicitly the Christian character of his doctrine. Still speaking the language of Aristotle but giving it the quality of Christian context found earlier in such fellow Dominicans as Albert the Great and Thomas Aquinas, he asserts that men are ordered to an end beyond nature, to a supernatural end (*finis supernaturalis*)—eternal life (chapter 2). Indeed, humans and all human natural society are by nature ordered to such an ultimate end. This supernatural end would pertain to the office of king were it possible to achieve it naturally. But since it is not possible to do so, the supernatural end requires another power which is capable of attaining it: divine power or authority. This kind of authority rests in Him Whose purpose is to direct men to the common supernatural end: the person of Jesus Christ. Christ achieved the possibility of men reaching their supernatural end through His own death; and He provided means for men to attain this end in the sacraments of the Church. Further, having removed Himself from this world, He left behind appointed ministers to act for Him in directing men to the supernatural end. These ministers of Christ are called priests (*sacerdotes*), and their function and exercise of power directed to the supernatural end of men is called priesthood (*sacerdotium*). Priesthood thus can be defined as "the spiritual power given by Christ to ministers of the Church for dispensing the sacraments to the faithful" (chapter 2).

Having defined the two focal concepts of kingship and priesthood, Quidort proceeds to relate these concepts to one another. First, he comments on the issue of whether all spiritual and temporal power is subordinated to a single supreme ruler in each sphere (chapter 3). He emphasizes the necessity of unity under one supreme authority in the spiritual sphere, just as there is one true faith and one Christian people. The supreme spiritual authority is the pope, and his authority as head of the Church derives from God directly, and not from any council or synod. The subordination of all ecclesiastics to one head, then, can be said to be by divine ordinance.

The case of temporal authority, however, is different. It derives from natural rather than from divine law, and nature expresses it as a kind of inclination. Men are led by a natural inclination from God to choose different types of temporal rulers and different types of rule. John goes into some detail concerning the natural pluralism of political society, listing several reasons why political power is naturally diverse in form, even though spiritual power is naturally of a strict unity. (1) While men are one as to soul, they differ physically and in respect to the climate and conditions in which they live; (2) political authority requiring the use of physical force cannot be exercised well over a vast area or over distant people, while spiritual authority can be exercised easily over the whole world; (3) material goods are privately owned and unlike ecclesiastical goods, which belong to a community, they do not need a common dispenser. John's approach to the nature and character of political society and its many forms shows him once more to be in the very concrete, matter-of-fact tradition of Aristotle; and he bolsters his position here by a direct appeal to Aristotle, as well as to St. Augustine.

The distinction John draws between the unitary character of spiritual authority and the natural pluralism of political authority is one fundamental aspect of the basis for his rejection of the doctrine of papalist supremacy. As long as unqualified acceptance was given to the principle that all things must be subordinated to one, there was no logical escape from the doctrine that the temporal must be subordinated to the spiritual, whose ultimate unitary embodiment was the papacy. As Ullmann has pointed out in his detailed investigation of the medieval papacy's claim to total authority, successful opposition to the papalist doctrine required that issue be taken with the claim that all power passed in a unitary way to the papacy through the commission given by Christ to Peter.[34] Earlier efforts to reject the papalist claims while accepting the general principle of subordination of the many ultimately to one single authority had been required to substitute the claim of the temporal ruler to exercise all power, including spiritual authority, for that of the pope.[35] And few Christians were prepared to take seriously the claim that the spiritual can be subordinated to the temporal, even though there was a tradition in Roman law that the supremacy of the emperor was absolute.

At the same time as John prepares the ground for a rejection of the papalist claims for supremacy, he breaks as well with any effort to formulate a unitary theory of temporal authority, and shows that he is not an imperialist in political theory any more than he is a papalist. His rejection of the imperialist system, however, is more explicit in his later comments on the consequences of the "Donation of Constantine" for papal authority in France (chapter 20). Speaking to the point that a single person should be ruler of the whole world, Quidort correlates his acceptance of the single leader (king) with his preference for a world made up of many states. He rejects the view that one man should rule the whole world, on the practical grounds that "the world certainly did not enjoy such great peace in the period when emperors ruled it as it had both before and since" (chapter 20).

Having contrasted kingship and priesthood in terms of their unity, John relates them to one another in terms of priority: priority in time, in dignity, and in causality. Here John addresses himself directly to the position developed in support of papal supremacy by Hugh of St. Victor in his *De Sacramentis*.[36] Following Honorius of Canterbury,[37] Hugh had maintained that the spiritual authority of the papacy as the ultimate expression of the priesthood was prior to kingship in both time and dignity. He asserted that the priesthood had been instituted by God Himself, and therefore antedated any human temporal authority. Hugh's second point as to how the priesthood could be said to be prior in dignity to kingship was a foregone one: it is prior in dignity insofar as the spiritual is prior to or superior to the material. This Victorine position had become an important ingredient in the formulation of the papalist doctrine, and Quidort's response to it is instructive for an appreciation of his methods for handling his opposition. He concedes one of Hugh's two points, contests the second, and adds a third level of priority to bolster his own position in the argument.

John asserts that kingship is prior in time to priesthood (chapter 4), provided one takes the meaning of priesthood in its proper sense. For Christ was the first true priest insofar as He was the first to offer true sacrifice. Kingship, however, existed before the time of Moses. Even if priesthood is accepted in the broad sense according to which it can be said that Melchisedech was a priest, it is still the case that the priesthood was not prior to kingship but concurrent, since the reign of Melchisedech as priest and king was concurrent with the earliest examples of kingdoms, those of the Assyrians and

Sicyonians before the Flood. In effect, then, Quidort simply ignores the claim that the priesthood is prior in time because instituted by God Himself.

The priesthood, however, is conceded to be prior to kingship in dignity (chapter 5), since it pertains to man's ultimate end, to which the end of kingship relates as a means. But superiority of the priesthood in dignity does not mean that the priest is superior to the king in all things; for the fact that secular power is lesser in dignity than the sacerdotal power does not mean that it is derived from the spiritual power of the priesthood. Amplifying this point, John makes the most crucial statement in the formulation of his position. He asserts that both spiritual and temporal power derive directly from a single higher power, and therefore are not subordinate to one another in any kind of simple gradation of superior and inferior. "The two arise directly from a single supreme power, the divine power. Wherefore, the inferior kingship is not subject to the superior priesthood in all things, but only in those things in respect to which the supreme power made it subordinate to the superior" (chapter 5). He clarifies this position by an example: in a household a teacher or instructor in morals is superior to a doctor, since the former directs his efforts to a superior, spiritual end while the doctor aims at a lower, material end: health for the body. It does not follow, however, that the doctor is simply and absolutely subject to the teacher or instructor in morals. Both are appointed by the head of the household, and both derive their authority directly from him. The single higher power gives legitimate authority to each in his proper sphere. John's conclusion is simply that "the priest is superior principally in spiritual matters; and, conversely, the prince is superior in temporal matters, although the priest is superior absolutely insofar as the spiritual is superior to the temporal" (chapter 5).

John's formulation of position here marks a point of view not previously found in Christian medieval speculation on the problem of church-state relations. Though all Christians and medieval thinkers on this point take their departure from the New Testament text of Matthew, where Christ speaks of "rendering unto Caesar," and while early Christian texts to which reference is made concerning the problem of church-state relationship accept and assert the duality of the two spheres of the spiritual and the temporal, the whole burden of development of a coherent doctrine of church-state relations always assumed the necessity, apparently logical and certainly consistent with the feudal type of western European society in which the speculation took place, of ordering all things ultimately under a single head or in a single line of development. Looked at this way, at least if the context was seen as this world, the problem could oscillate between insistence on subordinating the sphere of the temporal to the spiritual, or the opposite extreme of subordinating the spiritual authority ultimately to the temporal. Only these alternatives existed as logical possibilities within this frame of reference.

It is the virtue of John's position that it breaks through this set of limited and mutually exclusive alternatives. John rejects the principle of correlating the two spheres of spiritual and temporal to one another in terms of one of them as subordinate to the other in this world. In accepting the logical concept of unity as explanatory of plurality, he locates the unity outside this world, in God Himself. This enables him to give to the spheres of the temporal and spiritual positions of hierarchical equality rather than of subordination and superiority to one another. In this world the two spheres are not subordinate one to the other; they are on the same plane "causally" in that both are derivative directly from God, and not from one another.

John's formulation of doctrine on the relationship of spiritual and temporal powers is achieved basically at this point. What remains to be done is to specify the precise relationship between the two spheres of spiritual and temporal, and show what is meant by his denial that the two spheres relate causally in any way, but are formally distinct as not directly derivative from one another. The task remaining takes up the balance of the treatise, except for the last three chapters.

Kingship does not relate to priesthood in terms of causality, as has been said already (chapter 8), inasmuch as God directly is the cause of both. John expands this point further to bring out more clearly the interrelationship of one with the other. In showing that the kingship of temporal power is not caused by spiritual power, Quidort makes two points raised first as questions: (1) that the pope does not have dominion over temporal things, either those belonging to clerics or those belonging to laymen; (2) that the pope does not have jurisdiction over them either.

The distinction between having dominion and having jurisdiction is as follows: to have dominion is to have possession or property rights; to have jurisdiction is to have the right of determining what is just and unjust (chapter 6). According to John, the pope does not have dominion or property rights over any material things except those he possesses by virtue of his own efforts and those given him as personal possessions. He lacks dominion over ecclesiastical goods—that is, material and spiritual goods relating to the well-being of the Church—because such things are for the use of the Church as a whole, and not for any individuals as such. Consequently, no individual has property rights or dominion over ecclesiastical goods—not even the pope. He is "the universal dispenser of all ecclesiastical goods, spiritual and temporal" (chapter 6). The community of the universal Church is their general proprietor, while individual church communities are proprietors of church goods relating to their proper individual community functions. As will be seen, John now will have no difficulty denying the pope any dominion or proprietary rights over the goods of laymen.

Several important addenda (chapter 6) are drawn from the conclusion that the pope has no dominion over ecclesiastical goods, but only the power of dispensing:

(1) The pope cannot appropriate ecclesiastical goods merely as he sees fit; he could do so only if he were God.

(2) For the pope to make illegitimate personal appropriation of ecclesiastical goods is illegal, and a pope can be held to restitution in such cases.

(3) A pope can be deposed for wrongfully disposing of ecclesiastical goods for purposes other than the common good of the Church. (This is John's first mention of papal deposition, and he returns to it in detail later.)

(4) A pope cannot lawfully take action against any person who properly protests against papal abuse of the power to dispense ecclesiastical goods.

(5) It is incorrect to claim that God can give the pope power to act in this fashion, for such action is unnatural, and it would be contradictory for God to act contrary to nature.

(6) A pope cannot remove a power rightly exercised by any other ecclesiastical administrator unless that other person has sinned.

Correspondingly, the pope has no dominion over the goods of laymen (chapter 7). He is not even their administrator except in cases of extreme necessity for the Church, where these goods then can be considered necessary for the common spiritual good of the Church. In fact, neither prince nor pope has either dominion or jurisdiction over the goods of laymen in ordinary circumstances, since these goods belong by proprietary right to the individuals who have come to possess them through their art, labor, and industry. "Their owners can dispose of them as they see fit, without injury to anyone else" (chapter 7). In the same chapter several addenda are also offered by John on this position:

(1) Where no extreme necessity for the Church exists, the pope cannot coerce anyone to yield goods to him, although he can encourage such an action by granting indulgences to laymen who assist him in this way.

(2) The pope can exercise coercion or compulsion against rebels and dissenters, but only by way of ecclesiastical censure.

John amplifies further his insistence that the pope lacks jurisdiction over lay goods by asserting that Christ Himself had no such power, and that even if Christ had possessed this power, He did not transfer it to His successors, the popes. The argument is extended and somewhat complex. First, Quidort shows in what way Christ might be considered to have jurisdiction over temporal goods, in terms of the different ways in which Christ is called king (chapter 8). Secondly, he offers a series of four New Testament texts referred to by those who maintain that Christ has jurisdiction over laymen's goods, and replies to them (chapter 9). Finally, he argues contrary to fact, that Christ did not give temporal power to the popes even if He Himself possessed it (chapter 10).

Christ might be called "king" in three ways: as God, as man-God, as man. Obviously, only the third of these would entail the possible exercise of temporal authority over a state. However Christ could not properly be called a king in this fashion, and therefore He did not have temporal jurisdiction. And because He did not have this type of jurisdiction Himself, He could not transfer it to His successors. The four arguments John adduces in favor of the position that Christ had temporal jurisdiction are all taken from Matthew, and his response to each of them construes the text as referring to Christ as God and not man, and therefore as involving Christ's spiritual and not His temporal kingship.

The argument that Christ did not give temporal power to the popes exhibits a further sustained effort to insist that the spiritual and temporal powers are distinct.

(1) Even if they were not distinct in Christ, they are distinct in His successors, just as many things indistinct in their principle are distinct in their principiates.

(2) Christ did not confer on His successors all the powers He possessed: for example, He did not confer "the power of excellence," by which He was able to do such things as institute new sacraments or confer sacraments without a visible sign.

(3) Nor is there any scriptural basis for the contention that Christ conferred temporal powers on His successors, as there should be if He had done so.

(4) The very perfection of the spiritual sacrifice of the New Law also indicates the propriety of its being distinct from temporal concerns.

(5) Further, circumstances in which a single person has many different responsibilities indicate an imperfect situation; and Christ had a clear twofold purpose in separating these two powers in His successors. (a) Because of the mutual need and assistance members of the Church have for one another, separation of the two powers encourages the qualities of joy and charity between pope and prince which are the essential lubricants for fulfilling this need; (b) secondly, separation of the powers prevents priests and pope from becoming too much concerned with temporal affairs to the detriment of their spiritual responsibilities. And John repeats his view that "the two powers are distinct in such a way that one is not reduced to the other, but the temporal like the spiritual derives immediately from God" (chapter 10).

(6) Finally, he notes that the Donation of Constantine should be construed as a "giving back" to the Church rather than as a gift, if in fact the popes possess temporal jurisdiction from Christ. And he deals at length with the effort made by some of his contemporaries to distinguish between the pope's possession of temporal jurisdiction and the exercise of this jurisdiction, which is said by these men to belong to princes. The inconsistency of this distinction is dealt with in devastating fashion, with John offering nine different objections to it (chapter 10).

The balance of John's statement of position distinguishing the spiritual and temporal powers is taken up with his listing of many arguments adduced by those who attribute the ultimate authority in both spheres to the pope (chapter 11), and with his replies to these arguments (chapters 12–20). This portion of the *De potestate,* which contains a detailed presentation of John's theory of the so-called "indirect power" the papacy has over temporal rulers, has rightly received greatest attention.[38] The theory of *potestas indirecta* is a specification of Quidort's basic position regarding the distinction of the two powers, and is a reciprocal one in respect of the spiritual and temporal spheres. While the pope, and by extension other ecclesiastical authorities exercising legitimate authority, exercise indirect power over temporal rulers, these temporal rulers exercising legitimate temporal authority also exercise indirect power over spiritual rulers, including the pope.

The Doctrine of Conditional and Accidental Power

The specifics of this position are worth noting in some detail. John begins by detailing the types of legitimate power contained in the priesthood as a result of Christ's institution of the Church (chapter 12). These types of power are five (or six) in number, corresponding to what the nature of the priesthood requires for its function to be fulfilled. Once again Quidort exhibits the Aristotelian tendency to explain a thing in terms of its nature and function. The priesthood requires: (1) the power to sanctify and consecrate corporeal matter (the power of consecration exercised primarily in the Mass and in other sacraments of the Church); (2) the so-called "power of the keys," most often illustrated by reference to confession, the sacrament of penance; (3) the power to preach and teach the word of God, which involves authoritative knowledge and understanding of God's truth; (4) the power to punish and coerce wrongdoers; (5) the power to establish and maintain order among the clerics who minister to Christ's Church; (6) the power or authority to provide for the material needs of the ministers of God's Church.

Only the fourth-mentioned of these—the power to punish and coerce—is significant in any consideration of the priesthood's jurisdiction over temporal affairs (chapter 13). What power has the priesthood over temporal affairs in terms of its power to coerce and punish? The powers of consecrating and administering the sacraments, of preaching, and or ordering ministers of the Church are all purely spiritual powers, while that of providing for the material needs of the ministers of the Church is more a right than a power, and hence is not of real concern here. The power of coercion and punishment in the external forum, however, poses the whole difficulty, as John puts it; and he concentrates his attention on it.

He contends that this legitimate sacerdotal power has two facets: the power of intervention and jurisdiction, and the power of coercion. With respect to jurisdiction, John asserts that an ecclesiastical or sacerdotal minister has the power of jurisdiction directly only over spiritual matters. He has jurisdiction over temporal matters only where there is a question of right and wrong, and even here his jurisdiction extends only to the spiritual and ecclesiastical aspects of a temporal matter. In clarification he asserts that there are two types of wrong (or sin) regarding temporal matters: (1) a sin of opinion or error, the jurisdiction of which relates solely and properly to an ecclesiastical judge—the judgment, for example, of whether usury is or is not a mortal sin; (2) a sin of selling—for example, the sin of using or spending wealth belonging to another.

Jurisdiction over this latter type of "sin" belongs properly to the secular judge alone, "who judges according to human or civil laws which govern appropriations of things and sales" (chapter 13). An ecclesiastical judge, then, has jurisdiction properly only over the determination of whether or not a given temporal matter is a sin, a moral or spiritual fault. The secular judge has jurisdiction over temporal affairs in terms of determining the material or physical qualities of a given temporal action. The only exception to this general rule in favor of additional legitimate jurisdiction for an ecclesiastical judge is a set of circumstances where such jurisdiction has been conceded to him explicitly either by Christ or by some temporal authority.

With respect to the ecclesiastical power of coercion, John maintains that it is a purely spiritual power, "except conditionally and accidentally" (chapter 13). It is a "conditional" power, insofar as the ecclesiastical judge can employ physical, material, or financial coercion or punishment only to the extent that a sinner or penitent is willing to accept it; the ultimate penalty an ecclesiastical judge can impose directly is the spiritual penalty of excommunication. The power is "accidental" insofar as, for example, in the case of a prince's having committed an ecclesiastical crime and remaining incorrigible, the pope can act by imposing the penalty of excommunication on all who continue to obey this prince. Insofar as this kind of action by the pope would lead to the prince's being deposed it could be described in terms of the pope's direct act of excommunication of the incorrigible prince's subjects leading accidentally to the prince's deposition. The deposition itself would not be accomplished by the pope directly, but by the subject people.

Conversely, the prince can act accidentally to depose a pope who is wrongly exercising his authority and remains incorrigible. In such circumstances the prince could employ temporal or physical coercion directly against his own subjects with a view to their deposing a pope, or requiring him to yield his spiritual authority. In such an event, the people would directly exercise spiritual authority against the pope, while the prince could be described as exercising temporal or physical authority directly against the people, and spiritual authority accidentally or indirectly against the pope (chapter 13).

The examples John employs in chapter 13 to illustrate his position here are thought provoking. He refers to the pope's rights to exercise coercion accidentally against a prince when the prince has sinned in an ecclesiastical or spiritual matter: "in matters such as faith, marriage, and things of this kind." But he goes on: "When the king sins [*sic*] in temporal matters . . . the barons and peers of the kingdom . . . correct him." John concedes that "if the barons and peers cannot or dare not so act, they can request assistance from the Church; and. . . ." The distinction between a spiritual and a temporal crime is being preserved here by John; and it seems clear that in the case of the latter type of crime or wrong practiced by a temporal ruler, the pope's right of even indirect or accidental coercion is limited to his acceptance of an invitation to so act extended by temporal authorities subordinate to an erring prince or emperor. What the case would be should no such invitation be forthcoming is not specified, although John's terminology here differs from that employed in the parallel case of temporal authorities moving accidentally against an incorrigibly sinful pontiff. Nor is the distinction between a purely spiritual sin and a sin of a temporal kind clear. The examples of these two types of sin are clear enough; but the distinction itself is not.

John on Papal Deposition and Resignation

In the parallel case of a temporal ruler exercising power to excommunicate or depose a pope, John again employs the distinction between the commission of a temporal and a spiritual wrong. When the pope commits a temporal wrong, such as borrowing money in a usurious way or giving protection to usurers, the prince can act directly against him. When the pope commits a spiritual wrong and is incorrigible—for example, by conferring benefices simoniacally—he is to be admonished by the cardinals, who represent the whole clergy. If the pope proves incorrigible in such a spiritual matter,

"the cardinals have to call on the secular arm . . . then the emperor . . . would have to proceed against the pope to achieve his
deposition" (chapter 13). It seems here that ecclesiastical authorities subordinate to the pope are *required* to call upon the secular
authority for his indirect assistance in ridding the Church of an incorrigibly sinful pope.

Greater attention is paid to the matter of the pope's deposition
in the last four chapters of the treatise, and the additional points
made there can be summarized as follows. John's treatment of the
issue of the pope's deposition or resignation is customarily systematic. Action and judgment against a pope, he says, can be understood in four ways: with regard to his status, his power, his abuse
of power, and his personal defects (chapter 22). (1) Quidort asserts that the pope's status involves the issue of whether he has
been properly elected; and questions can certainly be raised about
this matter. (2) The same obtains in respect of personal defects,
which may preclude a given person being elected to the papacy.
Anyone improperly enjoying the status of pope must be required to
yield office, by the use of the secular arm if need be.

(3) Regarding the power of the pope, John contends that it
is as legitimate to inquire about its specific character, as it is to investigate (4) a pope's abuse of power and personal defects. He
does insist that in this respect "one must always interpret and accept
things in the best light," and guarantees the primacy of papal authority by denying that anyone can judge a pope by virtue of having direct authority over him. He contends, nonetheless, that a pope can
be judged by "simple judgment," although not by right of office of
any such judge. He can be judged out of the "zeal of charity," as
anyone is to be judged, and he can be "bound to fraternal correction
of any fault out of zeal of charity and the consequences entailed in
his own act."

He includes here a specific consideration of what attitude
should be adopted toward a pope who declares a man to be heretic
without calling a general council. John's example involves the pope's
declaring as heretic any man who claims that the king of France is
not subject to the pope in temporal matters. John's answer, in chapter 22, is that such a papal declaration must be interpreted in "a

sensible manner," in accordance with the Scriptures and the commonly held doctrine which holds that such a papal pronouncement cannot be taken literally. Literal acceptance of such a papal pronouncement would be "a kind of novelty," and contains a position that a pope should bring forward "only after very mature consideration, and after having previously called a general council and having discussion of it carried on everywhere by learned men." In other words, such a papal statement ought to be ignored. If a pope persists in such an "erroneous view," he ought to be tolerated patiently as long as possible. In the last analysis, however, "if there is danger to the state's good order because the people are being led into a wrong opinion and there is danger of rebellion, and the pope is unjustifiably influencing the people through an abuse of the spiritual sword, and where there is no hope of his ceasing otherwise," John insists that "the Church ought to be mobilized against the pope in this case, and should act against him." In such extreme circumstances the temporal authority can act to depose a pope, although of course its actions would be considered indirect or accidental. He cites the Old Testament case of Ehud killing King Eglon, the case of the people deposing Pope Constantine, and that of Henry deposing Pope Benedict IX.

John's final comments on papal resignation and deposition come in the last two chapters of the treatise, in response to eleven arguments he adduces in denial of any power for a pope to be deposed or even for him to resign voluntarily. All these arguments against papal deposition and resignation emphasize the supremacy of papal power over all human power, and its subordination only to God. Accordingly, only God can depose a pope, and the pope's authority, like Christ's priesthood, is meant to endure forever. The pope, then, cannot resign, not even voluntarily.

In response to these arguments, John cites, in chapter 24, historical examples of papal resignation, offers canonical justification approving of a pope resigning, and gives arguments of his own as well. Among these last, he notes that papal authority relates to its purposes; thus, when its purposes are being subverted or not being pursued adequately, the pope, seeing his own inadequacy, can resign, or those who are aware of the pope's inadequacies and crimes can require him to yield his office. "Therefore, it is not unreasonable to assert that the pope can be deposed and can resign when invited to and prevailed upon by the people." And John is explicit concerning the details of procedure in such a case: "For a resignation it is sufficient to allege a reason before the college of cardinals which represents the whole Church in such circumstances . . . it is fitting for a deposition . . . to be done through a general council . . . and absolutely the college of cardinals would be sufficient for a deposition."

In replying to the general principle in arguments contrary to his own position that the pope derives his authority directly from God, and therefore can be deposed or given the right to resign only by God, John accepts the contention that papal power in itself derives directly from God, but points out that it devolves on a particular person through "human cooperation, to wit, through consensus of the elected and the electing. Accordingly, it can cease in this or that individual person through a human consensus" (chapter 25, *ad* 1).

John is explicit also regarding the power of the Church as a whole and other facets of its administrative structure in relation to the papal power. "Although [the papal power] is the highest created power in a person, nevertheless equal or greater power exists in the college [of cardinals] or in the whole Church. Or it can be asserted that a pope can be deposed by the college, or rather by the divine authority in a general council, the consensus of which is supposed and presumed to be able to depose a man when there is clear evidence of scandal and incorrigibility on the part of the man holding [the papal] office" (chapter 25, *ad* 4).

Finally, John distinguishes between the eternal authority conferred on a pope through his priesthood—something he has in common with all ordained ministers and which cannot be removed from him any more than from any priest—and a pope's jurisdiction. This latter is removable because it is not eternal, not eternal because conferred through human cooperation and consent (chapter 25, *ad* 11).

John on Popular Consent

One important feature of John's doctrine given emphasis in his treatment of the issue of papal resignation and deposition is the role of the people: "popular consent." The attention Quidort pays to the point is slight in terms of the number of statements he makes about it, but its importance should not be scanted. John offers parallel comments on the role and function of the people in respect of the legitimate exercise of both ecclesiastical and temporal authority; while he does not develop either point in detail, it is nonetheless true that Quidort considers both spiritual and temporal authority to rest on a popular base in the consent of the people.

He asserts categorically that kingship is "from God and the people electing" (chapter 10); that "a king exists by the will of the people" (chapter 19, *ad* 33: citing Averroes as an advocate of the position); and that "kingly power is from . . . the people who give their consent and choice" (chapter 17, *ad* 21). He makes similar statements concerning the legitimate basis of imperial authority (chapter 19, *ad* 33; chapter 15, *ad* 9). Quidort also draws the correlative conclusion that withdrawal of the people's consent from a temporal ruler results in his deposition from office (chapter 13). Further, he attempts in some way to outline a function for the nobility of a realm, the "barons and peers," who exercise a power of expressing the popular will in both the establishment and the deposition of a king (chapter 12; chapter 14, *ad* 5), without however spelling out in any satisfactory way either the precise manner in which the people exercise their rights in this connection, or the precise procedural relationship between "barons and peers" and people.

A parallel statement is made with respect to the attainment and exercise of ecclesiastical office. "The power of prelates is . . . from the people choosing and consenting" (chapter 10). Withdrawal of this popular support leads to the removal of a man from ecclesiastical jurisdiction: "the relationship between a prelate and the Church can be dissolved when there is dissension between the person elected and the electors, the elements through whose consent the relationship is established" (chapter 25, *ad* 3). A role similar to that of the barons and peers in respect of the temporal ruler is also assigned to the college of cardinals, "who act in place of the whole clergy and the whole people" (chapter 13). The cardinals can compel the resignation of a pope when he has acted in such a way as to have lost the people's consent for his holding the office of the papacy (chapter 14).

John is not comprehensive or precise about the way or ways in which loss of popular support might occur. Indeed, his comments on this point in respect of both temporal and ecclesiastical rulers mention only circumstances in which the persons occupying these offices have committed wrongs and remained incorrigible. Moreover, there is certainly no indication that tenure of these offices is naturally and automatically subject to popular review in the absence of "crimes" on the part of their occupants. Nevertheless, the possibility of such periodic reviews is not precluded by the general, though admittedly vague, outline of principles which John sets down on this score. And John actually goes further in application of the principle of popular support to ecclesiastical jurisdictional structure. He advocates as the best system of Church government an Aristotelian blend of monarchy, aristocracy, and democracy: "Certainly this kind of rule would be best for the Church, with several men being elected by every province and from every province under one pope. In this way everyone would have his role to play in some way in the rule of the Church" (chapter 19, *ad* 35). Coupled with his insistence on the limiting role of the general council to be exercised over the papacy, this position is well advanced for the beginning of the fourteenth century. Unlike Marsilius of Padua, who was shortly to advocate a much stronger limitation of papal authority in both temporal and spiritual spheres of authority in terms of popular consent, John did not at all see himself as heterodox in putting forward such views. To this day, however, even the "winds of change" generated by the Second Vatican Council have not produced in the Catholic Church the kind of democratic and constitutional struc-

tures advocated by Quidort. It would be naive, of course, to make of
John a twentieth-century democratic constitutionalist. Yet it would
be equally false to him historically to deny him credit for having
pushed farther than any of his predecessors or contemporaries logical and valuable implications of the concept of popular consent as
applied to the exercise of ecclesiastical authority.

John and Aristotelianism

The basis for Quidort's emphasis on the element of popular
consent underlying the legitimacy of authority, both temporal and
ecclesiastical, is Aristotelian. And John is at pains to acknowledge
the fact. Indeed, much of Quidort's position owes its principles and
its formulation to Aristotle. This point is not without importance,
and leads to a consideration of John's overall use of Aristotle in
the development of his doctrine of church-state relations.

Certainly, the conception of the state or political society as
natural to man insofar as it constitutes the perfect or complete community directed to the fulfillment of individual needs by the provision of the sufficient life is Aristotelian in its origin; and John of
Paris is not unique in his own period in formulating the conception.
A forerunner like Thomas Aquinas and a successor like Marsilius
of Padua exhibit comparable dependence on Aristotelian political
theory. It would be erroneous, however, to identify completely the
views of Aquinas, Marsilius, and Quidort—or indeed of almost any
two medieval thinkers—on this point, or to call them all equally
Aristotelian with respect to it. Matters are scarcely ever that simple
when it comes to establishing the sources for medieval thinkers'
views or to making comparisons between them. In his magisterial
study of Marsilius of Padua, Gewirth has pointed out the care
needed in interpreting the Paduan's position if one is to avoid the
conclusion that his doctrine is self-contradictory; he cites Marsilius'
use of the Aristotelian conception of the "natural" character of

political society as a case in point.[39] In order to appreciate the overall complexity of his thought it is essential to see the use to which such a derivative concept is put, within the fabric of the whole Marsilian doctrine. And from this point of view the issue of whether or not Marsilius was Aristotelian is not particularly relevant.

The same is true of John of Paris, and his use of the Aristotelian conception of a natural society. The question of whether or not John is Aristotelian is perhaps a pseudoquestion, at least a misleading one. To be answered at all satisfactorily it requires a response on several levels. The same thing must be said with respect to any comparison between John's position and that of men like Thomas Aquinas and Marsilius of Padua. Quidort both agreed and disagreed with them on this same point. He agreed in the sense that, like them, he borrowed from Aristotle the concept of the state as a natural entity. Like them, however, he made of this concept something "fitted" to the exigencies of his own thought. Thus, while all three doctrines *use* the same Aristotelian conception of the state as natural, all use it in different ways. The result is three different doctrines (or, in fact, four different doctrines, if one includes the original doctrine of Aristotle himself). This is the kind of conclusion almost invariably reached when a close and systematic analysis is made of a medieval philosophical doctrine; and it is the basis for the generally accepted rejection of the myth of a medieval Scholasticism as a monolithic intellectual structure. The lesson, however, is always worth repeating; for there is a natural tendency in presenting a summary or brief interpretation of a doctrine at least to imply its identity or similarity with other doctrines sharing the same conceptual sources. To designate any thirteenth- or fourteenth-century thinker as Aristotelian (or Augustinian, for that matter) and let it go at that, is at best an almost meaningless oversimplification. Not infrequently it can be a dangerous distortion of the doctrine, because of the natural connotations the term Aristotelian implies.

John's doctrine of the natural character of political society was Aristotelian, but not in the same sense in which this can be said, for example, of such other medieval thinkers as Thomas Aquinas or Marsilius of Padua. Selection of Aquinas and Marsilius of Padua in this connection is not purely arbitrary, for their views can be said in some fashion to bracket those of Quidort both chronologically and in content. For Aquinas, the natural character of the Aristotelian political society is fully teleological, and thus relates directly to the central orientation of most of medieval political thought. The implications from this for a doctrine of a single ruler ultimately and comprehensively responsible for the total ordering of all political society were seen by Aquinas, and are made explicit in his acceptance of the ultimate power of the papacy as consistently emphasized in the universalist view of society.

Marsilius of Padua, on the other hand, does not connect the conception of the natural character of a political society and the teleological overtones already present in the Aristotelian origin of the concept with its logically consistent correlative of a universal authority embodied in one supremely virtuous man. Quite the reverse: Marsilius insists on giving a strong "popular" emphasis to the principle and adds to it the notion that the *sole* source of legitimate political power is the will or consent of the people. Further, he gives a unique emphasis to the value and necessity of coercive power in political authority, which appears superficially to be quite at odds with the teleological motif.

John of Paris seems to find both these positions extreme. While he does not follow fully the implications leading from the Aristotelian concept of the natural character of society into support for a single universal ruler, neither does he emphasize as strongly as Marsilius advocacy of the importance of efficient coercive power in the state and the need for expression of the will of the people. John's own view, with the use to which he puts the Aristotelian concept of the nature of political society, emphasizes the basic plurality of political authority, distinguishing ineradicably between the spiritual and temporal spheres, and also advocating the natural diversity of political states in conformity with diversity among groups of people in respect of language, customs, and climate.

In a sense John is the more Aristotelian in his preference for a middle position between the extreme of a single universal temporal authority, which is the logical entailment of the theory of the one best man type of political authority, and the extreme of insisting on popular consent as the irreducible minimum for the exercise of temporal power. Whether or not he succeeds, Quidort tries to have it both ways. On the one hand, he repeats frequently that a temporal ruler exercises political authority with the consent of the people, indicating that a temporal ruler may be (even should be) deposed when this popular consent is removed because of a ruler's faults. And he even extends the notion of popular consent beyond political authority into the ecclesiastical sphere of church organization. A pope or bishop also exercises legitimate authority on the basis of popular consent, and when this consent is removed he can be deposed. Furthermore, as already noted, John maintains that the Church would profit from greater application of the principle of popular government, contending that the best juridical structure for the Church is one exemplifying the characteristics of the Aristotelian mixed polity of monarchical, aristocratic, and democratic elements. On the other hand, John expresses admiration for a "one man" rule in the state, and invokes the authority of St. Augustine to bolster the Aristotelian concept of the desirability of political rule by the most virtuous man in the state.

John upholds both the value of one-man rule by a singularly virtuous individual and the value of popular consent. He attempts to apply the two notions simultaneously to the exercise of authority over both ecclesiastical and temporal jurisdictions. In so doing, he refuses to push the emphasis on one-man rule to the point of insisting on universal political authority; thus he declines either to advocate a doctrine of a single temporal ruler for the world as a whole or to attribute universal political authority to the papacy, which he accepts as the universal authority on spiritual matters. Conversely, John refuses to emphasize popular consent to the point of making it an explicit *sine qua non* of the exercise of either political or spiritual authority.

To charge John's position with inconsistency or contradiction because of his failure to push either of these two notions to such logical consequences, or because of his failure to correlate explicitly the two notions with one another is perhaps legitimate as an exercise in logic, but it shows little appreciation of his views. The major significance of his doctrine lies in the fact that it finds a middle ground between a pure exercise in logical speculation and a complete rejection of a theoretical approach to politics in more positivistic terms. On balance, it avoids advocacy of a single seat of universal authority, avoiding even the advocacy of a world ruler in temporal affairs, although such a view can claim to be a logical entailment of the Aristotelian doctrine of authority naturally resting in the naturally best. And in so doing, John also had to deal with what was for him as an orthodox Christian the necessity of accepting a univocal concept of religion and the reality of the spiritual given expression from a single, omnipotent God, Who provided mankind with a single true religion and an ecclesiastical structure ordered in a hierarchical fashion parallel with the divine hierarchy, and containing a single, supreme human authority who by direct divine commission stood on earth in the place of God Himself. Yet Quidort's position avoids the kind of positivism favored by Marsilius of Padua in the formulation of a theory of politics.

Influence of the De Potestate

The influence of John's *De potestate* has been traced with some care.[40] It does not seem to have enjoyed much influence in its own day, when political events themselves moved rapidly to resolve the immediate issue between Philip the Fair and Boniface in favor of the French monarch. And the manuscript tradition exhibits no rapid or widespread diffusion of the work. The two major early-fourteenth-century treatments of the problem of church-state relations, Dante's *De monarchia* [41] and Marsilius of Padua's *Defensor pacis,* take other lines of approach and offer formulations of view quite different from those found in John's work. Even John's name does not appear in the edited catalogues of medieval library listings of fourteenth-century authors of political treatises, although contemporaries such as Aegidius of Rome, James of Viterbo, Augustinus Triumphus, and Alvare Pela do figure there.

Nevertheless, some traces of his influence can be seen early in the fourteenth century. Speaking on the king's behalf at a gathering of French nobles and ecclesiastics brought together by Philip of Valois in 1329 to resolve jurisdictional problems between church and state, Peter of Cuignières employed the doctrine of the two distinct powers in a fashion that clearly shows the influence of Quidort's thinking.[42] The first explicit reference found to John as an authority on political theory is in Alberic of Rosata's commentary (*c.* 1340) on the Justinian Code.[43] Alberic refers to Quidort as an authority on civil law and cites long passages from his treatise, applying John's views on the monarchy to the imperial authority. John is cited also by the Dominican, Peter of Palud (†1342) in his *Commentary on the Second Book of the Sentences.*[44] Further, Quidort's arguments on papal deposition and a king's right to intervene in such a matter are reproduced by another Dominican, Guillaume de Peyse de Goden (†1326). William of Ockham and Raoul of Presle [45] also assert views that are close to some of John's positions, but without any attribution to John.

It is clear, then, that John's views were known and used in the fourteenth century, although for the most part he was cited anonymously and on particular questions and issues rather than in terms of his overall doctrine. In this period it seems that neither his followers nor his opponents had recognized the overall significance of his middle position between the papalists and the royalists.

Fifteenth-century discussions on the issue of the relations between pope and general church council occasioned by the Great Schism saw further employment of some of John's views. Nicholas of Clamanges used without attribution ideas on the origin of ecclesiastical property taken from John's *De potestate* in the beginning of his *De ruina et de reparatione ecclesiae (1400)*; and Pierre d'Ailz in his *De ecclesiae auctoritate* (1416) quoted at length from the Prologue and chapters 6, 7, 13, and 19 of John's treatise.[46] In fact, Peter argued for a resolution of the schism scandal on grounds taken directly from John, using Quidort's views on the superiority of a general council over the papacy as a foundation for his own conciliarist position. John Gerson followed the same approach with no explicit reference to John of Paris, developing John's views in a highly personal fashion.[47] Dependence on Quidort can be seen also in the writings of two other conciliarists, Jacques du Paradis and Denis de Chartreux.[48]

John's doctrine on clerical and lay property and on the right of clergy to levy tithes was repeated anonymously by Cardinal Turrecremata (†1468), in his *Summa de ecclesia,* and by the Franciscan J. A. Delfino.[49] It was not until the Gallican controversies of the sixteenth century, however, that John's views on the integrity of political authority came to be cited in detail and by direct attribution. Jacques Almain (†1515) reproduced long sections of the *De potestate* on the nature of ecclesiastical power and the kingship of Christ and mentioned John by name, as did Jean Lemaire (†1550).[50]

Robert Bellarmine made explicit reference to the *De potestate regia et papali* in his *De romano pontifice* (1536), and classified John as one of the proponents of the theory of "indirect power." He described this group of theologians as holding "sententia media et catholicorum theologorum communis," [51] as did other writers of this period. While there is some question about whether Bellarmine knew Quidort from a direct reading of the *De potestate,* and even more question about the significance he attributed to John's views, there is no doubt that Bellarmine's reference to John's position gave impetus to its being referred to by other writers of the period: Aubert de Mire, Oudin, P. Lelond, Boulay, Victoria, Molina.[52]

The polemics occasioned by the late-sixteenth-century religious wars saw even more attention given to John's views by French Catholic theologians, who found in him a fellow countryman who was at once orthodox and capable of strong Gallican interpretations. Jacques de la Guesle, a member of the royal council of state, publicly referred to John of Paris as an authority for the "two powers" doctrine in a speech given before the Faculty of Theology of the University of Paris.[53] Similarly, Cardinal Du Perron gave public homage to John in a speech to the Third Estate on the occasion of the coronation of Louis XIII.[54] Jean Savaion [55] and Rodolphe Boteius [56] were others who invoked the authority of John of Paris in defense of the French monarchy's independence from papal authority. Throughout the seventeenth century, in fact, the controversy over the theory of "indirect power" was a major item of contention among French theologians; and, ironically, John found himself appealed to by both sides in the continuing dispute. The Gallican writers, for the most part, tended to invoke Quidort directly as a supporter of their position. Bossuet, for example, summarized with approval the main theses of John's position, and he expressed admiration for theologians of earlier centuries who had been able to maintain freedom of judgment even in times of turmoil.[57] The papalists of the day, however, such as the author of the anonymous treatise *Cathediae apostolicae oecumenicae auctoritas*,[58] Schelstratz,[59] and Father Pena,[60] invoked Quidort's authority on their own behalf. This was possible only because John's treatise was in itself little known at the time, and accessible largely through intermediaries. In fact Fr. Pena, who admitted to knowing Quidort only through Alberic of Rosate, criticized John for denying the kingship of Christ, and others [61] simply identified John's doctrine with those of Gerson and Ockham.

By the eighteenth century John's doctrine was becoming progressively less well known, and progressively more subject to distortion, and it has only been very recently that the kind of careful research necessary for the task has succeeded in rehabilitating him, and giving him the place he deserves in the history of medieval political theory.[62]

John of Paris
on
Royal and Papal Power

On Kingly and Papal Power

Prologue

IT HAPPENS SOMETIMES that a person wishing to avoid a certain error falls into its opposite. Thus, as we read in Gratian's *Decretum 16, 1,* some maintain that because monks are "dead" to the world, they cannot give penances and spread Christianity, since this is inconsistent with their state as monks. Others,[1] wishing to avoid error or to oppose it strongly, have said that by reason of their having chosen a state of perfection monks ought to hear confessions, give absolution, and impose salutary penances. Sound doctrine is midway between these two errors, and holds that this power is neither improper to monks, nor does it belong to them by virtue of their state. Rather, it can pertain to them if it is committed to them by their ordinaries, to whom this power does belong by right. Similarly, the book *On the two natures and one person of Christ* shows that faith holds the middle position between the two errors of Nestorius and Eutyches.[2]

So, too, the truth about the power of ecclesiastical pontiffs holds a middle position between two errors. For the error of the Waldensians [3] was to deny dominion over temporal things to the successors of the apostles, that is, to the pope and ecclesiastical prelates, and to forbid them to possess temporal wealth. Accordingly, they maintain that the Church of God, the successors of the apostles, and the true prelates of the Church continued only up to the reign of Sylvester. They hold that the Roman Church began afterwards, as a result of the donation made to the Church by the

Emperor Constantine.⁴ And according to them this is not the Church of God. They claim that the Church of God has already failed except insofar as it is continued in them, or has reappeared through them. To substantiate their view they point to such texts as the following: Matthew 6: "Do not store up for yourselves any treasure on earth"; ⁵ Epistle to Timothy 6: "Having food and clothing, we are content," and "Those who wish to become rich, etc."; ⁶ Matthew 6: "You cannot serve God and mammon"; ⁷ Matthew 6: "Be not solicitous for your soul what you shall eat, nor for your body, etc."; ⁸ Matthew 6: "Notice the birds of the air: they do not sow, neither do they reap"; ⁹ Matthew 10, where Christ said to His disciples: "Do not possess gold or silver or money"; ¹⁰ Luke 14: "Unless a man renounce all his possessions, etc."; ¹¹ and Acts 3: "Gold and silver I have none, etc." ¹² They employ these texts in asserting that the prelates of God's Church, the successors of the apostles, ought not to have dominion over temporal wealth.

The other error was that of Herod who, hearing that Christ was born king, believed He was an earthly king.¹³ The opinion of certain modern thinkers ¹⁴ seems to be derived from this. They react against the abovementioned error by going to the completely opposite extreme, and claim that the lord pope, inasmuch as he stands in the place of Christ ¹⁵ on earth, has dominion, cognizance, and jurisdiction over the temporal goods of princes and barons. They also assert that the pope has this power over temporal things more excellently than a prince, because the pope has it by primary authority and immediately from God, while the prince has it mediately from God through the pope. They maintain further that, unlike the prince, the pope does not have immediate execution of this power, except in certain cases noted in *Extra, Qui filii sunt legitimi, per venerabilem.*¹⁶ These men, then, who otherwise have spoken against princes, speak in their favor on this point. Further, if the pope sometimes asserts that he does not have temporal jurisdiction, they maintain that this is to be understood with respect to regular and immediate execution, or because the pope wishes to preserve peace between princes and the Church, or so that prelates not be excessively prone to intrude themselves into matters concerning temporal goods and secular affairs. They say too that the pope has a different relationship to temporal goods than do princes and prelates, because he alone is the only true lord, such that if he wishes he can absolve a usurer from any obligation due to usury, and can take for his own use what otherwise belongs to someone else. And the action of a pope holds, even though he sins and should not act in this way except for a reasonable cause such as the defense of the Church or some such thing. Other prelates and princes, however, are not lords but custodians, procurers, and dispensers.

This opinion concerning dominion over things does not arise solely from the error of Herod, but seems also to infer the error of Vigilantius.[17] For everyone holds, and indeed it must be held, that nothing pertaining to evangelical perfection is repugnant to the lord pope by reason of his state. It is evident, moreover, that if the pope is lord of all things by virtue of his state inasmuch as he is pope and vicar of Christ, renunciation of ownership and rejection of dominion over temporal things is repugnant to him by reason of his state, since the very opposite belongs to him naturally; and therefore, poverty and lack of dominion over external things are not of evangelical perfection. This latter position, however, was what Vigilantius asserted, about whom Augustine stated in the work *On Christian Combat* that there are those who, though Catholics, strive for their own possessions, or who seek for glory from Christ's name itself as heretics, one of whom was Vigilantius, who arose a long time ago in Gaul, which formerly lacked the monstrosities of errors.[18] He presumed to equate the state of poverty with that of wealth, just as long ago in Italy Jovinian [19] seems to have preferred marriage to chastity. And this opinion has something in it of the pride of the Pharisees, who maintained that the people were not bound to pay tax to Caesar on tenths and on the sacrifices they offered to God, asserting such a position so that they might receive larger shares from these richer holdings, as Jerome says.[20] This opinion also seems dangerous because it would imply for persons converting to the faith that they transfer dominion over things they previously possessed to the supreme pontiff. In such a situation the faith of these persons is less freely given, and their faith is disparaged when the rights of possession are disturbed by it, as the Gloss on I Peter: 2 asserts.[21] One ought also to be apprehensive about this view for fear that Christ, stern and angry, would enter while business dealings were being conducted in the Lord's house, and would cleanse His temple even by the use of a whip, transforming it from a den of thieves into a house of prayer, as Chrysostom says [in his commentary] on Matthew.[22]

This is why I consider the truth to be midway between these two such contrary opinions. Everyone recognizes the first of them to be an error, insofar as it is not repugnant for prelates of the Church to have dominion and jurisdiction over temporal things,[23] a point contrary to the first erroneous opinion. Neither, however, does dominion over temporal things belong to prelates by reason of their state and by reason of their being vicars of Christ and successors of the apostles. But it can pertain to them to have such powers as a concession from or with the permission of princes, if something of this kind was conferred by princes out of devotion, or if church prelates possessed it from some other source.

I now declare that I intend to say nothing in any of my statements contrary to faith, good morals, or sound doctrine, or against reverence for the person or state of the supreme pontiff. And if anything of this sort does occur either principally or incidentally in what I have said or will say, I wish it to be held as not having been said. And I wish this disclaimer to hold and be valid as if I were to repeat it individually with respect to each statement that will be made.[24]

The procedure for handling the subject set down for examination will be as follows: chapter 1 will define kingly power, and show from what it has arisen; chapter 2 will do the same thing for priesthood; chapter 3 will deal with the order of ministers as they relate to one supreme minister, and will show that it is not as necessary for all princes to be subordinated to one as for ministers of the Church to be subordinated to one supreme authority; chapter 4 will show whether kingship or priesthood is prior in time; chapter 5 will show which of them is prior to the other in dignity; chapter 6 will show that the priesthood is not prior in causality, and it will show first the pope's relationship to external ecclesiastical goods with respect to dominion; chapter 7 will show the pope's relationship to the goods of laymen; chapter 8 will show that the pope does not have jurisdiction over laymen's goods from Christ, because Christ Himself did not have it; chapter 9 will pose arguments to the contrary, namely, that Christ has this power, and will offer replies to these arguments; chapter 10 will grant that Christ has this power, but show that He did not give it to Peter; chapter 11 will present contrary arguments of those who say that the pope has jurisdiction over temporal external goods; chapter 12 will present preliminary remarks for a resolution of these arguments, and material to show what authority over temporal goods the pope has from Christ, and in the first instance will describe the authority given by Christ to Peter and the apostles; chapter 13 will show that, according to this authority, ecclesiastical prelates do not have dominion or jurisdiction over temporal things, and that princes are not, because of this authority, subject to ecclesiastical prelates in temporal matters; chapter 14 will offer replies to the first six of the arguments given [in chapter 11]; chapter 15 will offer replies to the second six [arguments 7–12]; chapter 16 will offer replies to the third six [arguments 13–18]; chapter 17 to the fourth six [arguments 19–24]; chapter 18 to the fifth six [arguments 25–30]; chapter 19 to the sixth six [arguments 31–36]; chapter 20 to the seventh six [arguments 37–42]; chapter 21 will examine first the Donation of Constantine, and will show what powers the pope has through it; chapter 22 will show whether it is licit to dispute with and judge the pope concerning temporal matters; chapter 23 will develop the frivolous arguments of those who say that the pope cannot resign; chapter 24 will show that he can resign; chapter 25 will resolve the previous arguments [of chapter 23].

Chapter 1
What Kingly Rule Is, and from What It Has Arisen

CONCERNING THE FIRST TOPIC, it should be known that king-ship [1] properly understood can be defined as rule over a community perfectly ordered to the common good by one person.[2] "Rule" in this definition is taken as the genus; "over a community" is added to "rule" to differentiate it from that by which someone governs himself, whether this latter be by natural instinct, as in the case of brutes, or by reason, as in the case of those who lead a solitary life. "Perfectly" is added to differentiate community from a family group, which is not perfect because it is only sufficient for itself for a short while and not for a whole lifetime; and according to the Philosopher in *Politics 1*, the state is sufficient.[3] "Ordered for the good of the community" is put in the definition to differentiate king-ship from oligarchy, tyranny, and democracy.[4] In these, and particularly in a tyranny, the ruler intends only his own good. "By one" is meant to differentiate kingship from aristocracy, that is, preeminence of the best persons or aristocrats, where a few men rule according to virtue. Accordingly, some define aristocracy as rule according to the direction of prudent men or the decisions of a senate. "By one" also differentiates kingship from polity, where the people are ruled by popular ordinances.[5] For there is no king unless he alone is the ruler, as the Lord says through Ezekiel: "My servant David will be over all, and there will be one shepherd over all of them." [6]

This kind of power derives from the natural law, and from

the law of nations. For man is naturally a political or civil animal, as is said in the *Politics 1*,[7] and according to the Philosopher, this is shown by reference to food, clothing, and defense, in respect of which one person alone is not self-sufficient, and from speech, which is directed to another.[8] Therefore, it is necessary for man to live in a community, and in a kind of community self-sufficient for life. A household or village community is not sufficient for this, while that of the state or kingdom [9] is. For all the things needed for food, clothing, and defense and for a full life are not found in the household alone or in the village, while they are found in the state or kingdom. Moreover, every community is scattered when each individual person seeks his own interests, and it is dispersed into different paths unless directed to the common good by some one person whose task it is to be concerned with the common good, just as a man's body decays unless there is some common power in the body directing it to the common good of all its members.[10] Accordingly, Solomon wrote in Proverbs: "Where there is no ruler, the people will be dispersed." [11] This is the more necessary because what is proper to one man is not identical with what is common to all. Men differ according to what is proper; they are united in respect of what is common. Besides, different things have different causes. Therefore, in addition to what promotes the good proper to any individual, there must be something to promote the good common to many.

Moreover, rule over a community by a single person preeminent in virtue is more useful than rule either by many or by several persons who are virtuous. This follows on the one hand from the nature of power, for virtue is more unified and therefore greater when vested in one man than when dispersed among several.[12] It also follows in respect of what should be the purpose in ruling a community—unity and peace, which exist only when people are united and in concord.[13] Wherefore, if there were any such person possessed of these qualities and possessed of them in a superior way, such a single person exercising leadership through virtue would be the better able to keep the peace, and the peace of the citizens would not be disturbed so easily. It follows further because a single leader intending the common good has an eye for what is more common than would be the case if several persons were also to exercise authority according to virtue. For the more persons who are withdrawn from the multitude the less common is what remains, and the fewer who are withdrawn the more common is what remains. This is why the Philosopher said that the tyrant is the worst among those rulers who seek their own good; for he seeks his own good more, and has greater scorn for the common good.[14] The point follows again, because in a natural government we see the whole authority reduced to a single thing, as one element dominates in a mixed body: in the heterogeneous human body there is one principal member in the whole man, and the soul keeps all the elements together.[15] Even gregarious animals, for which it is natural to live in society, are subject to one king.[16]

From the foregoing it follows that it is necessary and useful for man to live in a community, and above all in a community which can be sufficient for the whole of life, as a state or kingdom is, and particularly that he live under one man called a king, who rules for the sake of the common good. It follows also that this rule is derived from the natural law, from the fact, namely, that man is naturally a civil or political and social animal, inasmuch as before Belus and Ninus, the first men to exercise political authority, men lived unnaturally without rule, not living as men but in the manner of beasts. Orosius describes some men as having lived in this fashion in the first chapter of his book *Against the Pagans*.[17] Tullius also mentioned similar things in the beginning of the *Old Rhetoric*.[18] And in the *Politics* the Philosopher says of such men that they do not live as men but as gods or beasts.[19] Since men of this type could not by common words be called back from the life of beasts to a community life that has been seen to be naturally suited to them, men who were better able to use reason and who had compassion on those who had gone wrong tried by reasoned persuasion to call them back to a common life ordered under some one person, as Tullius says.[20] And when these people had been brought back, they were constrained to live in communities by specific laws. These are the laws which can be called here the law of nations.[21] So it follows that this kind of rule is derived from the natural law and the law of nations.

Chapter 2
What the Priesthood Is,
and from What It Has Arisen

IN ADDITION we must consider that man is not ordered solely to the kind of good which can be acquired through nature, that is, to live according to virtue; [1] he is ordered further to a supernatural end, which is eternal life.[2] In fact, the whole community of men living according to virtue is ordered to this end.[3] Consequently, it is necessary that there be some one person to direct the community to this end. And if indeed this end could be achieved through the power of human nature, it would be necessary that it pertain to the office of a human king to direct men to this end; for we call a "human king" that man to whom is committed ultimate responsibility for direction of human affairs. But because man is not brought to eternal life by human but by divine power—as the Apostle wrote to the Romans: "Eternal life is a gift of God" [4]—it does not belong to a human king but to a divine king [5] to lead men to that end.

Rule of this type, therefore, pertains to a king who is not only man but also God, namely, to Jesus Christ, Who brought men to eternal life making them the sons of God. This is why He is called king, as Jeremiah says: "A king shall reign, and he shall be wise." [6] Moreover, this position is entrusted to Him by God the Father, and it is not to be destroyed. And because it is a king's responsibility to remove obstacles to the attaining of an end, and to provide remedies and aids for reaching it, in offering Himself on the cross to God the Father as both priest and sacrifice, Christ removed by His death the universal obstacle, the obstacle, namely, of the offence against God the Father rooted in the common sin of the human race. This is why, in Hebrews 5, He is said to be a true priest standing in the place of men.[7]

It is true also that insofar as a universal cause must be joined to particular effects, particular remedies had to be provided through which the general benefit might be transmitted to us in some way. These particular remedies are the sacraments of the Church, in which the spiritual power of Christ's passion is contained as the agent's power is contained in an instrument.[8] And therefore it was fitting that these sensible things be established, to provide for man according to his condition, which is to be led through sensible things to the possession of spiritual and intelligible realities, as we are told in Romans 1: "The invisible things of God through which they were done, etc.",[9] and that those instruments be proportionate to the Word Incarnate, whose power as principal agent they contain, just as they contain spiritual power under sensible signs.

Moreover, because the physical presence of Christ was withdrawn from His Church, it was necessary for Him to appoint ministers to dispense the sacraments to men. These men are called priests because they are givers of sacred things, or sacred leaders or teachers of sacred things, in all of which functions they mediate between God and men.[10]

Moreover, these ministers had to be men, not angels, possessing spiritual power conferred on them, as the Apostle says: "Every pontiff is taken from among men to serve men, etc.",[11] so that the ministers might be appropriate in respect to both the instrument, in which spiritual power is present under a sensible element, and the principal cause of man's salvation, the Word Incarnate, Who achieves our salvation through His own power and authority inasmuch as He is both God and man.

From what has been said, priesthood can be defined as the spiritual power given by Christ to ministers of the Church for dispensing the sacraments to the faithful.[12]

Chapter 3

Concerning the Order of Ministers to One Supreme Minister, and the Position That It Is not as Necessary for All Princes to Be Subordinated to One Prince as for Ministers of the Church to Be Subordinated to One Supreme Minister

FURTHER, as the Apostle said in the last verse of II Corinthians,[1] because this power was given to the Church for its establishment, it must endure in the Church as long as the Church has need of establishment—that is, until the end of the world. Hence, in the first instance power was given to Christ's disciples, so that through them it might be passed to others, among whom there must always be some higher and perfect ministers whose function it is to confer the priesthood on others through ordination and consecration. These higher ministers are the superintending bishops. And although they do not surpass simple priests in respect of their power of consecrating the true body of Christ, they do surpass them in matters pertaining to jurisdiction over the faithful.[2] For bishops are great and perfect priests inasmuch as they can make other men priests, something simple and lesser priests cannot do. In fact, some matters of difficulty in the care of the faithful are reserved for the action of bishops, by whose authority also priests have the power to perform the tasks committed to them. And in matters where priests act on their own, they employ things consecrated by a bishop: for example, a chalice, an altar, and altar clothes, as Dionysius said in *On Ecclesiastical Hierarchy,* in the chapter on priestly perfections.[3]

It is clear, however, that although people are separated into different dioceses and cities over which bishops preside in spiritual matters, there is still one Church for all the faithful, and one Christian people. Therefore, just as in every diocese there is one bishop, who is the head of the Church for the people in that diocese, so there is one person supreme in the whole Church and for the whole Christian people. He is the Roman pope, the successor of Peter. The Church Militant[4] is thus patterned in the likeness of the Church Triumphant,[5] in which one person rules over the entire universe. Wherefore Revelation 21 reads "And they shall be His people, and God Himself will be their God for them";[6] Hosea 1 reads "The sons of Judah and the sons of Israel shall be brought together equally, and they shall appoint one head for themselves."[7] Whence, too, in John 10 we read: "There shall be one flock and one shepherd,"[8] which cannot be understood to refer only to Christ, but also to the single minister who presides over all in His place. For after the physical withdrawal of Christ's corporeal presence questions concerning matters relating to the faith do sometimes arise. And the Church, which needs unity of faith for its own unity, might be divided by differing opinions about such matters unless its unity were preserved through the judgment of one man. The one person having authority in this respect is Peter or his successor. And he does not have this power through synodal ordination, but from the mouth of the Lord,[9] Who did not wish His Church to lack whatever was necessary to it. In the last chapter of John, He said specifically to Peter before His ascension: "Feed my sheep";[10] and in Luke 22, before His passion we read: "And do you, when once you have turned again, strengthen your brethren."[11]

This subordination to one supreme authority is found more frequently among ministers of the Church than among secular princes, because ecclesiastical ministers are particularly designated by God as a special kind of person responsible for divine worship. Consequently, the subordination of divine ministers to one minister is by divine ordinance.[12] But it is not the case that the faithful laity are by divine law subservient to one supreme monarch in temporal matters. Rather, they live civilly and in community according to the prompting of a natural inclination which is from God. Accordingly, they choose different types of rulers to oversee the well-being of their communities to correspond with the diversity of these communities. Moreover, the notion that all persons are subject in temporal matters to one supreme authority derives neither from natural inclination nor from divine law; nor is it as suitable in this area as in the case of ecclesiastical ministers.

This is so in the first instance because, just as there is a diversity among men in respect to their bodies but not their souls, all of which latter are constituted of essentially the same type because of the unity of the human species, so too secular power has more diversity in respect to differences of climate and conditions [13] than spiritual power, which varies less in respect of such things. Consequently, it is not necessary that there be as much variation in the latter as in the former.

Secondly, one man alone is not enough to rule the entire world in temporal matters, although one man is adequate to rule in spiritual matters. For spiritual power can easily exercise its censure, which is verbal, on all persons near and far; but the secular power cannot so easily apply its sword, which is manual,[14] to persons who are distant. It is easier to extend a word than a hand.

Thirdly, the temporal goods of laymen do not belong to the community, as will be shown below, but to whoever is master of his own property by virtue of having acquired it through his own efforts.[15] Therefore, temporal goods of the laity do not need a common dispenser; for the person to whom property belongs is its dispenser as he pleases. Ecclesiastical goods, however, belong to the community. Hence, there must be some one person to preside over the community as common dispenser and common disposer of the goods belonging to all. And there is no more need for a single person to have disposition over the temporal goods of the clergy than there is need for such a person to handle the temporal goods of the laity.

Fourthly, all believers are united in the one Catholic faith, without which there is no salvation. Nevertheless, it happens sometimes that questions arise concerning what pertains to faith in different regions and kingdoms. Accordingly, in order to prevent the unity of the faith being disrupted by a variety of controversies one person, as already noted,[16] must be supreme in spiritual matters, through whose pronouncements controversies of this type will be ended. But this purpose does not require that the faithful be united in any common state. There can be different ways of living and different kinds of state conforming to differences in climate, language, and the conditions of men, with what is suitable for one nation not so for another. The Philosopher makes the same point about individuals in *Ethics* 2, where he says that something is too little for one person and too much for another; [17] just as, for example, the consumption of ten minas or ounces would be too much for a beginner in athletic exercises but too little for Milo of Croton, who used to fell a bull with one blow, as the Commentator says.[18]

Therefore, it is not as necessary for the world to be ruled by one man in respect of temporal matters, as it is necessary for it to be ruled by one man in respect of spiritual matters. In addition it is not so set down in either natural or divine law. Accordingly, the Philosopher shows in the *Politics* that development of individual states and kingdoms is natural,[19] although that of an empire or a monarchy is not. Augustine, too, states in the *City of God* 4, that the state is better and more peacefully ruled when the rule of any one man extends only to the limits of his own territory.[20] He also states that a cause for the expansion of the Roman Empire was its own ambition to dominate, or its provoking foreign states to act unjustly.[21] Accordingly, the natural law does not prescribe that there be one monarch in respect of temporal things as there is in respect of spiritual things. The statement in the *Decretum* 7. 1, "In apibus," [22] to the effect that one and not several ought to rule, is not contrary to this position. That statement indicates that there is no advantage from several persons exercising authority in such a way that their respective powers are not delineated, and as an illustration it cites the case of Remus and Romulus, who ruled together without their powers being distinguished, the result of which was that one of them killed his brother. The same point is also made there through other examples.

Chapter 4

Whether Kingship or Priesthood
Is Prior in Time

NOW WE must see whether kingship or priesthood was prior in time.[1] To determine this it is necessary to know the proper meaning of kingship. The term designates control not only over a household or district but also over a state, in which is found the greatest sufficiency of the things pertaining to a complete life. If we speak of priesthood properly understood, kingship existed before priesthood. For, as Augustine says in the *City of God* 16. 17, the first kingdom was that of the Assyrians, which began before the Law was given.[2] Belus was the first ruler in Assyria, and he ruled for sixty-five years. And after his death his son, Ninus,[3] extended his rule throughout the whole of Greater Assyria, except for India. Ninus ruled for sixty-six years, and had ruled for forty-three years when Abraham was born. This was about 1,200 years before the founding of Rome. The kingdom of the Sicyonians began in Africa concurrently with that of the Assyrians. In the beginning it was not very large; its first king was Egyaclus, and his son was Europs. At this time the king of Salem, whom the Hebrews called the son of Shem, himself the son of Noah, ruled over the followers of the true God; and he is said to have lived until the time of Isaac.[4]

During this period, moreover, even as they had for a long time previously, true kings existed; but there was as yet no true priesthood. And there was no such thing until Jesus Christ came as mediator between God and men.[5] This is true in that, even though there were persons among the Gentiles called priests, they were not true priests because they did not offer true sacrifices; neither did they offer sacrifices to the true God, but to something thought to be the true God, as Deuteronomy 32 says: "They sacrificed to demons and not to God." [6]

Even though some persons from the Levitical tribe were called priests under the Law of God's people, they still were not true priests but symbols of true priests; their sacrifices were only symbolic, and their sacraments were not true sacraments but only symbolic ones, insofar as they did not cleanse from sin and did not open heaven. Rather, they served as symbols in cleansing certain irregularities and opening a man-made temple, through which was prefigured the opening by Jesus Christ of the temple not made by man. Nor did they promise spiritual things except under the species of temporal things, as the Apostle says to the Hebrews: "The light of future benefits remained in shadow." [7]

Certainly before the Law there was Melchisedech,[8] who was a priest of the most high God, and his priesthood was more perfect and more excellent than the Levitical priesthood. But even this was only a symbolic and not a true priesthood, for he was more perfect because he represented the priesthood of Christ in respect of that in which the priesthood of Christ excelled the priesthood of Aaron. Aaron's priesthood was deficient as a symbol of Christ's priesthood in the matter of uninterrupted continuation, because it is not written in Scripture that Melchisedech had a beginning or an end, just as Christ had neither. There are also many other matters mentioned by the Apostle in the *Epistle to the Hebrews* [9] on which Melchisedech excelled Aaron. Nevertheless, his priesthood was still only symbolic and not a true priesthood, just as the Levitical priesthood was not a true one. Accepting, therefore, the meaning of a true priesthood, there was no priesthood until the coming of Jesus Christ as mediator between God and men; and He made us participators and vicars of this priesthood.

Therefore, since before the birth of Christ kings were found among the Assyrians, the Sicyonians, the Egyptians, and others as far back as the time of Abraham—which according to Methodius [10] means for some two thousand years before Christ, and according to other authorities approximately this long—it follows that there were true kings for a long period of time before there was a true priest-hood: kings whose office was to care for the necessities of human civil life. These men were indeed true kings, even though those who were anointed in this respect symbolized Christ in His relationship to God's people.[11]

It must be noted, however, that if priesthood is taken broadly and improperly such that a legal priest or any other person who was a priest symbolically or was thought to be one is called priest, then priesthood and kingship arose and fell concurrently. For Melchise-dech was simultaneously king of Salem and priest of the most high God among the worshippers of God; and according to the Jews and the learned author of the *History*,[12] the priesthood was continued through his heirs down to the time of Aaron. Moreover, according to the Jews, Melchisedech begot Arphat two years after the Flood, and from this time until the seventieth year of Abraham's life, when the first promise was made to him, as we read in Genesis 12,[13] there were 370 years on a literal reading or, according to some, 430. Now for others the first kingdom was quite simply that of the Assyrians, as has been said, and its first king was Belus. His son, Ninus, succeeded to the kingship when the father died, and he constructed the idol called Baal, from which the idols of the other territories take their names, such as Beelphegor, Beelzebuth and such names; and Ninus established priests or priestly officials through whom sacrifices were offered to the idol. It follows clearly from what has been said that true kingship was concurrent with the priesthood as it is understood in this latter sense—namely, as a symbolic priesthoood or as what was thought to be priesthood—and that this priesthood had been in existence a long time before the true priesthood.

Chapter 5
Whether Kingship or Priesthood Is Prior in Dignity

FROM THE foregoing it can be proven easily whether kingship or priesthood is prior in dignity.[1] For what is later in time is usually prior in dignity, what is perfect is prior to what is imperfect, and the end is prior to what relates to the end.[2] Therefore, we say that priestly power is greater than kingly power, and excels it in dignity; for we always find that that to which the ultimate end pertains is more perfect, and directs that to which a lesser end pertains. Kingship, however, is ordered to the end that a community be brought together and live together according to virtue, as has been said [chapter 2]. And this in turn is further ordered to a higher end, the enjoyment of God, the direction of which was entrusted to Christ, of Whom priests are the vicars and ministers. Therefore, priestly power is of greater dignity than secular power.

This is commonly conceded: *Decretum* 96, "Duo quippe sunt": "By as much as gold is more precious than lead is the priestly order higher than kingly power."[3] And in *Extra, De majoritate et obedientia*, in the chapter "Solite" it is asserted that just as spiritual things are to be preferred to temporal things, and the sun to the moon,[4] in the same way, etc. Hugh of St. Victor stated in On the Sacraments 2. 4: "By as much as spiritual life is more worthy than earthly life, and the spirit more worthy than the body, is spiritual power more excellent in honor and dignity than secular or earthly."[5] And Bernard wrote to Pope Eugene, Book I: "Which seems to you to have the greater dignity, the power of remitting sin or of dividing estates? There is no comparison." [6] This is the same as saying that spiritual power is greater; hence it excels the other in dignity.

However, if the priest is greater than the prince in dignity and absolutely, it is not necessary for him to be superior in all things; [7] for the latter secular power does not relate to the higher spiritual power in such a way that it arises or derives from it. [8] This is how the power of the proconsul relates to the power of the emperor; and the latter is greater in all things because the proconsul's power is derived from the emperor. The relationship, rather, is like that between the power of the head of a family and that of a master of soldiers; one is not derived from the other, but both are derived from some superior power. Therefore, secular power is greater than spiritual power in some things, namely, temporal things; and it is not subject to the spiritual power with reference to them in any way, because secular power does not arise from spiritual power. The two arise directly from a single supreme power: the divine power. [9] Wherefore the inferior is not subject to the superior in all things, but only in those things in respect of which the supreme power made it subordinate to the superior. [10] For who would say that, because a teacher of literature or an instructor in morals orders everyone in a household to a more noble end, namely, to the knowledge of truth, a physician who is concerned with a lesser end, the health of the body, is therefore subject to either of these in the preparation of his medicines? This simply does not follow, since the head of the household, who appointed both to his household, would not for that reason subordinate the physician to one who has a higher purpose. Hence, the priest is superior principally in spiritual matters; and, conversely, the prince is superior in temporal matters, although the priest is superior absolutely insofar as the spiritual is superior to the temporal.

Examples from previously mentioned authorities show this too. For lead does not come from gold as its cause, even though gold is more precious than lead. The same point also is stated expressly in [*Decretum,*] 2. 7, "Nos si incompetenter, Cum David." [11] Nevertheless, it must be understood that what has been said applies to the true priesthood of Christ. [12] For the priesthood of the Gentiles and the entirety of their divine cult were directed to temporal goods ordered to the common good of the multitude, whose care is the responsibility of the king. Accordingly, the priests of the Gentiles were subordinate to kings, and kingship was superior to the priesthood, in the same way as the power whose concern is for the common good is greater and superior to the power whose concern is only for a particular good. Similarly, the priesthood of the Old Law promised only temporal goods immediately, even though these were to be provided for the people by the true God and not by demons. Consequently, the priesthood of the Old Law was also lower in dignity than kingly power, and was subject to it; for the king was not directed by the priest to anything higher than the good of the community, whose care fell to his own charge. The opposite, however, is the case in the New Law.

One must consider, then, how marvellously Divine Providence functioned in the case of Rome, a city God chose to be the principal seat of the Christian priesthood. The custom grew there gradually of the rulers of the city voluntarily submitting themselves to priests more so than in other localities. This occurred even though there was no obligation in justice for the leaders to do this, since absolutely they were greater than priests. They did it as a sign of the excellence of the future priesthood, to whom a greater excellence was to be granted. Valerian says: "Our state always placed all things after religion, even those things in which the honor of the highest majesty wished to show itself. Wherefore the rulers did not hesitate to subordinate civil matters to sacred ones, considering that if they served the divine power well and faithfully, they would retain charge over human affairs." [13] Because it would also happen that in France [14] as in many other places the religion of the Christian priesthood would flourish, it was divinely ordained that there also be priests among the Gallic peoples. They were called druids, and were found throughout the whole of Gaul, as Julius Caesar wrote in his book *On the Gallic War*.[15] Therefore, Christ's priesthood has greater dignity than kingly power.

Chapter 6

That the Priesthood Is not Prior in Causality,[1] and How the Pope Relates to External Ecclesiastical Goods[2] in Terms of Dominion[3]

NOW BECAUSE some wish to raise the excellence of the priesthood above the kingly rank in order to assert that the priesthood is superior not only in dignity, as has been said [chapter 3], but also in causality,[4] and to assert that secular power is contained within priestly power and is constituted from it, it remains to be seen whether the pope, who holds the highest place among the priests of Christ, does or does not possess this power. Wherefore, first it will be shown how the pope relates to external goods in terms of dominion over things; and secondly, granted that he is not a true lord over external goods but a dispenser of them absolutely or as circumstances warrant, it will be shown how in fact he possesses basic and primary authority as superior, and as a person exercising jurisdiction.

Regarding the first of these points, it must be seen initially how the pope relates to the goods of ecclesiastical persons insofar as they are ecclesiastics. Here it must be understood that ecclesiastical goods, as ecclesiastical, are used for communities and not for individual persons. Therefore, no individual person has property rights and dominion over them; but the community alone, like the church at Chartres or of some such place, has dominion and property rights over such goods as belong properly to it.[5] Moreover, an individual person who has a right of use [6] over such things to sustain him according to his need and the decency of his person and status does not have this right as an individual but as a part and member of the community. Nevertheless, a differentiation is to be made here. For one man—for example, a simple canon—is a member as a simple member; and such an individual has only the right just described. Another man, however—for example, a bishop—is a member as principal member and as head of the community. For there would not be one congregation, nor would it be ordered, unless there were one head and principal member. This latter type of person has not only the use of community goods according to the needs of his status in the aforementioned manner, but also the administration and general dispensation of all the goods of the community. He appropriates what belongs to anyone from him, according to a proportional obligation in justice; [7] and he dispenses in good faith for the common good of the community what seems to him to further it. The bishop of any cathedral church is such a person.

This is true not only because any congregation of ecclesiastical men is one in a spiritual unity, but also because all ecclesiastical congregations have a certain general unity insofar as they are one Church, which is connected to a single principal member, the lord pope, to whom falls the charge of the general Church. As the head and supreme member of the universal Church, therefore, he is the universal dispenser [8] generally of all ecclesiastical goods, spiritual and temporal. He is not, however, lord [9] over them. Only the community of the universal Church is lord and proprietor over all goods generally, while communities and churches individually have dominion over the goods appropriate to them. Similarly, while principal members have only the power of dispensing, individual persons still do not have dominion, however this term is taken, except insofar as they produce their own fruits from their own efforts according to the demands of person and status. Or perhaps something might be appropriated to one or other of them by the universal dispenser so deciding and determining in good faith, according as the laws established by the pope distinguish four types of ecclesiastical goods in *Decretum* 12. 2.[10]

From what has been said, it appears to be wrong to assert that no individual other than the pope, no group or community, has right and dominion over the goods of the Church. To state that the pope alone has this power, since he is not only the universal administrator and dispenser, but also the true lord and proprietor of the goods of the Church, and that he can order them and distribute them as he pleases, and that he can retain this right even if he sins, unless he makes disposition of it for some sufficient cause, while other prelates and even princes and communities do not have dominion, but are only procurers, keepers, and dispensers of such goods would be false according to what has been said before. The pope is not the lord of all ecclesiastical goods generally, any more than lesser prelates are with respect to the goods of their own group. The pope, however, is the universal dispenser and disposer of goods, and he even makes his own, according to the requirements of his personal status, a richer portion of the fruits from common goods than lesser prelates, who are called to a share in solicitude and not to the plenitude of power.[11]

This is why, when speaking to Boniface about prelates, Augustine includes all of them generally when he says: "If we possess privately what is sufficient for us, these things are not ours; rather we see to the management of these things. Therefore, let us not by a damnable usurpation claim property rights for ourselves." [12] And the Apostle does not exclude Peter or the pope when he says in I Corinthians 4: "Let man see us thus as ministers of Christ and dispensers of God's mysteries." [13] And speaking of temporal goods, Bernard said to Pope Eugene, in book II: "Whatever the reason is for you to be engaged in buying and selling, it is not by apostolic right, since He could not give you what he did not possess. Silver and gold, He said, are not mine. What He had He gave, namely, care over the churches but not domination. Hear Him: Not as dominating, He said to the clergy, but as directing force over the gathered flock." [14] This is what Bernard held.

From this it is evident also that it is not repugnant for clerics as clerics or for monks as monks to have dominion over external goods at least in common, because their vows do not make them incapable of dominion in particular and in common, as is the case with some religious. Where the founders of churches directed that dominion and property rights over the goods they gave transfer firstly and directly to the community of a group, that is, to a given church, for the use of the servants of the Lord and not for the lord pope, it is clear that the community itself has immediate and true dominion over these goods, and neither pope nor any lesser prelate has it. For otherwise the mode of life of clerics would not differ with respect to this kind of exterior goods from the mode of life of the friars minor, who by their own peculiar vows are incapable of dominion over external goods in particular and in common. Friars minor have only the use of work, as Pope Nicholas says.[15] And to prevent the scattering and disordering of the goods collected for them, which are ecclesiastical goods insofar as they are conferred on ecclesiastical persons, the lord pope takes right and dominion over them to himself and to the Church. However, there is no mention that a different situation obtains with respect to external ecclesiastical goods for clergy and for certain types of religious. For Pope Nicholas also states in the same decretal that the monk in the monastery and the servant of the Lord acquire right and dominion in some manner.[16] Therefore, the pope alone is not lord, Rather, he is the general dispenser; and the bishop or abbot is a special and immediate dispenser, while the community has true dominion over goods.

Further, it cannot be said that the pope lacks right and dominion over such goods as a private person, but has them as a public person and vicar of Jesus Christ,[17] to Whom all such goods belong as principal lord, and to the pope as His vicar general. To say this proves nothing, because Christ as God is not lord only over ecclesiastical goods, but over all other goods as well. As man,[18] however, He does not have communication and corporeal conversation with persons who are in the Church. Nor do those who confer goods on the Church intend to transfer right and dominion to Christ either as God, because all things are His in this way, or as man, because He does not have to use those things now. Rather, they transfer right and dominion to Christ's ministers. Hence, these goods belong to the

Church by property right, and to prelates as dispensers, as has been said.[19]

From this it follows also that the pope cannot freely appropriate ecclesiastical goods in order to keep whatever he wishes. This would be true if he were God. But since he is the dispenser of the goods of a community, and good faith is required in such a role, the only power he possesses with respect to these goods relates to their being necessary or useful for the Church as a whole. Whence it is said in II Corinthians 13 and 10,[20] that God gave to prelates the power to build and not to destroy. Therefore, if he were to appropriate anything freely without having good faith, his action is not binding in law. And not only is he to be held then to punishment for sin as for an abuse of his own possessions, but he acts unfaithfully and is bound to restitution if he still possesses anything from his own inheritance or from what he has taken, since he would be defrauding with respect to things which do not belong to him.[21]

And just as even a monastery can act to depose an abbot, or a particular church can act to depose a bishop, if the abbot or bishop appears to be dissipating the goods of the monastery or the church and disposing of goods unfaithfully and for private and not for the common good, so too can a pope be deposed,[22] provided he has been admonished and does not make amends, if it appears that he is unfaithfully disposing of the goods of the Church for other than the common good which as the supreme bishop he is charged to maintain. Decretum 11, chapter "Si papa" states: "He who is the judge of all is to be judged by none, unless he be observed to be in error on a matter of faith." [23] On this the Gloss comments: "If he is observed to be at fault in any matter whatsoever, and does not act to correct himself when admonished to do so, and gives scandal to the Church, the same action can be taken." [24] Some argue, however, that this can be done only through a general council: Decretum 21, chapter, "Nunc autem." [25]

And if indeed the pope knows that some men, whether they be ecclesiastics or laymen, are protesting in possible and legitimate ways against him for an unwarranted dispensation, he cannot by rights remove them or take away what belongs to them in any fashion whatsoever, since he does not have authority from God for this kind of action. And those who claim that the pope's will is in such confusion commit an affront to heaven and do injury to the most holy pontiff, our father. For it should be assumed that the will of so great a father is not contrary to rights, and that he will not take what belongs to anyone from him without reasonable cause. For he cannot by rights act otherwise.[26] In fact God does not will to remove or to have removed from anyone what He has given him unless a sin intervenes; for as the Apostle says to the Romans: "The gifts of God are irrevocable." [27] It is because of men's sins that He also says: "I regret that I have made man." [28] It was on account of sin also that He made over the spoils of the Egyptians to the Hebrews.[29] However, He wishes to take nothing from the just man, or to have nothing taken from him: Job 36: "Judgment favors the poor, does not take his eyes from the just man, and places kings on their thrones for eternity." [30] Therefore, even though God gave the dispensation of goods to Peter or the pope in good faith and not contrary to the express will of God, the pope cannot lawfully take away the power of administration which a person has rightly and properly received, without there being a clear fault intervening. This, therefore, is the type of power the pope has in respect of ecclesiastical goods.

Chapter 7

The Relation of the Supreme Pontiff to the Goods of Laymen

FROM WHAT has been said the relation of the pope to the goods of laymen is clear: he has much less dominion over the external goods of laymen than over those of clerics. He is not even their administrator, except in circumstances of most extreme necessity for the Church; and even here he is still not an administrator but a proclaimer of what is right.

To establish this point one must acknowledge that the external goods of laymen are not given to a community as ecclesiastical goods are. Rather, they are acquired by individual persons through their art, labor, or their own industry; and individual persons as individuals exercise right, power, and true dominion over such goods. As lord over such goods, a person can order, dispose, keep, or transfer what is his as he sees fit, without injury to anyone else. These goods, therefore, have no order and relation among themselves, nor are they ordered or related to any one common head [1] who has them to dispose of and dispense; for everyone can do with his own possessions as he sees fit. Thus, neither prince nor pope has dominion or administration over such things.

Now it sometimes happens that these external goods lead to a disturbance of the general peace, as when someone usurps what belongs to someone else, or when men desire excessively what is theirs and do not share it as the needs or use of the country require. This is the reason why the people name a ruler: to govern, to act as judge of what is just and unjust in such matters, to punish injustices, and to be the measure in receiving goods from individuals according to a just proportion for the needs and use of the community. Indeed, as general shaper of faith and morals the pope is, as it were, not only head of the clergy but also of all the faithful insofar as they are faithful. And, therefore, in circumstances of extreme necessity [2] with respect to faith and morals, when all the goods of the faithful—even the chalices—belonging to churches are common and to be shared, he has the power to dispense and determine what is to be turned over for the common needs of the faith, which otherwise would be subverted by an invasion of pagans or some such thing. And so great and evident a necessity could exist that he could exact tithes or specified portions of their property from individual members of the faithful, conceding however that this must be done according to a just assessment, so that no person be unreasonably burdened more than others in aid of the common needs of the faith. An order of this kind from the pope would be nothing less than a declaration of right.

The pope can also coerce rebels or dissenters by the use of ecclesiastical censure.[3] And he can even use the same measures in a parish where there are so many new faithful that the old revenue is no longer sufficient to maintain the priest in charge of the parish, and he suddenly finds it necessary to maintain many new chaplains as assistants. In such a situation the pope can require the faithful of that parish to increase contributions from their goods to an amount needed for a sufficient income. And in such circumstances this kind of order is a declaration of right.

Except for cases of this kind, however, where there is the necessity of the common spiritual good involved, the pope has no disposition over goods of the laity, but each individual person disposes of what is his as he sees fit; and in cases of necessity the ruler disposes for the common temporal good. Now in cases where there is no necessity but some spiritual use, or where it happens that material goods of the laity are not collected for such use or necessity, the pope does not have the right to coerce anyone, although he can grant indulgences to the faithful for giving assistance.[4] And in my view nothing else is to be granted to him.

Chapter 8

That the Supreme Pontiff Does Not Have Jurisdiction over the Goods of the Laity from Christ because Christ Did Not Have It

NOW HAVING property rights and dominion over external goods is not the same as having jurisdiction, that is, the right of determining what is just and unjust with respect to them. Accordingly, just as a ruler has the power of judging and ascertaining with respect to the goods of those under his authority without, however, having dominion over them, it remains to be seen whether the pope has jurisdiction and power from Christ, as some assert. To show that he does not have them from Christ, it will be shown first that Christ Himself did not have them as man; secondly, conceding that Christ had them as man, it will be shown that He still did not consign them to Peter.

To understand the first point, then, it is necessary to appreciate that Christ can be understood to be king in three ways: in one way insofar as He is God and one with the Father. He was a true king in this way, not only of men but of all creatures; for all creatures are subject to Him. Ecclesiasticus, I: "There is one creator of all, the most high, omnipotent king." [1] And He did not confer this kingship or power on any creature, for He did not confer on Peter the power of being a creator.

Christ can be considered a king in another way, as man-God. And He is called a king of men in this way also, insofar as through the things He did in the flesh He brought us to participation in the kingdom, not indeed a kingdom of the world, but the higher kingdom of heaven. Wherefore He is not only called priest but also king, as Jeremiah says: "He shall reign as king, and He shall be a wise man." [2] Whence, too, a loyal priesthood is derived from that, according to Peter's statement: "You are the race of the elect, the royal priesthood." [3] And what is more, all the faithful are called kings and priests,[4] inasmuch as through faith and charity they are His members and as it were one with the head, Christ. The Gloss on the text just cited implies this.[5] And the Apocalypse states: "You have made us a kingdom for our God, and priests in Your blood," [6] that is, through belief in Your passion. Ecclesiastical ministers, however, are more fully participants in this royal priesthood inasmuch as they not only offer sacrifice to God interiorly with a penitent and contrite spirit, as all just men do, but as has been said above [chapter 2] they also offer both for themselves and for the people external sacrifices, in which divine power is contained in a spiritual manner. Further, they direct others to a participation in the kingdom of heaven through teaching and administering the sacraments, doing so by virtue of their office and not only by the zeal of charity.

If, however, Christ is understood to be king in the third way, insofar as He was a man, that is, king of a temporal kingdom having as it were direct or usable dominion over temporal goods, this is completely false. For He accepted our poverty, along with certain other irremovable defects, as Damascene says in Book III.[7] Wherefore we read in John 18: "My kingship is not of this world"; [8] and the Gloss gives Augustine's comment: "Hear, Gentiles and Jews, I offer no impediment to your domination of this world." [9] And Chrysostom is quoted in the same text [10] as saying that He does not possess kingship as earthly kings in this world do, but that He who is not human but someone much greater and more excellent, holds power from above. Pope Leo in his Epiphany sermon asserts: "The Magi thought they were seeking a king in the human sense, who was a ruler of a kingly state; but He who had taken the form of a servant and had come to minister and not to be ministered to chose birth for Himself at Bethlehem and passion at Jerusalem." [11] Wherefore, hearing that a king was born, Herod was mistaken to fear that the king would be someone who would usurp his own dominion over temporal things. And accordingly, commenting on Matthew, Chrysostom writes: "Herod did not correctly interpret the prophecy of Micah: 'And you, Bethlehem, of the land of Judah, are in no way least among the principalities of Judah; for from you a king shall rise, who will feed my people, and his day shall be for all the days of eternity.' [12] For someone who realized that He whose day was for all the days of eternity was not an earthly king, would not have become excited into making so great an error." [13] This is why Eusebius declared that the Herodians were mistaken in asserting that He was anointed to be king over temporal goods.[14] For He was not anointed with a material ointment as the kings of this world are, but with a spiritual ointment, to wit, the oil of gladness in consequence of His participators. Therefore, He is not a king of this world, but is of that kingship of which the prophet David spoke: "His is an eternal power, and His kingship is incorruptible." [15] Further, it is stated in Luke 12 that someone from the crowd spoke: "Master, speak to my brother so that he may divide his inheritance with me. But He said to him: Man, who made me judge or divider over you? See and beware of all avarice." [16]

It follows from what has been said that, according to the holy writers, Christ did not have authority or judgment over temporal things; rather, He had to give witness to virtue. Accordingly, in explaining this authority to Eugene in Book II, *On Consideration,* Bernard writes: "It will not be shown," he says, "Where at any time any one of the apostles sat as a judge of men or as divider of boundaries or distributor of lands. Indeed, I read that the apostles have sat to be judged, but I do not read that they have sat as judges. That will be; but it has not been." [17] And later, in showing what power Christ had over earthly things he asserts: "So that you may know, He said, that the Son of Man has the power of forgiving sins, etc. . . ." [18] Further, commenting on the text of Matthew 22: "Render unto Caesar the things that are Caesar's, etc.," [19] Jerome says that He paid tribute for Himself and for Peter, and returned to God the things that are God's, doing the will of the Father.[20] And commenting on the same text Hilary says: "He commanded us to give our riches to Caesar, but to retain the innocence of conscience for God." [21]

If it is claimed that Christ was not obliged to pay tribute but paid only because he wished to avoid scandal, as is said in Matthew 27, regarding payment of the didrachma,[22] the objection is of no value. For the didrachma was not paid by the firstborn of Israel in favor of Caesar but in favor of the temple on account of the death of the firstborn of Egypt. It was because they thought Jesus was the firstborn of Joseph and Mary and considered Peter to be the principal and as it were first among Christ's disciples that the didrachma was sought from them both. But Christ was not obliged to pay, since He was not Joseph's son, and Peter was not obliged to pay, since he was not by virtue of being the principal disciple the firstborn of his father. Accordingly, Christ paid the didrachma only to avoid scandal. However, payment of tribute to Caesar, which Christ so many times ordered to be paid, is something different. Pope Urban also adduced this authority concerning the didrachma found in the fish's mouth to show that all clerics and churches are bound to pay tribute to the emperor regarding material goods: *Decretum,* last question, "Tributum." [23]

It follows from these arguments that, since Christ as man did not have dominion over temporal goods, no priest as vicar of Christ has power over such things from Christ. For Christ did not confer on them what He did not possess Himself. Christ Himself said, in John: "Amen, amen, I say to you, no servant is greater than his master, and no apostle is greater than He Who sent him." [24] And Matthew 10 states: "The disciple is not greater than the master, nor the servant above the lord." [25]

Chapter 9

Arguments that Christ Had Jurisdiction over the Goods of Laymen and Replies to Them

PERHAPS, HOWEVER, there are some who assert the contrary, taking an argument from Matthew 21, where it is said that Christ drove the buyers and sellers from the temple with a whip,[1] something He would not have done unless He possessed that power. Wherefore it is said in *Decretum* 1. 3, "Ex multis," [2] that He spoke to declare the authority of His own rule when He said there: "Do not make the house of My Father a place of business." [3] Again, it is written in Matthew that He sent His Disciples to bring an ass and a colt and they did so, saying that the Lord has work for these things.[4] Again, that He sent the demons into swine, which immediately threw themselves into the sea,[5] and He did not seek out the master of the swine. Again, in the last chapter of Matthew, He asserted that after the resurrection "all power in heaven and on earth is given to Me," [6] on which the Gloss comments "to Him Who formerly was dead and crucified." [7] Further, they appeal to the verse of the Psalms containing the Father's words to the Son: "Ask Me and I shall give You the people as Your inheritance, etc., and the lands of the earth as Your possession. Kings you shall break them with a rod of iron, etc." [8] These are the arguments by which they maintain that Christ as man had power over temporal things.

But all these arguments can be resolved easily if one considers that something is owed to Christ as God which does not pertain to Him as man,[9] although this point applies differently to the respective texts. For what is said about the removal of the sellers is answered in *Decretum*, 10, "Quoniam idem," [10] and in the Gloss, where it is stated that Christ did some things as emperor but other things as priest; [11] in the section of *Decretum*, II, "De consecratione, Sacerdos," which maintains that the same person does not and ought not exercise those two offices, but that He did this to show that both powers proceeded from Him insofar, namely, as He was God.[12] In fact these two, supreme authority in a state and the priesthood, do derive from the same principle, as stated in *Authentica, Quomodo oporteat episcopos*, Coll. II, primo.[13] Commenting on Matthew, Chrysostom states that Christ, having as it were authority as God, did this to show that none but spiritual ministers who bear God's image and not the image of an earthly man ought to be found in God's temple, so that there will not be any business dealings or greed for gifts in God's house: in this way Jesus will not enter it angry and stern, and will not purify His temple otherwise than by use of the whip, and transform it from a den of thieves into a house of prayer.[14]

Similarly, a reply can be made with respect to the ass, asserting that Jesus had authority as God. Accordingly, the Gloss on that text reads: "The Lord has this task. The Lord speaks absolutely and without qualification, to imply that He was lord not only of beasts of burden but also of men, and it is to Him that all things are subject." [15]

The same reply can be made regarding the swine, although perhaps they were wild swine and had no master inasmuch as there was nothing about swine accruing to men's use, since the Jews were not accustomed to eat the flesh of swine. Now to the statement "all power is given me in heaven and on earth," [16] the response of Jerome can be made, that this does not mean that all temporal power but that all spiritual power is given Him. Accordingly Jerome writes: "The power in heaven and on earth was given Him so that He Who previously reigned in heaven would reign on earth through the faith of believers." [17] Now just how He will reign through the faith of believers will be explained immediately in the argument which follows. One can also offer the view of Remigius [of Auxerre], who stated that all power was given in the Incarnation to Him Who died, to wit, that He be God, Who is all powerful.[18] Certainly this was evident on earth until after the Resurrection, when He sent preachers to announce the word of God, and to preach that Christ was the all-powerful God. Therefore, all power in heaven and on earth was given to Him at that time through the communication of idioms, although not insofar as its reality was given then, since He had this from the beginning. Rather, evidence and knowledge of it were given at that time.

To the text "Depart from me, etc." I reply that this refers to the kingship which directs us through faith to heaven. So, too, with the text, "I shall give the people to You as an inheritance." It refers to the people adhering to "You" through faith.[19] Similarly, with respect to the text "Kings over those in inflexible bonds," the Gloss comments: "In inflexible justice," [20] which is through faith; for the just man lives by faith. "And you shall break them into pieces like a clay vase," [21] [is a text which] the Gloss interprets as "By cleansing from sin and from the filth of carnality." [22] For this is how the yoke of the Law and of sin is removed by Christ from His members, according to the Gloss. And one should not understand that Christ reigns in men through faith as if something thus converted to faith is thereby a subject of Christ's vicar in respect of temporal goods in the way men are accustomed to be subject to their kings. For in this way Christ would alter an earthly kingship in the way Herod feared. Rather, He is said to reign through faith because believers subject to Christ what is supreme and principal in men, to wit, intelligence, conquering it in the submission to faith. And this is the saints' understanding. Wherefore Christ is said through faith to reign over hearts and not over possessions.

Chapter 10

Christ Did Not Commit Jurisdiction over the Goods of Laymen to Peter Even if He Possessed It Himself

GRANTING THAT CHRIST as man possesses this authority and power,[1] He still did not commit it to Peter. Consequently, this power does not belong to the pope by reason of his being the successor of Peter. Rather, the episcopal and temporal powers are distinct not only in themselves, but with respect to their subject.[2] And the emperor[3] is the greater in temporal affairs, having no superior over him, just as the pope is the greater in spiritual affairs.

Indeed, this can be shown from a comparison of the Church with Christ. For Christ is the head of the Church: Ephesians 5.[4] And according to Ambrose,[5] He is not to be understood as head of the Church according to divinity only, but also according to humanity. However, things indistinct as to head are sometimes distinguished as to subject in their members, just as it is true that all the senses are in the head, but not all are in each of the other members. It is normally true that certain things are more distinct in their principiates than in their principles, more distinct in their effects than in their cause, and more distinct in inferiors than in the superior.[6] Therefore, even if Christ as man had both powers, it does not follow that He conferred on Peter both of the powers He had received from God. He conferred only spiritual power on Peter, and gave corporeal power to Caesar.

This position also can be shown by examination of the major. For Christ as man did have a certain power over spiritual things, which He was able to confer on Peter and the other ministers of the Church. Nevertheless, He did not confer the power theologians call "the power of excellence," which was in Christ as man alone, the power namely to confer a sacrament's effect without the sacrament or without a vocal sign, or the power to confer sacraments in His name, or the power to institute new sacraments.[7] Now He could have conferred on Peter this power over spiritual things, as the theologians assert,[8] and He did not. And in the book *On the Remission of Sins,* Richard says that Christ was able to eliminate sins, but we are able only to forgive them.[9] Therefore, even if Christ had power over temporal things, so much the more was it not necessary that He confer it on Peter: particularly so since this point is not found expressed anywhere, but reference is made to the spiritual power by which Peter can only absolve from sins. Accordingly, all the arguments which attribute something to Peter because Christ possessed such a power even insofar as He was man are of no worth, unless something is found expressed on the point.[10]

This also follows from the perfection of the sacrifice of the New Testament; for the very perfection of a thing is a measure of its distinctness from other things. We see this in plants where sex is not so perfect as in animals. Accordingly, there can be male and female elements in the same plants, and they are not distinct in subject as is the case with animals, among which the sexes must be distinct in subject unless there is an error in nature, as in the case of hermaphrodites.[11] Now in the Old Testament, where the priesthood was less perfect, the kingly and sacerdotal powers were distinct both in fact and in subject.[12] So much the more, then, did God wish them distinct in subject in the New Testament.[13]

This also appears from a comparison between the Church instituted by God and works of art. For a household seems to be imperfect, and to have a dearth of things, and to be insufficient in itself for life if one person is occupied with several tasks. Wherefore the Philosopher says in Politics 6 that poor people use their children and wives as helpers because they do not have a supply of servants, and are not well supplied with the things needed for the perfection of a household.[14] Now the Church of Christ is called a household according to the text: "O Israel, how great is thy household." [15] And in Matthew we read: "My household will be called a household of prayer." [16] Therefore, since the Church was sufficiently instituted by God, it is unfitting that such diverse ministries as the priestly office and the kingly office, in which kings also minister to God, be committed to one person. Romans 13 states: "For he does not carry the sword without cause; he is a minister of God." [17] Moreover, it is inconsistent for us to posit that any one of the things instituted by God is unbecoming in comparison with the works of art and of nature. For the Philosopher said in Politics 1 that nature does nothing comparable to what the workers who made the Delphian sword used to do.[18] For among the Delphian people swords were made for the poor such that one sword was used for several offices. But nature does not act in this fashion, and much less does the Author of nature. Accordingly, the Philosopher says that the organ performing work best is the one which performs only one and not many actions.[19]

This point is also clear if we consider what profit or harm results [from combining the two powers in one person]. For God had two purposes in willing that these two powers be distinct in subject and object, so as not to be in one and the same person according to primary authority. One purpose is that, because of the mutual need and assistance members of the Church [have for one another], the qualities of joy and charity without which members of the Church do not live might be fostered in circumstances where the prince has need of the priest in spiritual matters, and the converse is the case in temporal matters. And this would not occur if one person held both powers. The Apostle implies this in Romans 12, saying: "We are all one in Christ, but we are individual members one to another, having different gifts." [20] "For if the whole [body] is the eye, why the hand; and if the whole body is the hand, why the eye?" [21] The other purpose is to avoid a situation where concern for temporal authority renders a priest or pope less solicitous for the concerns of spirituality.[22] The Apostle touches on this, too, when he instructs

Timothy: "Let no soldier of God involve himself in secular affairs, etc." [23] For these reasons the Most Wise Ordainer willed that these two powers be distinct in object and subject.

Moreover, Cyprian touches on both reasons in *Decretum* 10, "Quoniam idem." [24] And Pope Nicholas says almost the same thing in *Decretum* 96, "Cum ad verum." [25] And in Matthew 20 the Savior says: "The princes of the people are their lords, but you are not." [26] Again, all the apostles received the same power along with Peter: Matthew 28.[27] And this is asserted in *Decretum* 21, "In novo," where it is said that Peter was the first to receive the power of binding and loosing, with the other apostles receiving with him; [28] but it is not said that they received these from him. And in conferring this Christ did not place any restriction on anyone other than Peter, although it appears from the manner of speaking that He wished Peter to be the more primary and as it were head of the Church, in order to preserve the unity of the Church.[29] The same situation must be understood to obtain now as it did then for the apostles; whatever one of them such as Peter willed, the others willed. So, too, now from common law: [30] whatever the pope can do any bishop can do, with the qualification that the pope can act anywhere, while other bishops can act only in their own dioceses. But no one claims that as vicars of Christ and successors of the apostles other bishops have authority and dominion over temporal goods, and that a call can be made by a prince to a bishop of a given place for a temporal matter, or to the pastor of a parish, who some say has in his parish the power which a bishop has in his diocese. Accordingly, no one should make this general assertion about the pope.

Again, when the disciples asked who would be greater in Christ's kingdom, understanding kingdom as His kingdom in this world, He replied: "The kings of the people rule over them, and those who have power over them are called 'generous ones.' You, however, are not so named." [31] And explaining this statement, Bernard said to Pope Eugene, in Book II: "It is plain that absolute power is forbidden to the apostles. Therefore, how dare you usurp it either as master of the apostles or as an apostolic lord? Plainly you are forbidden both. How else do you think you are exempt from a place among those men about whom the complaint is made: 'They exercised authority, and not from me; princes have appeared and I have not recognized them.'" [32] Further on: "The apostolic form is this: domination is forbidden; ministry is proclaimed." [33] And further on: "Go out, Eugene, go out into the world. For this world is your land to be cultivated, and it is on loan to you. Go out into it, not as lord but as steward." [34] The pope, therefore, does not have absolute power from Christ or from his vicar, Peter. Bernard repeats the same position in Book IV: "Your power lies in hearts, not in possessions; for you have received the keys of the kingdom of heaven because of the former, not the latter." [35] And further on: "Kings and princes have their own judges in such matters. Why, therefore, do you enter on foreign territory? Not because you are unworthy, but because it is unworthy of you to be concerned with such matters. Surely you should be occupied with more important things." [36]

Further, the supreme pontiffs assert that these aforesaid spiritual and secular powers are distinct in subject: *Decretum* 10, "Quoniam," [37] and *Decretum* 96, "Cum ad verum" [38] and "Duo quippe." [39] And they are distinct in such a way that one is not reduced to the other; but the temporal, like the spiritual, derives immediately from God.[40] Accordingly, imperial authority is from God alone, as is maintained in *Decretum* 23. 4, "Quaesitum." [41] And the pope does not have his sword from the emperor, any more than the emperor has his sword from the pope: *Decretum* 96, "Si imperator." [42] For the army creates an emperor: *Decretum* 93, "Legimus." [43] And what belongs to a prince concerning temporal matters is not licitly applied to a pope, and temporal affairs do not fall within the pope's jurisdiction, as Alexander says: *Extra, De appellationibus, si duobus,*[44] and *Extra, Qui filii sunt legitimi, Causam.*[45] Further, there is an appeal from a bishop to a prince about temporal matters: *Extra, De foro competenti, Verum;* [46] for a bishop insofar as he is a secular judge has jurisdiction in such matters, *Extra, De judiciis, Ceterum;* [47] and *Authentica, Quomodo oporteat episcopos,*[48] at the beginning of the first *Collatio.* The Church also pays tribute to the emperor according to *Decretum* 11. 1, "Magnum," [49] where Ambrose invokes the example of Christ Who paid tribute, and the saying of the Apostle: "Let every soul be subject to the governing powers, etc."; [50] and the statement in I Peter, 2: "Be subject to your masters or to the king, etc." [51] The same point is made in the same question, *Si tributum.*[52]

Many similar arguments can be adduced to show that the lord pope does not have both swords, or jurisdiction over temporal matters unless this be granted to him by a prince out of devotion.[53] And interpreters of canon law who have held office in the Church assert the same view, even in a case where it seems less obvious. For Hostiensis, on *Extra, De hereticis, Vergentis,* enquires about circumstances where the lord pope orders the goods of heretics to be confiscated: What has the pope to do with temporal goods? And along with his own lord, Innocent, he replies that possessions are nothing to him, but that he did this with the emperor's consent, and the emperor, who was then in Padua, agreed. It also seems surprising that the Emperor Constantine is said to have given political authority over Italy and the entire temporal jurisdiction to the Church, and that the Church received this as a gift, if it also held this by right.[55] For [in this view] the Donation would not have been given to Saint Sylvester, but what was his would have been returned to him. And the Church maintains just the opposite: *Decretum* 96, "Constantinus." [56]

Now some think to evade some of the above arguments through a fine distinction. They assert that although secular power is the pope's possession immediately and according to primary authority, he does not possess the direct exercise of this power; rather, he relinquishes this power to the prince. The secular prince, then, ought to acknowledge that while the power he exercises derives from the pope, its exercise belongs to him. Some persons attempt to resolve some of the previous arguments in this fashion [see the Prologue].

Still other writers assert that the pope has temporal jurisdiction according to his primary authority, but not its exercise: the emperor has its exercise not from the pope, but from God. And they try to interpret the above statements in this fashion.

This evasion, however, is completely absurd, and does not agree with the statements of these men. For if the Church acknowledges the exercise of power by a secular prince, then the secular prince must be judge of the exercise of power owed to the pope, and can take such exercise out of the pope's hands. But those who argue in the above fashion do not assert this, since they maintain that the pope cannot be judged by anyone. Again, if God gave secular power to the pope according to primary authority but not its exercise, because this is improper for the pope, how does the pope receive from the prince what God judges cannot or should not belong to him? And how does the pope give to a prince what he receives back from him? Again, if the pope has secular power directly from God and the prince has its exercise directly from the pope, then the prince is a minister of the pope, just as the pope is a minister of Christ. But this seems to be contrary to canonical writings. For on the subject of king and prince the Apostle said To the Romans, 13: "If you have done wrong, beware. For he does not carry the sword without reason. For he is a minister of God, the deliverer from wrongs in anger, etc." And later: "Therefore, you shall be responsible for taxes." For he is a minister of God. Paul does not say minister of the pope, but of God. "For in this they are His servants"; [57] on which the Gloss comments, "God's." [58] Again, kingly power in itself and in exercise existed earlier than papal power [see chapter 4], and there were kings in France [59] before Christians. Therefore, kingly power is not from the pope either in itself or in respect to exercise, as previously maintained [see chaps. 2, 5]; it is from God and from the people electing [60] a king in a person or family. For to say that kingly power was immediately from God in the beginning and afterward from the pope is completely ridiculous, as this cannot be unless Christ gave to Peter the power of conferring kingly dignity. Wherefore it is indubitably from God, as previously stated. Accordingly, the Gloss on Peter, II, "Be subject to every creature, etc." [61] states: "Faith and religion do not disturb the rights of a situation." [62] And in the Gloss on Romans, XIII, "Let every soul, etc.," [63] Ambrose states: "Although the faithful as faithful are one in Christ, there is a difference in their situation." [64]

Further, the power of lesser pontiffs and guardians also seems to be more through the mediation of the pope than kingly power, insofar as ecclesiastical prelates are more immediately dependent on the pope than upon secular princes.[65] The power of prelates, however, is not from God through the mediation of the pope, but immediately from God and from the people choosing and consenting.[66] For Peter, whose successor the pope is, did not send the other apostles whose successors the bishops are. Neither did he send the seventy-two disciples, whose successors are the carefully prepared presbyters. Rather, Christ sent them immediately: Matthew 10 and Luke 10.[67] Nor did Peter breathe on the other apostles to give them the Holy Spirit and the power of forgiving sin; it was Christ Who did so: John 20.[68] And in *Decretum* 21, "In novo," [69] it is said that all received the same and equal power simultaneously from Christ. Paul also said that he did not receive his apostolate from Peter, but from Christ or from God immediately. "Paul," he asserted, "Apostle not by men or through a man, but through Jesus Christ and God the Father." [70] And later: "For I did not receive this from a man, nor was I taught it." [71] And later he says that he did not see Peter for three years after having been called to the Gospel himself, when he came to Jerusalem to see Peter.[72] Therefore, kingly power derives much less from the pope in any way.

Further, although it sometimes happens that a person has the power to do something but because of impediments can not perform the act (for example, a person has the power of consecration but it is impossible for him to perform the act because of a defect of matter such that he has no bread, or because of suspension of the power, or because of a physical defect such that he is mute and unable to pronounce the words) nevertheless, these are impediments coming unexpectedly into conflict with the power. For no wise man confers the order of the priesthood on someone while knowing him regularly to possess any of the aforesaid impediments. Therefore, it does not seem that the pope can be said to have the power of the secular sword directly from God without its exercise belonging to him regularly. For in this way God would be more superfluous in His activities than nature, which gives power to nothing without act. For what has power also has act, as is said in *On Sleeping and Waking*.[73] God then would be more foolish than man.

Moreover, they cannot take this distinction from any canonical text, unless perhaps they wish to take the statement of Saint Bernard that the pope has the material sword at his command.[74] And clearly that statement, along with the fact that it has no great authority, is more contrary than favorable to their position since, as will be asserted later,[75] Bernard expressly states that the pope has the material sword at his command because the emperor must exercise secular jurisdiction for the necessity of a spiritual good where the pope instructs him to do so. But if the emperor is unwilling [to exercise authority], or if it does not seem to him to be expedient to do so, there is nothing else the pope can do. Accordingly, Bernard asserts that only the emperor and not the pope has this power by right.[76]

One can also relate to this problem the text of I Corinthians 6: "Accordingly, in respect of secular judgments, if you have contemptibles in the Church, appoint them to act as judges." [77] From this it seems to follow that clerics have to appoint contemptibles, that is, laity,[78] to see to secular matters. But that text in no way supports the views of these men. For the Apostle is not speaking particularly to clerics or ecclesiastics but to the faithful in general, to reprimand them because they were appointing contemptible persons —that is, inexperienced persons—to see to secular matters. Accordingly, the faithful were being compelled to fall back on the judgment of infidels, as if there were no wise man among the faithful who could act as judge. Now the Gloss explains the term "appoint" as follows: "That you act in this way is meant to be taken ironically and not hortatively, that you act in such a way as to appoint such contemptible and ignorant men, and so compel the faithful to fall back on the judgment of infidels; as if what I say is to your shame, as if there was not a wise man among you, etc." [79] And so the Apostle intended that the faithful laity should also appoint industrious persons to judge on secular matters. Consequently, the Apostle's statement has nothing in it of the meaning proposed above.[80]

But, even granting that Paul was speaking to ecclesiastics, it is still not to the point. For he did not intend that ecclesiastics should appoint judges for secular matters indiscriminately, but only in circumstances where jurisdiction over temporal affairs is given them by a prince. Then ecclesiastics ought for such matters to establish contemptibles, that is, lay persons, to judge these matters, just as today they appoint secular bailiffs. Therefore they ought not to intervene directly in these matters. Accordingly, the Apostle does not say "since" but "if" you have secular concerns, implying that such judgments do not belong to ecclesiastics unless handed over to them or permitted them by a prince. And when this is the case they ought to judge through contemptibles, that is, lay persons, but according to the meaning of existing laws and the weight of earthly law. Hugh says this explicitly in *On the Sacraments*, 2. 2. 7, as follows: "It should be noted, nevertheless, that earthly princes sometimes cede to the Church the use only, and sometimes the use and the power, over earthly possessions which are theirs either through their subjects or not through their subjects. They cede use without power when they decree that the fruit of possessions is to be transferred to the Church's use. But they do not permit the transfer of the power of implementing justice in such a possession to the Church's jurisdiction. Sometimes they cede both use and power, although the Church cannot exercise the power of implementing justice through ecclesiastics, nor can it make secular judgments. The Church, however, can have ministers, namely, lay persons, through whom it enacts laws and judgments pertaining to temporal power according to the tenor of laws and the obligations of earthly law.[81]

Indeed, the position of those who say that princes have the exercise but not the power from God rather than from the pope is not reasonable. It is not reasonable that God should give power to anyone without the ability to act either himself or through another, and that He should give the exercise of this power to someone else without that person having either the power or the authority. For us no opinion would be more contradictory than that one, because according to its minor there is no appeal from the prince to the pope.

Chapter 11

Arguments of Those Maintaining the Contrary
Position, That the Pope Has Jurisdiction over
External Material Goods

NOW WE MUST see the fundamental positions which support
those persons who say that priests, and particularly the pope, have
primary power and that this power devolves on the prince from the
pope.[1]

[1] They advert to a text of Jeremiah 1 found in the *Decretum, De majoritate et obedientia,* "Solite," a statement concerning
the priesthood of Jeremiah and relating to the sacerdotal and not
the royal tribe: "Behold I have placed you over peoples and kingdoms that you may level and destroy, and build and sow."[2] From
this they assert that the pope, who is the highest in the rank of
ecclesiastical priests, has power over the kings of the earth to remove and appoint them.

[2] Again, there is the statement to Peter in Matthew 16 and
18: "Whatever you shall loose on earth shall be loosed in heaven
also, and whatever you shall bind on earth shall be bound in
heaven."[3] This statement they assert to be an unqualified one.

[3] Again, [I] Corinthians 6 states: "Do you not know that
you shall judge angels,"[4] on which the Gloss comments: "By so
much more [shall you judge] secular matters."[5]

[4] Again, Genesis 1 reads: God made two sources of light,[6]
the sun, to wit, the pope, to preside over the day, that is, over

spiritual matters; and the moon, that is, the emperor or king, to preside over the night, namely, over temporal matters. But the moon only presides over the night insofar as it borrows light from the sun. Therefore, emperor and king possess the power to preside over temporal affairs by virtue of power received from the pope.

[5] Again, Pope Zacharias deposed the king of the Franks, and put his brother, Pepin, in his place: *Decretum* 15. 6, "Alius." [7]

[6] Again, Pope Nicholas states in *Decretum* 22. 1 that Christ yielded or committed to Peter the rights of heaven and earth.[8]

[7] Again, the emperor swears allegiance to the pope, as stated in *Decretum* 63, "Tibi Domino." [9]

[8] And the pope deposes the emperor: *Decretum* 15. 6, "Alius." [10]

[9] Again, the pope transferred the imperial power from the east to the west: *Extra, De electione, Venerabilem.*[11]

[10] Again, the pope sometimes legislates in spiritual and in temporal affairs: *Extra, Qui filii sint legitimi, Per venerabilem.*[12] Again, an appeal is made sometimes from a secular judge to the pope: *Extra, De foro competenti, Licet.*[13]

[11] Again, he has absolved soldiers from [their] oath, and in some instances absolved all the Franks from the oath of allegiance: *Decretum* 15. 6 and 4, "Quia praesulatus." [14]

[12] Again, the pope has jurisdiction over every wrong.[15] But it happens that a wrong can be committed regarding temporal matters, as when someone sells to another what does not belong to him; therefore, etc.

[13] Again, when one prince is wronged by another in a base matter,[16] the injured party can complain to the supreme pontiff. And in such a case the pope has jurisdiction in temporal matters.

[14] Again, it is said in Matthew: "If your brother sins against you, etc." [17] And later: "But if he does not listen to you, tell the Church; moreover, if he will not listen to the Church, let him be to you as a Gentile and a publican." [18] Therefore, the Church has to judge without qualification in cases where an injury is denounced to it.

[15] Again, the Emperor Theodosius stipulated, and Charles confirmed the position, that without any doubt a person having a

case for litigation could, if he so chose, immediately elect the presiding priest of a holy place to sit in judgment, even if the other party was opposed to the judgment of bishops: *Extra, De judiciis, Novit.*[19]

[16] Again, it is said in Deuteronomy [20] and upheld in *Extra, Qui filii sint legitimi, Per venerabilem,*[21] that if you find any difficulty and uncertain case arising in your midst between one kind of homicide and another, one kind of legal right and another, one kind of assault and another, and you see judgment vary within your gates, come to the priests of the tribe of the Levites, to him whose office it is to be judge at the time, and he will assess the truth of your judgment; and you shall do whatever they say who preside over the place God chose, and follow their judgment, etc.

[17] Again, he who has power over the greater also has power over the less. Since the pope has power over spiritual matters, accordingly, he has power also over temporal matters.

[18] Again, temporal things are ordered to spiritual things, and sometimes relate to them. Therefore, the pope, who has the care of spiritual things, also has to judge or order with respect to temporal things, at least insofar as they relate to spiritual things.

[19] Again, the pope changes and confers legacies which have not been arranged for. And it even pertains to him to make restitution concerning the goods of the dead, when there are unknown persons to whom something is owing. Therefore, temporal goods pertain to him.

[20] Further, some [22] argue in this way: corporeal things are ruled through spiritual things, and depend on them as on a cause, a position they demonstrate in different ways. For heavenly bodies are guided by angels; [23] and in the same way, as in the case of man, the soul rules and moves the body.[24] Wherefore, similarly, spiritual power has causality over temporal power, and temporal power depends on spiritual power as on a cause, since temporal power is directed more to the guidance of bodily life. And Hugh of St. Victor seems to hold this position in *On the Sacraments* 2. 2. 4, where he states: "How much more worthy is spiritual life than earthly life, and the spirit than the body, inasmuch as spiritual power takes precedence over earthly or secular power in honor and dignity." [25]

[21] Spiritual power has to institute earthly power for the latter to exist, and has to judge whether or not it is good. But spiritual power was instituted in the first instance by God, and if it errs it can be judged only by God.

[22] It is written: "The spiritual man judges all things, and he is not judged by anyone." [26] Accordingly, spiritual power institutes and judges secular power.

[23] Again, they argue the same point from the order of ends. For, among ordered arts the art to which the ultimate and principal end pertains rules the other arts to which secondary ends pertain. But secular power is directed to the good of the multitude, which is to live according to virtue: an end that can be achieved through the power of nature and the things supported by nature. Spiritual power, however, is directed to the supernatural good of the multitude—namely, to eternal beatitude—and leads to that end. Moreover, a supernatural end is stronger and more principal than any other end. Therefore, spiritual power, which is found in the ministers of the Church, is superior not only in dignity but also in causality to secular power, and prescribes to it how the latter ought to be used.

[24] Further, they conclude from the above argument that the pope hands over to princes the laws according to which they ought to execute and exercise jurisdiction, and secular princes cannot accept laws from any other source unless they have been approved by the pope.

[25] They also assert that spiritual power, therefore, is called royal priesthood,[27] because Christ is king and priest, and His vicar has kingly and priestly power because through him kingly power is instituted, ordered, sanctified, and blessed.

[26] For this reason they also assert that in the Old Testament the priesthood was instituted by God first, as Hugh says,[28] and kingly power was instituted later through the priesthood; and this was done at God's command. And even in the Church, priestly dignity sanctifies kingly power through blessing, and shapes it through instruction.

[27] They also show this by citing Augustine, *City of God,* 2. 21,[29] where he says that there cannot be a kingly state without true

justice. But there is no true justice where Christ is not the ruler. Otherwise, there is no rightful and true state, the type of state the state of the Christian people should be; and in it governing power is found by right only in the pope, who is Christ's vicar. Accordingly, they assert that the pope has both jurisdictions immediately from God.

[28] They say further that things which are from God are ordered to one another. But both powers are from God: Romans 13.[30] Accordingly, they are ordered to one another in this way, that the secular is mediated [31] by the spiritual, and is not immediately from God.

[29] Again, since there is one Church and one Christian people and one mystical body,[32] it seems reasonable that there be one head on which the members depend spiritually and temporally. Therefore, they say that all power in the Church, whether spiritual or temporal, depends on the person in whom both powers reside. And this person is the pope, the successor of Peter and the vicar of Christ.

[30] Further, they appeal to Bernard's statement to Pope Eugene, 1. 4 to support them. It reads: "Why do you attempt again to seize the sword which you were ordered once to keep in its scabbard, even though he who denies it is yours does not seem to have sufficient regard for God's statement which says: "Replace your sword in your scabbard." Therefore it is yours, and it is to be sheathed: otherwise it would not pertain to you in any way. And to the position of those who assert that there are two swords here, God did not reply that this is enough, but that this is too many. Both swords, then, the spiritual and the temporal, belong to the Church. But one, the sword of the priesthood, is indeed for the Church, and is to be used by the Church; the other is for the soldier's hand, but is to be used sensibly at the will of the priesthood and at the command of the emperor." [33] It follows from these statements that the pope has both powers immediately inasmuch as he is the primary authority, although the exercise of the material sword pertains to the emperor.

[31] Further, in addition to the above arguments, a certain man of Cremona,[34] a man learned in the decrees as he says, argues

that God ruled the world Himself from its beginning, and that He
punished Eve and Adam and Cain, and acted in this manner until
the time of the Flood. And after this time He ruled through Noah,
whom He ordered to construct and command the ark. And Noah
himself was a priest, this man argues, because he built an altar
to the Lord and offered sacrifice. Moreover, God ruled later through
Abraham and the other patriarchs, who were priests offering sacrifices to God. Accordingly, Abraham twice built an altar to God and
was a priest in name: *Decretum* 94, the last chapter.[35] Afterward
God ruled through Moses and Aaron, who punished the Pharaohs,
and ruled over the people in the desert in both spiritual and
temporal matters. Whence the Psalms read: "Moses and Aaron were
His in priestly matters, etc." [36] It seems, therefore, that the priests
of the New Law, who are not of lesser authority, have command
of both areas.

[32] Again, he who has dominion over the end has dominion
also over the things which pertain to the end. But temporal things
are ordered to spiritual things as to end, and the pope has dominion
over spiritual things; therefore, etc. And the abovementioned
Cremonan argues to the same conclusion in this way: God gave
souls to Peter, but the body is for the sake of the soul and is subject to it.[37] Indeed, external temporal goods are for the sake of the
body, and are subjects in respect to it. Therefore, from beginning to
end, all things are subject to the pope. And the Apostle also seems
to say the same thing, in I Corinthians: "All things are yours, but
you are Christ's, while Christ is God's." [38] The Gloss comments on
this text, that nevertheless He does not commission anything for
Himself: "All things whatsoever in the world are yours." [39]

[33] Again, this man asserts that, if emperors had any right
of authority from the beginning, nevertheless because of the sins
they have committed against the saints in killing them, and particularly against the supreme pontiff, they have been deprived of
the right of authority, and the right of authority has been transferred to the Church, because a privilege deserves to be taken
away from someone who, having been granted it, willfully abuses
it: *Decretum* II. 3, *Privilegium.*" [40]

[34] Again, he says: the dominion the Church now has and

did not have a long time ago was prefigured in Luke 14, where it is said that when the feast was prepared, the head of the household sent his servant into the highways and byways to tell those who were invited to come; and when he had done this the head of the household said again to the servant to go out into the highways and byways and compel them to come in that his house might be filled.[41] And the Church in the beginning is signified in the servant's first condition, when he did not have authority to compel, because the Church was in subjection. But the modern state of the Church is signified in the second condition, in which it has full authority to compel and rule over everything, as Augustine says: *Decretum* 23. 4, "Displicet." [42]

And some men adduce similar things from the text of the Psalms: "Why are the people plotting in vain," [43] where in the first instance the Gentiles and the Jews are said to be plotting against Christ—this signifies the first condition of the Church. Afterward, it is said: "We shall break their bonds, and throw them from us, etc." And later: "And now, kings, understand, take knowledge of Him who will judge, etc." "Be warned lest He be angry, etc." [44] The condition of the modern Church is signified here; and in this condition the pope, the vicar of Christ, has dominion over the kings of the earth, who should be totally subject to him, even though he did not have this power from the beginning. Some men [45] add also that in the beginning the Lord converted Peter and Andrew by calling [them], but He converted the last of the apostles, Paul, by knocking him to the ground. And they interpret these facts in a way similar to that used in the preceding arguments.[46]

[35] Again, as an argument for lessening kingly power and elevating papal dignity, some add that from the beginning the Lord established the priesthood for his people but not a king, and yielded to their petition, as He says in Deuteronomy 17: "When you have said: I shall establish a king over me, etc." [47] And the Lord, Who was offended at their petition, granted it, as is shown from what He said to Samuel in Kings I; "They have not rejected you but Me, so that I might not rule over them." [48] It follows from this that God did not willingly accept kingly rule, but only permitted it after having been offended, and it was more acceptable to God for the

world to be ruled in all things through the pontiff alone. Whence the remark is made about kings in Hosea 8: "They have exercised royal authority, and not from Me; princes have come into being, and I have not known it." [49]

[36] Again, to lessen kingly power and hand over the rule over temporal things to the pope, they appropriate the statement in Genesis 47, that when Pharaoh purchased the territory of all the Egyptians during a time of famine and brought it under his control, he still furnished the priests with the necessities of life in such a way that they lost neither their possessions nor their freedom.[50] as if priests in all nations should be free from then on as a result of the Lord's statement. And the words of Pope Urban in Decretum 23, last Question, "Tributum," [51] are taken in the same way, to prove that the temporal possessions of clerics do not seem to be subject to imperial exactions.

[37] Again, if the pope summons the bishops of any region to the curia, and if the king from whom they hold feudal rights [52] asserts that he needs them and wishes to retain them, they are bound to obey the pope. Accordingly, at least in such a case, they are not bound to a prince, but the pope seems to free them: *Decretum* 23. 8, "Reprehensibile." [53]

[38] Again, they declare that the pope can take from kings the possession of prebends, which are said to belong to kings customarily by right of patronage.[54] They prove this assertion in a variety of ways: on the grounds that the possession of prebends, like the law of tenths, is in some sense spiritual or connected with what is spiritual, and therefore does not fall to the laity; on the grounds that the Church's burden should not be onerous; on the grounds that custom does not prejudice public right, and in fact the ordering of ecclesiastical benefices belongs by public right to an ordinary and not to a lay person on the grounds that harmful or injurious circumstances or customs are held not to apply to the substance of a contract, and hence since such a custom is harmful, it has to be considered inapplicable; on the grounds that the Church "rejoices" in the rights of minors, and therefore when it considers these to have been infringed by certain arrangements and by negligence it can demand restitution of the whole. In this way the

pope in place of the Church can demand prebends back, and can take steps to prevent kings from conferring the aforementioned benefices.

[39] Again, these men say in confirmation of their position that the pope must be perfect in both the active and the contemplative life,[55] much more so than any other prelate. But he cannot be perfect in the active life unless he has direct or useful dominion over temporal things, because the administration of temporal things pertains to the active life.

[40] Again, they say that clerics are more vigorous in reason and intellect than lay persons, and ought to rule in both areas.

[41] Again, they say that those who assert the opposite are speaking in favor of princes from hope or fear, and not according to conscience.

[42] Again, that man from Cremona says that those who claim that the pope does not have power everywhere regarding temporal things are to be judged as quasi-heretics, because what they are saying is that the Church cannot coerce heretics through the secular arm.

These are the arguments I have been able to hear or collect in support of this position.

Chapter 12

Preliminary Remarks to Be Set Down before Solving the Foregoing Arguments, and for Understanding What Authority the Pope Has from Christ over Temporal Things. First Are Set Down What Authorities Were Granted by Christ to Peter and the Apostles

FOR CLARIFICATION on how to resolve these difficulties one must set down first what power the apostles and disciples of Christ, and among them bishops and priests, received from Christ. For, as the Gloss on Luke 10 says, there is an order of presbyters of the second order among the seventy-two disciples just as there is an order of bishops among the apostles, and every priestly power is reduced to these two orders.[1]

Therefore, as is apparent from what has been said previously in chapter 2,[2] one must consider that the priesthood is nothing but the spiritual power brought together in the ministers of the Church to dispense to the faithful the sacraments containing the grace by which we are ordained to eternal life. Moreover, just as nature is not lacking in necessary things,[3] and therefore does not give power to anything unless it gives that thing sufficient aids through which the power can translate into action and into its own operation in a suitable manner—wherefore the Philosopher maintains that it is inconvenient for nature to give a power of the soul to anything without giving it an organ through which the power of the soul is to be completed [4]—in the same way when God, Who is not less deficient than nature, gives spiritual power to priests, He gives them the things necessary for the convenient exercise and assertion of this power. And there are five such things, without which they cannot exercise this power.

[1] The first relates to the sacraments, to wit, the sanctification and consecration of corporeal matter. For according to Hugh [5] and the master of the *Sentences*,[6] a sacrament is a sensible element sanctified and consecrated by the word of God. In addition, there are two things which relate to the faithful to whom the sacraments are administered.

[2] One of these is the necessary knowledge or erudition in respect of doctrine, so that the faithful might know how they ought to live in order worthily to receive the sacraments; for these are conferred only on persons who are properly disposed.

[3] The other is the punishment of the condemned, so that whoever is not swayed by the disgrace present in sin, or by admonitions and salutary instructions, may be frightened away from disgrace by the penalty imposed by judges. Two things are required of ministers inasmuch as they are the persons who administer the sacraments.

[4] One is their distinction and proper order. For if the multitude of ministers was not ordered and distinguished in relation to one who has authority in this respect there would be confusion, and the common benefit would be neglected if any minister whatsoever could exercise his own jurisdiction anywhere. For men are not accustomed to being as solicitous about what is common as about what is appropriated to themselves.[7] There would be matter for dissension also among the people and among the ministers, if every minister had charge indiscriminately over the whole people, as was the case in the early Church, where one said: I am from Paul, and another: I am from Apollo. This is why a distinct order of ministers is necessary, an order related to some one man who has authority in the matter.

[5] The second requirement here is the maintenance of ministers in respect of the necessities of life.

And according to the words of the Gospel, we learn that there are six [8] powers brought together in the apostles and disciples of Christ, and in the successors, the ministers of the Church. [1] The first is the power of consecration, which is sometimes called the character or power of orders. The Lord conferred this power on the disciples at the Last Supper when, giving them His body under the species of bread, He said: "Do this in commemoration of Me." [9]

[2] The second is the power of administering the sacraments, and especially the sacrament of penance. This is the power of the keys,[10] or of spiritual jurisdiction in the forum of conscience, and consists in the authority to loose and in the power to absolve from sin and change an almost eternal condition into an almost temporal one. And this power in the spiritual forum was promised to Peter: Matthew 16: "I shall give you the keys, etc."; [11] and it was promised to all where it was said in Matthew 18: "Amen I say to you that whatever you bind, etc."; [12] and confirmed again in John 20: "As the Father sent Me so I send you. And when He had said this, He breathed, saying: Receive the Holy Spirit: whose sins you shall forgive they are forgiven them, etc." [13]

According to some, this power is, in respect of the nature of power, one with the power of consecration,[14] differing according to different acts in respect of the true or mystical body of Christ, and is the complement of priestly power. Wherefore, the very same words are pronounced in the ordination of simple priests as in the ordination of bishops, who are great priests, to wit, the words: "Receive the Holy Spirit, whose, etc."

[3] There is a third power or apostolic authority, the authority to preach, which the Lord gave to them when He said in Matthew 10: "Go out and preach, saying that the kingdom of heaven has arrived"; [15] and in the last chapter of Matthew: "Go and teach all nations." [16]

[4] A fourth power is the judiciary power of correction [17] in the external forum, through which sins are corrected almost from fear, especially things which are scandals for the Church.[18] This power is given in Matthew 18, where it is stated: "If your brother

has sinned against you, etc., . . . and if he will not heed, tell the Church; if he will not heed the Church, let him be to you a Gentile and a publican." [19] The Gloss says of this text: "So that the reproof of many might correct him." [20] And there follows: "Amen, I say to you that whatsoever you bind, etc.," [21] on which the notation is: "Authority to investigate in the external forum is given to the Church when it is said: 'Tell the Church,' so that it will know; and authority to coerce or punish through ecclesiastical censure [is given] when it is said: 'If he will not heed the Church, let him be to you a Gentile, etc.'" [22] And in confirmation the two are brought together in the statement: "Amen, I say to you, whatsoever you bind, etc.": in the Gloss, *vinculo anathematis*.[23] And it is particularly to be noted that, in respect of these three [*sic*] activities, priests have complete power to exercise jurisdiction over the people of the faithful, namely, by enlightening through teaching, by cleansing through correction, and by perfecting through administration of the sacraments.

[5] There is a fifth power, namely, the power of disposing ministers in such a way that certain of them determine ecclesiastical jurisdiction so as to avoid confusion. This power resides in Peter and his successors, according to *John 21*, where the remark is made to John: "Feed my lambs." [24] For the power of the keys and the power of jurisdiction reside equally in all, and without determination. And any one of them could effectively use these powers against any sinner, since the sinner is the matter needed on which the act of jurisdiction or absolution has to fall, just as unleavened wheat bread is the matter on which the act of the power of orders falls. Wherefore, Saint Paul proselytized the people everywhere without restriction, as is clearly seen by anyone reading his Epistles. And because confusion could result thereby, as has been said, accordingly the Lord anticipating this conferred on Peter [25] and his successors authority to place ministers of the Church and determine jurisdiction. He said: "Feed my lambs" as a directive to the chief shepherd, to whom the disposition and general control of the sheep and sheepfold belong. And this statement was not made to anyone else.

Some [26] assert, however—and reasonably—that only the repen-

tant sinner and not just any sinner is the matter on which actions
of the keys of the power of jurisdiction can effectively fall; and that
therefore this power has no effect on a sinner unless one presup-
poses a subjection which makes the man to be the matter needed,
on which the power can have its action take effect, just as the power
of orders has no effect except on wheat bread. And this jurisdiction
or supervision over the whole Church was given to Peter through
subjection of the faithful to him when it was said to him: "Feed
my lambs," that is, be shepherd and supervisor; and I commit the
Church to you as shepherd, and set it under you. Whence Theo-
philus asserts: "He gave the commission to Peter and to no one
else." [27] Gregory also says the same thing or something similar.[28]
And therefore, even if all the apostles possessed the same power
from Christ and equal power of the keys and of jurisdiction, still
only Peter and anyone to whom he wished to commit it is possessed of the jurisdiction or subject matter. And according to the
manner prescribed in the words: "Feed my sheep," the power to determine jurisdiction is not settled on Peter as something formerly
possessed by all. Rather, jurisdiction is given solely to Peter, although he did divide the power later among others, calling some
of them to this task out of solicitude.

Now, according to a first opinion, the view that no bishop
can perform absolution outside [his] diocese stems from the order
of Peter or of the Church to determine and prohibit, since a bishop
would have the power elsewhere without a specific prohibition. And
thus if he were to act the action would hold, since he has the power,
from his own ordination, and the necessary matter, to wit, a sinner.
He would, however, act wrongly in going against the regulations of
the Church, just as a Latin [priest] reciting the words [of conse-
cration] over leavened bread would accomplish [the act], although
he would commit a sin in going against the regulations of the
Church prescribing unleavened bread for him. The position also
agrees with that respecting dominion over temporal things. Hence,
just as appropriation of things is solely through the decision of men
—and when it has been removed I cannot say "this is mine," but all
things are common—so too when a church regulation is removed,
a given group of people no longer are one bishop's rather than an-

other's. They are indifferently the charge of any priest, and can be absolved by anyone. Moreover, appropriation is made through the Church from the authority given to Peter in the text: "Feed my sheep."

According to a second opinion, however, the position that no bishop can give absolution outside his own diocese follows not only from the regulations of the Church, but also from a defect in the matter, since he does not have any people subject [to him] outside his own diocese. Wherefore, he would not perform absolution outside his own diocese even though he intended to give absolution and, even though he pronounced the words of consecration over a stone or over bread that was not wheat, he would not accomplish anything.

Further, there are three men who assert that in the statement "Feed my sheep" [29] only the power of teaching and building proper to prelates was given to Peter, while its exercise was set down previously when it was said: "Go, teach, etc." Whence the Gloss reads: "Feed my sheep, by word, example, corporeal food." [30]

[6] There is another, a sixth, power which seems to belong to priests from the obligations of the preceding ones. This is the power to receive the things necessary for the sustenance of a suitable life by the persons through whom spiritual things are administered. And this power is given, or rather is declared to be owing, to Peter and the apostles in Matthew 10, where after He had commanded: "Go and preach, etc.," [31] He linked this with an explanation of how they were to relate to temporal things, saying: "You have received freely, give freely." [32] The Gloss comments: "Just as I give you such power without price, so too should you give it freely, lest the gift of the Gospel be corrupted." [33] And there follows the statement: "Do not possess gold or silver or money in your moneybelts"; [34] on which the Gloss comments: "That you may exhort others to a contempt for riches." [35] And there follows the statement: "Neither scrip for the road, nor two tunics, nor shoes nor staff"; [36] with the Gloss commenting: "He cuts off the aid of a walking staff, which is very much like the necessities of life, lest those who teach the king all things concerning God have care for the morrow." [37]

And the power granted them is described: "The worker is worthy of his food"; [38] on which the Gloss comments: "Wherefore He prescribed that they take nothing because everything was owing to them." [39] And the Gloss says: "Take only the necessities sufficient for what is necessary, and from then on you will be better freed to seek eternal things." [40] Other texts on the power of receiving necessities for the maintenance of life are also to be found in the last chapter of Matthew,[41] and in Luke 10.[42]

Therefore, these are the powers the apostles received from Christ. And they received from Christ no other power in addition to these six except that of working miracles to confirm the faith. And bishops and priests do not necessarily succeed them in this, because the confirmation of our faith is so manifest that it does not now need to be confirmed by miracles.

Chapter 13

According to the Authorities Cited, Ecclesiastical Prelates Do Not Have Dominion or Jurisdiction over Temporal Things; nor Are Princes Subject to Ecclesiastical Prelates in Temporal Matters [1]

NOW THAT these things have been stated, we must see what power bishops and priests have in temporal matters and over princes from the powers granted to them. And it seems that from none of the aforesaid powers do they have power directly [2] over temporal things or temporal jurisdiction, except insofar as they can receive things necessary to sustain life. Such a position can be seen by reference to these powers individually.

[1] It is certainly clear in respect of the first power, that of consecration, since this power is totally spiritual and exists equally in all, bishops and priests, even those degraded, suspended, and deposed. This last point follows from the fact that when such ecclesiastics become reconciled, they are not reordained. Accordingly, one can conclude that ecclesiastical prelates have no jurisdiction or dominion over temporal things from this power.

[2] The second power, to wit, the power of the keys in the forum of conscience, is totally spiritual. Wherefore, Chrysostom commenting on John 20: "Receive the Holy Spirit, etc.," [3] says: "Only the spiritual power to forgive sins was given to them." [4] And the pope cannot do anything regarding temporal matters through this power, except when he induces and imposes reparation in the forum of conscience, imposing corporeal penances along with other penances. However, no one is subject to him in this way absolutely, but under multiple circumstances: as, for example, if a person has sinned and wishes to do penance. And even if the sinner wishes to do penance, the pope cannot coerce [5] him through this power in the way a secular judge can impose a fine or a correction on even an unwilling subject, and compel him to accept it.

[3] The third power or authority, that of preaching, is wholly spiritual; and [the pope] does not have dominion through it, since it is not the power of dominion but the authority of a teacher, as the Apostle says: I Timothy 1: "I, an Apostle, am placed in the position of preacher and teacher to the Gentiles." [6] Bernard [writing] to Eugene [states]: "Absolute power is forbidden to the apostles or to apostolic men": [7] and again "You shall tame wolves, and you shall not dominate sheep." [8] And the apostle Peter asserts: "Do not be domineering over your charge, but be an example to your flock." [9] Ecclesiastical prelates, however, can have power indirectly [10] over temporal things through the power of teaching, inasmuch as they induce men to penance, to a restoration of what belongs to another, and to the disposition of temporal things as the order of charity demands.

[4] The whole difficulty concerns the fourth power, judicial power in the external forum. And because of the difficulty one must understand that this power involves two things: to wit, the authority to intervene or have jurisdiction, which is meant in the text: "Tell the Church"; [11] and the power to coerce, [which is meant] in the text: "Let him be to you as a Gentile, etc." [12] For these are the two keys in the external forum. Of the first, indeed, it must be understood that the ecclesiastical judge as such has jurisdiction in the external forum only over spiritual matters, which are called ecclesiastical. He does not have jurisdiction over temporal matters except where a wrong has been committed. And even if it is understood that there is a wrong, it is not necessary for an exception to be made on this account, since the Church has no jurisdiction over any crime except insofar as the crime relates to what is spiritual and ecclesiastical. For two kinds of sin can be committed regarding temporal things: one is a sin of opinion or error, as when it is held that usury, or the keeping of what belongs to another, or the selling of any title whatsoever, is not a mortal sin, or when anyone has doubts about whether according to God such things are licit or illicit. And since all these matters are determined by divine law, according to which an ecclesiastical judge must give judgment, there can be no doubt that the jurisdiction over such things pertains only to an ecclesiastical judge.[13]

The other type of sin [14] is the sin of selling, to wit, the sin of using or spending what belongs to another as if it were one's own. Jurisdiction over such matters pertains to the secular judge alone, who judges according to human or civil laws, which govern appropriations of things and sales, lest things needed for human uses be neglected as they would be if they were common to each and every individual, and in cases where things are held in common without distinction as to individuals, and so that peace might easily be kept among men. This is the reason, accordingly, why appropriation of things of this type is made through the emperors, as Augustine said in his *Commentary on John*,[15] and as is maintained in *Decretum* 7, "Quo iure": "Remove the laws of the emperor, and you cannot say these things are mine. For according to the natural law, there is a single freedom for all men and the possession of all things is common." [16] This is why the secular judge and not the ecclesiastical judge has jurisdiction over sin [17] in temporal matters, unless perhaps jurisdiction was conceded or permitted the ecclesiastical judge by Christ on some other basis.[18]

Bernard noted this when he said to Pope Eugene: "Your power is not in possessions but in hearts," [19] as was argued above and in chapter 10. And in explanation of the text in Matthew 18: "So that every word be confirmed by the evidence of two or three," [20] the Gloss says: "In order for you to prove that this is a sin if it is said not to be a sin. For if one is not satisfied, it is necessary to tell the Church, which judges of sin, and not otherwise." [21] There is also Decretum 96, "Duo sunt," where the pope speaks to the emperor and says: "You know that you value the judgment of those men, namely, priests," [22] to which the Gloss adds: "With respect to spiritual matters." [23] And the supreme pontiffs make the same point: *Extra, Qui filii sunt legitimi, Lator,* where it is asserted that the secular judge or lord should always decide matters dealing with heredity.[24] And in the chapter "Causam" the pope says: "We tend to think that it pertains to the king and not the Church to pass judgment on possessions of this kind, lest we seem to detract from the right of the king of the Angles, who asserts that judgment in such matters belongs to him." [25] And in *Extra, De judiciis, Novit* the pope says: "We do not intend to pass judgment on a base matter; this relates to the king himself, unless by chance in common law, etc." [26] It is asserted in *Extra, De appellationibue, Si duobus,* that there is no appeal to the pope from a secular judge except in a territory subject to or conceded to the Church.[27]

Now to say that the supreme pontiffs teach and write such things from humility [28] is completely pernicious and an affront to heaven. For in *Ethics 4* the Philosopher attributes this to the vice of dissimulation, which is the opposite of truth.[29] He also says that men exhibiting this kind of humility are not virtuous, but timid and flatterers. And in the work *On the words of the Apostles* Augustine makes the following comment: "When you lie for the sake of humility you become a sinner in the act of lying, if you were not a sinner before you lied." [30] And, commenting on John, he says: "Do not be so cautious about arrogance that you relinquish truth." [31]

And Gregory asserts: "Those who entangle themselves in lies are humble in a very careless way." [32]

Now concerning the power of ecclesiastical correction or censure, one must know that directly it is nothing but spiritual, because it can exact no penalty in the external forum except conditionally and accidentally.[33] For although it is the function of an ecclesiastical judge to lead men back to God, and to lead them away from sin and correct them, he has this power only in the manner in which it was given him by God, that is, in respect to separating [the sinner] from the sacraments and from fellowship with the faithful, and things of this kind which pertain to ecclesiastical censure. And I say "except conditionally" insofar as the penitent must wish to repent and accept a pecuniary penance. For an ecclesiastical judge cannot impose a corporeal or pecuniary penance for the commission of a crime in the way a secular judge does, but can do so only if the wrongdoer is willing.[34] If a person does not wish to accept such a penance, an ecclesiastical judge compels him by excommunication or some other spiritual penalty. This is the ultimate penalty [35] an ecclesiastical judge can impose, and he cannot do anything more.[36] I also say "accidentally" because, where there is a prince who is heretical and incorrigible and contemptuous of ecclesiastical censure, the pope can do something among the people to have this man deprived of secular honor and deposed by the people. The pope would do this in the case of an ecclesiastical crime,[37] jurisdiction over which is held by the pope, by excommunicating all who are obedient to the wrongdoer as lord. In this way the people actually would depose him, and the pope would do so accidentally.

Similarly too, in an opposite case, if the pope were criminal and gave scandal to the Church and was incorrigible, the prince could excommunicate him indirectly and depose him accidentally, to wit, by admonishing the pope either himself or through the cardinals.[38] And if the pope refused to acquiesce, the prince could do something through the people to compel the pope to yield or be deposed by the people.[39] For the emperor has the power, by way of appropriating possessions or punishing persons physically, to employ anything and everything to ensure that no one obey or serve such a pope. In fact each can do this to the other. For both pope and emperor have universal and ubiquitous jurisdiction,[40] although one has spiritual jurisdiction and the other temporal.

A distinction, however, must be made on this matter. For when a king is derelict in spiritual matters—in matters such as faith, marriage, and things of this kind—the jurisdiction of which pertains to ecclesiastical judgment, the pope in the first place must admonish him. And if the king is found to be obstinate and incorrigible, the pope can excommunicate him, and can do nothing more except accidentally inasmuch as the pope could act through the people if the king were recalcitrant, as has been said. But when the king sins in temporal matters, the jurisdiction of which does not pertain to ecclesiastical judgment, then the barons and peers of the kingdom [41] —not the pope—are the first to correct him. If the barons and peers cannot or dare not so act, they can request assistance from the Church; and then, when requested by the peers to assist in upholding the law, the Church can admonish a prince and proceed against him in the manner described above.

Similarly, when the pope is derelict in temporal matters, the jurisdiction over which pertains to the secular prince—as, for example, if he were to borrow money in a usurious way or gave protection to usurers—and particularly in matters prohibited by the civil law, the emperor, if there were one, would have the right to be the first to correct him by admonishing and punishing him. For it pertains to the prince in the first place to correct all wrongdoers: Romans 13: "For not without reason does he wield the sword; he is a minister of God, the punisher of wrongdoers in wrath." [42] The Gloss on that verse reads: "And for that reason you are liable for tributes. He says that they were established for this purpose, that good men be praised and evil men be punished." [43] And Jerome, commenting on Jeremiah,[44] and *Decretum* 23. 5 say: "The office of kings is properly to make judgment and justice, and to free from the grip of their attackers the victims of force, and travellers, orphans, and widows, who are easily oppressed by the powerful." [45]

This is why, and commendably so, the emperor Henry deposed two men quarreling over the papacy, using not only canonical but imperial censure, as is written in the *Chronicles of the Romans*.[46] And I say that by right in the first place the emperor has the right to correct a pope immediately in the case of a specifically civil crime. As for the privilege possessed by clerics [47] of being judged only by their bishops, this privilege was granted by princes, and was first obtained by Pope Julius, the second pope in line from Sylvester, while Constantine was still living, as the *Chronicles* state.[48] Nevertheless, some say that this power belongs to clerics by divine right and not as a privilege from princes; and they cite the words of the Psalms: "Do not lay hands on my anointed," [49] which they take to mean priests. Others, however, explain this text as referring to kings, who were anointed at that time.[50] And so we find in Kings 1 that David killed Doech because he said that he had killed the anointed of the Lord, that is, Saul.[51]

If, then, the pope is delinquent in spiritual matters, by conferring benefices simoniacally, by destroying churches, by freeing ecclesiastical persons and chapters from their own laws, or by thinking or teaching badly about the things pertaining to faith or good morals, then in the first place he is to be admonished by the cardinals, who represent the whole clergy.[52] And if he is incorrigible and they cannot eliminate the scandal to the Church by these means, then in pursuance of the right the cardinals have to call on the secular arm. Then the emperor, as required by the cardinals inasmuch as he is a member of the Church, would have to proceed [53] against the pope to achieve his deposition. For the Church possesses the secular sword in some manner, not indeed in its hand or at its command, but with its assent and at its request, as Bernard says to Eugene: "So, too, are the two swords kept for mutual assistance out of a common charity which unites the members of the Church." [54] And agreement on this point is found in *Decretum* 94, "Cum ad rerum," [55] and 23, 5, "Principes saeculi" and the following chapters.[56] This is why we read in the *Chronicles* that, when Constantine II had caused many scandals for the Church because of his own ambition, he was deposed by the princes and was deprived of his eyes through the zeal of the faithful.[57] Similarly, John XII was deposed from the papacy by emperor and clergy, because he was a sinner and a dangerous man, who had been admonished frequently for his own correction and had not reformed; and Pope Leo succeeded while John was still alive. This is the reason, too, why it is said that when the priests received offerings from the people for the making of repairs to the buildings of the temple and did not make them, King Jehoash forbade any more offerings to be made, and placed his own servants in a position to receive the offerings, and it was in this way that he repaired the buildings of the temple from the money received, distributing the money to the workmen.[58]

It follows from what has been said that the whole ecclesiastical censure is spiritual, to wit, by excommunication, suspending, interdicting; and there is nothing further the Church can do except indirectly and accidentally, as has been said. And what is found in Matthew 18 proves that the whole censure is spiritual: "If he will not heed the Church, let him be to you as a Gentile and publican." [59] The Gloss on this text reads: "So that reproof of many might bring about his correction." [60] And the statement follows: "Amen, I say to you, whatsoever you bind, etc.," [61] on which the Gloss reads: "In the bonds of anathema." [62] Chrysostom comments on the same text: "See how he bound the incorrigible person to two necessities, to wit, by a penalty here and now, namely, expulsion from the Church, which He noted when He said: "Let him be to you as Gentile and publican"; and by future punishment, which is to be bound in heaven, so that the fault of a brother might be corrected in a variety of judgments." [63] This is the position of the Apostle in I Corinthians 5, where he says: "He who is called brother among you and is a fornicator, an avaricious man, a worshipper of idols, an evildoer, a drunkard or a robber—do not eat with such a man." [64] Notice here that the Apostle does not go further than excommunication for grave crimes. And instructing all bishops he says in Titus 3: "Avoid the heretical man after a first and second correction, knowing that such a man is self-condemned." [65] It should be noted here that he does not say "burn," but rather "avoid." From this it follows that the aforesaid power is spiritual; and for this reason princes are not subject to it except as has been said. Similarly, concerning the power given to Peter in the words "Feed my lambs," it follows that this is spiritual only, and there is nothing from it applicable to princes, whatever explanation is given for the first, second, or third types of power.

[6] Now the sixth power—that of receiving the things needed for the necessary sustenance of life—is temporal and ought rather to be called a certain right owed to ecclesiastical prelates as a contribution to their livelihood. But princes are not subjects in this respect but only debtors, like the other faithful who receive spiritual things from priests. And although this is owed to them, the apostles nevertheless did not seek this right through a mode of authority, but rather by supplication. The pope, however, can decide that this is owing to ecclesiastics, and they can ask for it in terms of what is owing to them from the abundance of one's possessions; sometimes the pope even compels rebels to pay it by applying ecclesiastical censure.

Chapter 14

Replies to the First Six Arguments

[1] THEREFORE, when Jeremiah is cited in the first instance: "Behold I have placed you over peoples and kingdoms, etc.," [1] I reply: this is to be explained in two ways. Some say this was said in the person of Christ insofar as Jeremiah is interpreted as being the exalted of the Lord.[2] For many things are said in this way about Solomon, which were verified in some sense in Christ as signified through Solomon, as Augustine showed in the *City of God* 17.[3] Therefore Christ Himself, as signified through Jeremiah, was placed above the peoples and the kingdoms of the world and of the devil, when He was placed on the mountaintop and despised the things offered Him.[4] Or else He was placed above those things in His members who, adhering to Him through faith, conquer

the cruelty of kings and kingdoms by their suffering, armed with the constancy of faith, according to the text, "The blessed have conquered kingdoms by faith," [5] and the text of Solomon: "The wise man is better than the strong one." [6]

On the other hand, if this text is understood to refer to the person of Jeremiah, it is well known that he deposed no king from his throne for any reason whatever. Rather, it is to be understood to mean that he is placed over peoples and kingdoms, having authority over them as it were in announcing and preaching truth, in the same way as David and Christ are spoken of in the Psalms: "Moreover, I am set by Him as king on His holy hill, preaching His precepts," [7] although he was also placed over peoples and kingdoms as vanquishing them through patience, when he took a chalice filled with pure wine in his hand, and was ordered to drink for all nations.[8] And therefore the remark follows: "So that you may dash them into pieces," [9] to which the Gloss adds: "Evil things, and that you may blot out and destroy." [10] The Interlinear Gloss reads: "The devil's kingdom, and you shall build," [11] and adds: "Indeed, you shall not scandalize the Church, and you shall plant," adding again: "Good deeds." This is how the saints explain the task, not as a tearing down and a destruction of the kings of the world and their replacement by others, but as the destruction of vices and the establishment of faith and morals, as we learn from I Corinthians 3: "You are God's building, God's agriculture." [12] Wherefore, this is also said about priests but not kings, because this task was not achieved by kingly and secular power, but by spiritual power. Therefore it can be said also that the reply can be interpreted as referring to the priests who lived in Anatoth,[13] because they concerned themselves more with matters concerning faith and morals than with exercising authority over secular power. Accordingly, too, it is asserted there first that the Lord touched His mouth and put words into that man's mouth,[14] because the foregoing statements relate more to what priests do as teachers employing language and doctrine than to what they do as lords employing physical labor and power. This explanation also is confirmed in Bernard's statements to Eugene, Book II, where he explains the character of the papal power: "Gird yourself with your sword," he said, "to wit, the sword of the spirit, which is the word of God." [15] And further on: "For so will you tame wolves, and you shall not dominate sheep." [16]

[2] When it is asserted in the second argument: "Whatever you shall loose on earth, etc.," [17] I reply as follows: according to Chrysostom and Rabanus [18] the only thing meant here is the spiritual power of absolution—absolution, that is, from the bonds of sin. Moreover, it would be foolish to understand that this text gives power to absolve from the bonds of debt. Further, according to Jerome,[19] this power is not to be understood as having effect when the key is wrongly used. Wherefore, he says that priests and bishops who do not understand this text take to themselves something of the pride of the Pharisees when they condemn the innocent or think to banish persons harmful to them, since according to God ordinary life is dealt with by the judgments of those responsibile for such matters and not by the judgments of priests. Jerome makes this point in the same text by an example showing how priests of the Old Law did not cleanse or make unclean, but according to their office were judges of who were cleansed and who were unclean. Richard of St. Victor explains this text in the work, *On the Remission of Sin,* chapter 11, as follows: "The Lord does not say: whatever you wish to bind or loose, but whatever you have bound or loosed. However, the judgment of the priest either binds or absolves just matters, not unjust ones." [20]

[3] When the third argument maintains "Do you not know that you will judge angels?" [21] this is my reply: according to Ambrose [22] and other holy commentators [23] the Apostle is not speaking here about clerics in particular but about the faithful generally, who in scandal to our faith were choosing unbelievers to act as judges in secular matters, and as if there were no wise men among the faithful to act as judges. And he rightly criticized this practice.

[4] Where the fourth argument states "God made two great sources of light, etc.," [24] I reply: the explanation is a mystical one. Moreover, according to Dionysius [25] mystical theology argues nothing without taking its proof from some text of Scripture, since mystical theology is not argumentative. Further, the aforementioned

mystical interpretation is not found among the saints, but precisely a contrary one is. Accordingly, Isidore says in the Gloss, commenting on Genesis, that kingship is to be understood as the sun, and priesthood as the moon. Wherefore, he says: "The splendor of the sun represents the excellence of kingship, with the people submitting to the king, while the splendor of the moon represents the synagogue and the stars its leaders; and all things are based on the stability of kingship as on a firm foundation." [26]

Even granting that the text means what has been assumed, the argument is in our favor. For even though the moon does not illumine the night unless it receives light from the sun, nevertheless, the moon has its proper power given it by God, the power to cool and moisten, which the sun does not possess.[27] The same can be said in respect of the text cited in the interpretation given it. For the prince has knowledge of the faith from the pope and the Church, but he still has a power distinct and proper to him, which he does not receive from the pope but immediately from God.

[5] When the fifth argument maintains that Pope Zacharias deposed the king of the Franks and put Pepin in his place,[28] I reply: the Ordinary Gloss explains that in this case the pope gave consent to those doing the deposing.[29] For it is not written that Zacharias deposed the king of France. But we do find the *Chronicles*[30] saying that Hildericus was completely inactive and inert in exercising rule over France, while Pepin alone governed as leader of the Franks, and was called lord of the household, while his brother Charles lived as a monk. Therefore, the barons of France sent for Pope Zacharias to resolve for them the question of who should be king, the man to whom because of his inactivity the power to rule was given in name only, or the man who bore the entire burden of the kingship. And inasmuch as the lord pope gave as his reply that the man who exercised more usefully the governing powers of kingship ought to be king, the Franks immediately put King Hildericus and his wife away in a monastery, and established Pepin as their king; and Saint Boniface, the ranking archbishop, anointed him king. Martin's *Chronicles*[31] tell the same story. Other *Chronicles*,[32] however, relate that after Hildericus had reigned for four years, he became tonsured as a monk for reasons of piety, and

then Prince Pepin was ordained and anointed king through an election of the barons and exercise of the pope's authority to resolve a doubt among the nobles, even though for sufficient reason the nobles had the power to do this without the pope's assent. It follows from these statements that the pope never deposed the king of France, unless the explanation given is that he consented to the act of those doing the deposing, as the Gloss explains.[33]

Nor is it proper to consider that arguments can be offered based on individual cases which sometimes occur out of devotion to the Church or to some person, or for the sake of a favor or for some such other cause, and not out of obligation to the law. For we find in the same *Chronicles*[34] that Boniface, the sixty-fourth head of the Church, obtained the right for the Roman Church to be chief among all the churches from the Emperor Phocas, because the church at Constantinople was describing itself in writing as the first among them. And from these facts a similar argument can be developed that it pertains to the emperor to transfer the rank of primacy among churches, and to pass ordinances concerning churches.

It is also recorded by Sozomenus, writing in the *Three-Part History*,[35] that the Emperor Constantine intervened at a council of clerics, as Rufinus relates in his *Ecclesiastical History*,[36] where he also says that, when the bishops from almost every land were brought together and quarrels had broken out among them on different issues, disturbances were frequent and petitions were being made by individuals among them. Recognizing that the purpose of this high-level conference was being frustrated by such quarrels, Constantine set a certain day by which all the bishops were to defer to him if they still had any complaints. But when this was done and the council had reconvened, he continued to receive petitions from individuals. Accordingly, keeping all the petitions together in his lap, and without opening them to see what they contained, he said to the bishops: "God has constituted you priests and has given you power to judge us, and we are judged rightly by you. Moreover, you who have been given to us by God are of God, and cannot be judged by men, because it is not fitting that man judge what relates to God. But you should expect God's judgment among yourselves, about which it is written: 'God stood in the synagogue of the gods, etc.' Therefore, lay aside these quarrels which have been present up to now, and desist." And when he had said this, he ordered all the petitions of complaint to be burned together. Does it follow from this, therefore, that similarly it is proper for a prince to intervene in councils of clerics and determine their disagreements and their cases?

Hugh of Florence also said in Book V [37] that Constantine sanctioned and established in his own will [38] that all things pertaining to the ecclesiastical order be under the jurisdiction of the bishop of Rome. And in Constantine's letter to all the Catholic bishops, which Saint Isidore transcribes, Emperor Constantine wrote: "Settling the issue, we decree that the Roman see is to be primary among the four special sees of Antioch, Alexandria, Constantinople, and Jerusalem." [39] And in the same Constantine's will, which the Holy Church so joyfully embraces and places in the body of the *Decretum*,[40] he asserts and ordains that the Roman pontiff, for the time being and whoever he may be, is to be considered superior to all other priests in the world, and to have disposition over all things relating to the worship of God and the faith of Christians and to be procured for their maintenance. Do we therefore assert that because of such things the Roman Church has primacy from the emperors over churches and disposition of these things? Not at all.

Further, on the question of legal rights, it is recorded that at the first Council of Jerusalem, after much controversy thither and yon, Peter rose and gave reasons why the yoke of the Law ought not to be imposed on the faithful, whereupon James with pontifical authority offered a clear statement to the effect that this issue had been settled in the church of Jerusalem, of which he was bishop, and that it could not be transferred to another church except by way of appeal. And James made the point as follows: "I judge, etc." [41] Do we assert, therefore, that although the Roman church is the head, it does not have the exercise of such jurisdiction over churches belonging to other bishops except in cases of appeal? Certainly not.

It is also written that, during the reign of King Henry, the

Romans swore not to elect a pope for themselves without Henry's permission.[42] What inference, accordingly, is to be taken from this? None. I have introduced the point, however, so that it is apparent that one cannot adduce arguments in law from such individual facts as can occur in various circumstances.

[6] To the sixth argument concerning Pope Nicholas,[43] saying that Christ handed over the laws of the heavenly and the earthly empire, I reply: where there is a question about the pope's power in temporal matters, the testimony of the emperor on the pope's behalf is useful, and the pope's testimony on his own behalf is of no greater value unless the pope's statement is bolstered by the authority of a canonical writing.[44] This is especially so in a situation where the emperor and other popes as well assert a clearly opposite view, as is the case here. Such a papal statement is not to be taken seriously.

Nevertheless, the words of the Lord Nicholas can have a true meaning in many ways. One is that the pope can declare what the faithful must do to respond to a common need for a spiritual good, in the manner mentioned above [chap. 7]. And this is so not only with respect to the goods of clerics, but also those of laymen. It can be true in a second way, because the statement can be taken to mean that the Lord consigned the laws of the heavenly and the earthly kingdoms to Peter inasmuch as He gave him power to absolve and bind on earth, whose sentence, absolution, and binding are approved in heaven as long as the key is not used in error, as is expressed in the statement made to Peter concerning the handing over of the keys: "Whatsoever you bind on earth will be bound also in heaven, etc." [45] And the Glosses on Matthew 18 [46] explain the text in this fashion. But it does not seem that the lord pope meant his statement to be interpreted other than through the words of the Lord to Peter: "And I shall give you the keys of the kingdom of heaven," [47] particularly when the lord pope says that, "I shall make Peter the bearer of the key of the kingdom, etc.," as if alluding to the words by which the power was given to Peter. And therefore, since the saints do not attribute to Peter through those words any power other than what has been mentioned, namely, spiritual power, as all the interpreters of this text and of

Matthew 10 [48] assert, it cannot be maintained that the lord pope intends otherwise.

There is, however, a third way in which the lord pope's statement can be taken, which can be verified by various means: namely, that therefore Christ is said to have given to Peter the laws of the heavenly and the earthly empires, because He gave him the spiritual power of joining earthly states to the heavenly empire. And it is in this sense that Maximus speaks of Christ in his Epiphany sermon, saying: "He is that great king who came to unite the earthly kingdom with the heavenly empire." [49] There are some men learned in the law who interpret Nicholas's statement in still a fourth way, as follows: Christ conceded the laws of the heavenly and earthly empires to Peter, by which is meant the law for ruling heavenly and earthly subjects, that is, clergy and laity, who are as it were two equal parts of the Church, over both of which the pope rules in spiritual matters.

Chapter 15
Replies to the Second Set of Six Arguments

[7] NOW WHEN it is asserted in the seventh argument that the emperor swears allegiance to the pope, I reply: Emperor Otto did not swear allegiance to the pope except with respect to the kingdom of Italy, which he had received in fief from the pope or from the Church.[1] Moreover, he swore to hand back the territory of St. Peter if he held it. And this has no significance for other parts of the world, which either do not belong to the empire [2] or do not fall under the Donation of Constantine.

[8] When it is maintained in the eighth argument that the pope deposes the emperor,[3] I reply: it is true that the pope does so for sufficient reason in the case of a man who has received a fief from him. Such arguments, however, are factual ones, and assert what is fact; but they do not describe what ought to be done. Moreover, many arguments for the converse can be adduced from fact, as was said above [4] in the resolution of the fifth argument.

[9] Now what is said in the ninth argument, that the pope transfers imperial power,[5] can be resolved in the same way as above.[6] Nevertheless, it can be said that Constantine never gave imperial power to the Church absolutely. Rather he gave the Church the City and certain western provinces, and the imperial symbols, to remove them from the other provinces; and he transferred his seat [of government] to Constantinople, along with the entire dignity of the imperial power. And so when it is said that the pope later transferred the imperial power from the Greeks to the Germans, I reply: he did not transfer its reality, but only its name. For the Romans considered it an insult that the imperial power or the name "empire" had been transferred from them to Constantinople. This is why they heaped praises on Charles, and gave him the title of emperor when they called him to their defense; and he was victorious. And from that time on it was as if the imperial power was divided,[7] with two men called emperor.

Further, this was not done by the pope alone, but through the acclaim and action of the people, to whom it belongs to subject themselves to whomever they wish,[8] without prejudice to any other. Again, this was done for the necessary and sufficient reason of defending themselves against unbelievers and pagans, when it did not appear they could be defended by any other. And this the people could do by right, for the people establish a king, and the army an emperor. And what about other facts in the case? This was done with special advice from God for the defense of the Church, as was shown to Constantine, the first emperor, and urged on him through an angel who appeared to him in the form of an armed soldier. There is no reason, moreover, why things called for by private law should be arranged by public law. Now all these things pertaining to this deed are set down in the book *On Cosmog-*

raphy[9] and in Hugh of Florence's *Chronicles,* book V[10] and in the *Chronicles* of Sigisbert.[11] Whatever was done in this case notwithstanding, however, the pope did not legislate except insofar as authority to do so had been given him by Constantine. And this I concede can be done by right.[12]

[10] Now to what is said in the tenth argument, that the pope legislates in temporal affairs,[13] I reply: he can grant dispensations in temporal affairs in his own territory,[14] where he has jurisdiction, but elsewhere by way of consequences only, as John notes.[15] Or rather, he cannot legislate even by way of consequences in territory not subject to him. And where the Decretal says that, in granting dispensation with respect to spiritual matters the pope dispenses indirectly by way of consequences in respect of temporal matters,[16] this is to be understood to mean in territory subject to him where, it being conceded that he has the greater power, one should understand it to be also conceded that he has the lesser power as well insofar as he possesses both powers. Beyond these limits, however, he has no power except in spiritual matters, and the Ordinary Gloss notes this in the same place.[17]

I think, however, that if there were persons illegitimate because born from the marriage of illegitimate persons in contravention of the Church's prohibition, the pope can grant a universally applicable dispensation in such cases, and can legitimate[18] such persons in respect of both temporal and spiritual goods, insofar as he can ratify the marriage and make the persons legitimate with respect to this kind of contravention. But if they were illegitimate by reason of a marriage of persons illegitimate in contravention of the natural or divine law, the pope cannot grant a universally applicable dispensation legitimating them with respect to temporal matters.

[11] When it is said in the eleventh argument that the pope sometimes absolves soldiers from their oath of allegiance,[19] I say that this is an argument from fact.[20] Nevertheless, I make the following reply to what is mentioned in this respect regarding the Frankish soldiers. The action referred to was more a declaration of right—to wit, that the oath in such a case was not binding—than it was absolution from the act of swearing fidelity. For it was

done with the consent of the king, who was very aware of his own incompetence and anxious to void his own oath of office and who chose to take up the monastic life. And in this case the barons [21] were able to proceed to the election of someone else, with the pope as it were deciding and declaring the legitimacy of such a course.

One must consider, however, that a vassal has a twofold obligation to his natural lord: one in virtue of what he has received from the lord with the honor of vassalship and under determined conditions, the other in virtue of the bonds of the oath. Now the pope cannot absolve from a natural bond, although in a situation where, for example, a prince is a heretic he can declare that the vassal is not bound to follow the lord but must relieve himself of his obligations and return his fief. The pope, moreover, can absolve a person from the bonds of an oath for a sufficient and clear reason,[22] and in good faith. And relieving a person of his obligation is not valid in the eyes of God under any other conditions since, according to the Apostle, power is not given to the pope for destroying but for building, as has been said above.[23] Moreover, whenever an oath has been taken, a natural obligation always remains and accompanies the deed, unless the fief is returned.

[12] When the twelfth argument asserts that the pope has jurisdiction over wrong,[24] I reply: it follows from what was said above in the beginning of chapter 13 that this is true where there is a question of sin; if, for example, the issue is whether a given action is or is not a sin, is or is not licit. For these things are determined by the natural or divine law, and for this reason are ecclesiastical concerns. But the pope does not have jurisdiction over crimes of commerce, which are determined according to human laws. On the other hand, the pope may be understood to have jurisdiction over every wrong in the forum of conscience, where he must believe the person who confesses.

Chapter 16

Replies to the Third Set of Six Arguments

[13] NOW REGARDING what is said in the thirteenth argument concerning denunciation, the pope made a reply in the same place.[1] For denunciation does not give the pope jurisdiction, because in this way the jurisdiction of princes could be annihilated completely, since every case could be denounced by one party to the pope. But as the pope said there, he did not intend to pass judgment on a base matter, about which it is the province of the king of the Franks to pass judgment, except in a case where in common law something is set aside through special privilege or contrary custom. However, he did intend to make decisions concerning what is sinful, the jurisdiction over which undoubtedly belongs to the pope, as he asserts. And the arguments he adduces support this view.

[14] When it is said in the fourteenth argument: "If your brother has sinned against you, etc. . . . . speak to the Church,"[2] I reply that Chrysostom explained this as follows: "To the Church, that is, to those who rule the Church."[3] Now if the community of the faithful generally is called the Church,[4] and the term "church" is not taken to mean only a group of clerics, the ecclesiastical judge presides over the Church in spiritual matters and the secular judge presides in temporal matters. Or it can be claimed that Chrysostom is speaking of a situation where a sin is involved. Accordingly, the Gloss on this text reads: "So that in the mouths of two or three, etc., if he asserts that there is no sin, they may establish that there is."[5] For it is in this way that, if a man will not accede, it must be reported to the Church, which passes judgment on sin.

[15] To what is said in the fifteenth argument concerning Theodosius,[6] I reply as follows: as jurists [7] have noted on this point, the Theodosian law has been abrogated. But that is precisely why Innocent adduces it, since the reason for the law still has value; and knowledge of the reason is useful for a realization of how much affection the legislator had towards the Church. And the words "whoever has life" are inserted into the body of the *Decretum* 11. 1 [8] to show this. We can also extend the argument further by an appeal to a statute of princes, according to which it can happen that an ecclesiastical judge has jurisdiction over such matters. But if this power belongs to the pope according to a statute of princes, one cannot conclude that it belongs to him naturally inasmuch as he is the vicar of Christ. Rather, the contrary can be concluded; and one can say that although they are not obliged to, princes can revoke from ecclesiastical judges and their predecessors the privileges and powers they grant, just as conversely popes revoke, or can revoke, from princes privileges they have granted.

[16] When it is stated in the sixteenth argument concerning the text of *Deuteronomy:* "If it is difficult, etc.," [9] I reply: there is one special case in which appeal can be made from a secular to an ecclesiastical judge. This is when a doubt exists concerning whether the case is a secular one, particularly where there is a question of sin.[10] It can also be asserted that recourse is not only to a priest, but also to the person who was judge at the time, by which is meant a secular judge. Accordingly, one man will judge of spiritual matters, another of temporal matters. Wherefore, the text says significantly: "To the priest of the tribe of Levites, and to the judge"; and this is how the Gloss expresses it.[11]

[17] To what is stated in the seventeenth argument: "The pope can command the greater, etc.," I reply: that is true in itself with respect to major and minor orders, so that a bishop can give orders to a priest, and accordingly to a deacon as well. However, it does not apply to cases where there are diversities of order or kind, such that if my father can beget a man, so too can he beget a dog; or if a priest can absolve someone from sin, so too can he also absolve [him] from a debt of money.[12]

[18] To the eighteenth argument, that temporal things are ordered to spiritual things, etc., the reply follows from what has been said above in chapter 7.

Chapter 17
Replies to the Fourth Set of Six Arguments

[19] WHEN MENTION is made in the nineteenth argument of legacies and restitutions,[1] I reply: insofar as legacies are made for pious causes they pertain to ecclesiastical law, which is spiritual, as ecclesiastical men say. This is the case particularly when legacies are totally unspecified; then they can be settled by ecclesiastical judgment within the terms of the expressed will of the testator. I do not see, however, that [the pope] can lawfully change the will of a testator in such a way that, if the testator wills a hundred pounds to the poor of the city or the diocese of Paris, the legacy can for some lack of specification be given to the poor of Caen. However, this kind of transfer and grant could be made for a sufficient reason by a prince, who rules over both dioceses or provinces. For he is someone who belongs to the diocese named, and not someone from outside.

Moreover, regarding making restitutions I do not see why they cannot be made through the foresight of any good men for pious uses to the advantage of the country where an imminent necessity exists or as utility demands, and particularly through the foresight of the prince, whose responsibility it is to see to the common benefit. This is the manner in which monies are to be paid out for the common need or benefit in circumstances where individual beneficiaries are not known. Moreover, even though an ecclesiastic has jurisdiction over the sin of usury, and for this reason is the one to judge it a sin and to decide that restitution must be paid, it sometimes pertains to the prince as the embodiment of justice and protector of the just man to impose restitution and punishment for reasons already shown. The case is the same for other contracts in which jurisdiction over heirs seems to pertain even less to an ecclesiastical judge: *Extra, De hereticis, Ad abolendam,*[2] and the following chapter: *Vergentes.*[3] It is the case, however, that princes are to be reprimanded and punished by the pope for negligence in carrying out this responsibility. As Innocent notes, this is done with the consent of the reigning emperor. Sometimes, too, in cases where the testator has not designated any one person to carry out a settlement, the bishop of the district has from the emperor the faculty of demanding and appropriating goods from the executor and the person actually carrying out the settlement: *De sacrosanctis, Nulli licere;*[4] it being the case, however, that when a bishop acquires money from such a source, he must make known to the ruler of the district the amount and the period of time during which he has received such monies. The same text makes this point.

Further, too, the law, *De petenda hereditate, Hereditas,*[5] to which the canonists refer on their own behalf, asserts that the defense and execution of last wills and such other things as pertain to pious causes pertain not only to pontifical authority but principally to the prince, and maintains at the end that heirs are to be compelled to comply with a last will by princely and papal authority, that is, by the authority of prince and pope. What is more, in some cases where restitution is to be made of what belongs to someone else, the problem seems to pertain more to issues of justice than to those of piety. For all these reasons I do not think it follows that such restitution is to be done by ecclesiastical authority alone. It pertains more to the prince, even though it can be done by chance through the foresight of certain good men.

[20] When it is claimed in the twentieth argument that corporeal things are ruled through spiritual things and depend on them as on a cause,[6] I reply: the argument as formulated in this way has many weaknesses. First, because it supposes that kingly power

is corporeal and not spiritual, and that it has care of bodies and not of souls. This is false, as has been said earlier [chaps. 1, 2], since it is not ordered to any common good whatever of states, but to the common good of living according to virtue. The Philosopher asserted in the *Ethics* that the purpose of the lawmaker is to make men good, and to lead them to virtue.[7] And he maintained in the *Politics* that just as the soul is more perfect than the body, the lawmaker is more perfect than the doctor: for the lawmaker has care of souls, the doctor care of bodies.[8]

Secondly, the argument fails because not just any peculiar power is established, moved, and directed by just any spiritual power. For in an organized household the teacher of morals, whose power is spiritual, does not direct the doctor, but both are directed by the head of the household [see chap. 5]. Nor does the teacher of morals direct the doctor inasmuch as he is a doctor; he directs him only accidentally insofar as he wishes to be chaste or to become literate. Thus, the pope does not direct the king, but each is directed in his own way by God. Nor does the pope direct the king essentially inasmuch as he is king, but only accidentally insofar as it is proper for the king to be a believer, direction in which comes from the pope by way of faith and not by way of kingship. Accordingly, the king is subject to the pope in those matters in which the Supreme Power subjects him to the pope: namely, in spiritual matters only.

It also follows that the argument is defective and more in our favor than against us if we take some examples. For, although heavenly bodies are moved to their proper end and are guided by angels,[9] they are not made by angels but immediately by God. Accordingly, one should conclude that terrestrial power is immediately from God, although it is to be directed to the happy life by the spiritual power.

[21] When the twenty-first argument appeals to Hugh's statement that spiritual power institutes temporal power,[10] it can be asserted that Hugh's words are not authoritative and carry a modicum of value. Nevertheless, it can be said following Augustine in the *City of God* that it is the custom of Sacred Scripture to assert that something can be done when that thing has been made mani-

fest.[11] By so much the more, then, did Hugh assert that the spiritual power institutes kingly power, not indeed by bringing the latter into being, since this is from God and the people who give their consent and choice, but because anointing makes manifest that the man has been selected and chosen.[12]

[22] To the twenty-second argument, that "the spiritual man judges all things and is not judged by anyone," [13] I reply: although that authority is frequently and in different cases assumed to be the authority of the pope, this point is not pertinent because the spiritual man referred to in the text is not so called by reason of the spiritual power an ecclesiastical judge possesses. For sometimes a person having this power is an "animal" man, as asserted in the text, since a man is called "animal" in respect to either life or the senses. Now a life is called animal when the person's life is led with lasciviousness of soul and contains no ordering by the spirit; and a man who is animal in respect to the senses is one who judges of God according to the images of bodies or the letter of the law or physical causes. A man is said to be spiritual in terms of life and science. A life which possesses the spirit of God and rules the soul in an orderly way is called spiritual; while a life which judges of God most certainly and faithfully, not according to the human senses but as subject to the Holy Spirit through faith, is called a life of science. This kind of man, accordingly, judges all things as the Gloss puts it: "In certain faith of things which are hidden"; and such a man is judged by no one.[14] The Gloss adds: "That is, it is known whether he judges well or ill; or he is judged by no one, that is, he is reprimanded [by no one]." [15] And Jerome and Augustine [16] explain the text in this way; and any man who follows the words of the Apostle knows this.

[23] I reply to the twenty-third argument concerning the order of ends [17] as follows: it has many weaknesses. First, the art to which a higher end pertains does not move and rule absolutely the art to which a lower end pertains, but only insofar as it relates to the former according to the necessity of its own final end. And this is partly conceded in the argument above [chap. 27, *ad* 20].

This argument has a further weakness, because the superior art does not always rule the inferior necessarily by moving it according to the mode of authority and by directing it. It sometimes rules the inferior only according to the mode of direction. This is how the doctor directs the druggist, and judges of him whether he mixes drugs well or ill; but he does not correct or punish the druggist. There is someone such as the king or the lord of the state superior to both doctor and druggist, to whom the whole order of the state belongs. And it is this man who must correct or punish the druggist who does not mix drugs in a manner acceptable to the doctor. And so in the argument proposed the whole world is as it were one state in which God is the supreme power which directs both pope and prince, etc.

The aforesaid argument is defective in a third way because, although it has some appeal where what pertains to an inferior art does not possess the nature of the good or appetible in itself but only as it is ordered to a higher end which the superior art aims at —just as the mixing of medicines which the druggist performs relates to health which the doctor intends—nevertheless, the aforesaid argument has no appeal where what pertains to the inferior art possesses in itself the nature of the good or appetible according to its own nature. And to live according to virtue is of this kind. For there are many things good and appetible in themselves which nevertheless are orderable to something else, as the Philosopher says of friendship in *Ethics,* 8.[18] He says the same thing about knowing and seeing and such things in *Book X.*[19]

A fourth weakness in this argument stems from the fact that even if one grants its validity in certain particular circumstances where the inferior end does not lead to the superior end except in a determinate way (and hence to be deficient in respect to that determinate way is to be deficient absolutely and to remain useless in respect to that end) nevertheless, where the inferior end has various connections with the superior, it does not follow that deficiency in one of these connections renders useless the power contained in the inferior. For there is another connection between the inferior and the end, a connection perhaps known only to the Supreme Power; and it is on account of this connection that He wills the inferior to continue to be useful. This is how it is with kingly power, because the people are not only directed to God by it insofar as a king uses this power as king, but also insofar as a king uses it as a tyrant, to the extent that the tyranny of princes exists as a punishment for sins, as Job says: [20] God makes a hypocrite to reign because of the sins of the people, or to test the patience of those in subjection, or to compel them to take refuge in God, Who alone can change the hearts of kings for the better, according to the words of Solomon: "A king's heart [is] in the hand of God, and He will incline him in whatever way He wishes." [21] God can also change by way of conversion tyrants whom He considers unworthy, according to the text of Wisdom: "God had destroyed the thrones of the proud rulers, and has made the humble to sit in their places." [22] And He says through Ezekiel: "I will free My flock from the mouths of those who have charge of them." [23]

[24] When it is maintained in the twenty-fourth argument that it is the pope who hands over laws to princes, and that the prince cannot make laws or use them unless they have been approved by the pope, I reply that this is false, as Pope Leo asserts explicitly in a letter to Lotharius Augustus: *Decretum* 10: "Concerning your imperial chapters and precepts and those of your predecessors, they are to be kept without any change and obeyed insofar as we value them; and we give them the value of Christ. And we decree that they are to be kept in every way both now and always. And if perchance anyone has told you differently or will tell you so, you will know that he is certainly a liar." [24] Nor did he ever derogate laws through the canons except for spiritual reasons; nor can the pope remove laws unless they are in his forum, as John and others say.[25]

To assert, moreover, that those masters maintain that the pope hands laws over to princes and that the prince cannot in any way enforce laws unless they have been approved by the pope is to destroy kingly and political power totally, and to fall into the error of Herod, who feared and tried to destroy the earthly kingdom of Christ. For according to the Philosopher in *Politics* 1,[26] a leader is called kingly only when there is someone preeminent according to laws which he himself has established. Indeed, when he is not preeminent according to his own judgment but according to laws which the citizens or others have established, he is said to be a civil or political ruler, not a kingly ruler.²⁷ Therefore, if no prince rules except according to laws handed over by the pope and approved by him first, no one would exercise leadership as a kingly or political ruler but only as a papal ruler. And this destroys kingship and nullifies every former leader.²⁸

Chapter 18
Replies to the Fifth Set of Six Arguments

[25] WHEN THE twenty-fifth argument asserts that the priesthood is called royal because priests are kings,¹ I reply: it follows from what has been said [chaps. 2, 8, and 9] that the priesthood is not called royal from the kingdom of the world but from the kingdom of heaven, to which it orders and directs. Either that or, according to the intention of Saint Peter, the text has reference to all the just faithful who are kings and priests in Him ² inasmuch as they are one with Christ the head, attributing to the members what belongs to the head according to the law of Tichonius.³ Or else they are designated in terms of kingship because Christ their king reigns in them, and they are called priests because they offer to God a sacrifice of praise and anguish of spirit as do all just men.

[26] When the twenty-sixth argument refers to the Old Law in which the king was anointed ⁴ by the priest, I reply: it is not necessary for secular power to be anointed, for persons like Moses and Joshua and their successors, through whom God provided [for His people], were leaders of this people before kings were anointed. Neither is it from necessity that a king who has more perfect authority [than these men had] be anointed, since other peoples

have kings who are not anointed. Among that people, however, kings were anointed as a mystery and as a symbol of Christ,[5] Who was to be born from that people, and Who was anointed with the oil of grace and exaltation in advance of His participators. I say that "signed by oil" refers to the oil by which kings were anointed by that people. The same thing may also be observed among Christian kings, who consider themselves members [of the body] of Christ. For it is not unsuitable that kings among God's people be true kings, and nevertheless also be symbols of a higher king, as Augustine says: "This anointing of kings was surely done by the priesthood in anticipation and to symbolize that He Who would be at one and the same time king and priest, namely Christ, would be born from that people."[6] But the things instituted among that people were not to be handed down to the Christian people, since many of them were symbols. Wherefore, we do not read in the New Testament that priests should anoint kings. Nor is this even done among all Christian kings, as witness the case of the kings of Spain.[7] Therefore the argument is worthless for the point at issue.

Further, that anointing was a consecration. But according to the law of Papius,[8] to consecrate is to give to God. Therefore, it follows that one cannot conclude from this that the priesthood is greater than kingly power in temporal matters and in worldly concerns, but that it is greater only in the concerns of God. In the same way, the fact that the sins of kings are expiated through offerings made to priests does not prove that the priesthood is greater than kingly power except in those things which relate to God, as is said in *Decretum 2. 7,* "Nos si incompetenter,"[9] That the argument is not conclusive follows, moreover, from the fact that the priests of the Old Law who anointed kings were undoubtedly subject to kings.

[27] When argument twenty-seven asserts that there cannot be a kingly state without true justice,[10] I reply: it must be asserted that the moral virtues can be acquired perfectly without the theological virtues [11] and that the former are not perfected by the latter except by a kind of accidental perfection, as Augustine suggests in the *Book of Sentences of Prosperus.*[12] Therefore, the true and perfect justice a kingship requires exists without the reign of Christ,

since kingship is ordered to the life of acquired virtue, to which it is accidental that it be perfected by any other virtue whatsoever. Either that [is his position], or Augustine declares that no true justice exists where Christ is not the ruler not because there cannot be true justice [without Him] but because not even acquired virtue could be found among those who believed they were serving justice by serving demons and idols; and Augustine says against them that they did not serve true justice.

It can also be said that the state of a Christian people is not ruled rightly unless the pope rules, since he is the vicar of Christ in spiritual matters, and that justice is not maintained otherwise than by his being obeyed, since he is just in spiritual matters.

[28] When the twenty-eighth argument asserts that it is necessary for those powers to be ordered in a certain way from God,[13] I reply: they have an order according to dignity but not according to causality, as has been said [chaps. 5, 6], since one does not derive from the other. In the same way all the angels are made by God according to a certain order of dignity, inasmuch as one thing is always more noble than another among natural things: but no order of causality exists there by which one derives from another, since all are created immediately by God.[14] Moreover, the meaning of the Apostle seems to refer to the order of things according to their own proper ends, and not to the order of one thing to another. This follows from the fact that he submits himself to the prince because a minister of God is bound, etc.

[29] Now when the twenty-ninth argument brings forward the concept of one head, the reply can be made that there is one church, one Christian people, and one mystical body.[15] However that one head is not Peter or Linus; Christ alone is properly and supremely head of the Church, and it is from Him that both powers are distributed as distinct according to different grades—Ephesians 2: "He made all things subject under His feet, and He gave them a head over the whole Church, which is His body." [16] Ambrose commented on this that He is head according to humanity; [17] and in Ephesians 5 it is asserted that Christ is head of the Church.[18]

Nevertheless, it can be said that the supreme pontiff is head with respect to the external behavior of ministers inasmuch as he is

chief among ministers, and that the whole order of ministers depends on him in spiritual matters as the principal vicar of Christ as
[it depends] on a high priest and architect. So too the Roman church
undoubtedly is head among all the churches.[19] He is not, however,
head in respect to rule over temporal matters or in the disposition
of temporal affairs. Rather, whoever is king is the head of his own
kingdom in these matters, and the imperial monarch, if there is one,
is head of the world.[20]

One must also consider here that some men try to show that
kings and princes are subject to the supreme pontiff in temporal
matters according to an ecclesiastical hierarchy that must have one
supreme ruler, namely, the supreme pontifl. The result is that both
spiritual and temporal power reside in the supreme pontiff. These
men proceed to this conclusion in different ways.

In truth, however, the contrary of their position can be learned
from that ecclesiastical hierarchy. For according to blessed Dionysius,[21] the laity who are as it were imperfect are in the lowest grade
in the ecclesiastical heirarchy, along with their kings. They are, however, perfectible. Above them are the perfect, and above these are
the more perfect still: ecclesiastical men. In the highest rank is the
supreme monarch of all: the pope. The doctrine of the same Dionysius, however, asserts that the lowest are not reducible to the
highest except through the middle ranks.[22] Furthermore, the highest ranks of the hierarchy do not relate to the lowest directly, but
rather through the mediation of the middle ranks. The supreme
pontiff, therefore, does not exercise general and immediate power
over the laity except through the middle ranks: for example, bishops
or abbots exercise that power by virtue of an immediate and more
contracted hierarchy. For although the supreme monarch, God, can
have a relationship to the lowest angel in the angelic hierarchy because there can be no medium in relation to Him in terms of the
act of creation and the act of reducing [them] to nothing, nevertheless He does not possess this power in terms of the hierarchy, but
insofar as He is God, the creator.[23] Since, therefore, some among
those in the middle more perfect ranks do not possess both spiritual and lay power but only spiritual power over the laity, it is
clear that in terms of his position in the hierarchy the supreme

pontiff possesses only spiritual power according to the concept of rank in an ecclesiastical hierarchy, even though he possesses more general power to the extent that it operates everywhere.

This is why, when dealing with the hierarchical order in Book III of his letter to Pope Eugene, Bernard gave no power to the pope which he did not give to lesser prelates, although he did give the supreme power to the pope. "Wherefore," he says, "You are mistaken if you consider that your apostolic power as supreme power is therefore also the sole power instituted by God. If you think this, you dissent from him who says: "There is no power except from God." [24] Similarly, what follows asserts: "He who resists power resists what is ordained by God, even if he does it principally but not entirely on your behalf." [25] And he says the same thing again: "Every soul is subject to more sublime powers." [26] He does not say to "*a* more sublime power," as if referring to one person, but to "more sublime powers," as if referring to many persons. Your power, therefore, is not the only one from the Lord: there are also middle powers, and lower powers." [27] Notice in that hierarchical order [Bernard] clearly gives no power to the pope which he does not give to the middle prelates, although he gives the pope supreme power. It follows from this that since these middle powers do not have any power from Christ except spiritual power, it cannot be that the pope alone has temporal power by virtue of his supremacy in the hierarchy of the Church.

And the saints assert this. It is said in Matthew 16 [28] in the very same words, that Christ did not give any power to Peter which He did not give to the other apostles and bishops and priests, although Peter is said particularly to have received the keys because of the leadership he received from Christ, as Rabanus [29] and the Gloss [30] assert. Because of this, too, what was said of Peter in particular in Matthew 16 [31] was also said in the same terms of all in Matthew 18: "Whatsoever you shall bind, etc."; [32] and in John 20 it is said of all: "Receive the Holy Spirit, whose sins you shall remit, etc.," [33] on which Chrysostom comments that only their spiritual power was specified.[34] I have made this digression here, however, because many great men have tried to show by an appeal to the unity of the ecclesiastical hierarchy that the pope has both swords.[35]

It should also be pointed out that when Bernard argues from the aforementioned order of hierarchy to reprimand the pope for disturbing that order by claiming that abbots and lesser ranks of bishops are directly subject to himself, the point [Bernard] is making is not found in the celestial hierarchy on which the ecclesiastical hierarchy is modelled. Bernard seems to think that the papal action [he is condemning] cannot even be done legally, inasmuch as the Lord said to the pope through Moses: "Look and act according to the example shown you on the mountain." [36] For he suggests that this text involves a dispensation but not a destruction, since dispensation and not destruction is credited to the pope. However, I do not agree with the whole of Bernard's position here.

[30] Where the thirtieth argument refers to the two swords: "Behold two swords here," [37] I reply: this is only a kind of allegorical interpretation from which no valid argument can be made. For, as has been said elsewhere,[38] according to Dionysius mystical theology is not argumentative. And Augustine says in his letter to Vincent that an allegory is not sufficient to prove a point unless some clear authority can be found to support it.[39] I can also say that the two powers being discussed here are not to be understood mystically from those two swords, particularly since none of the saints whose doctrines have been approved and confirmed by the Church have explained them mystically in this way.[40] Rather, everyone understands the word of God as symbolized mystically by those two swords, according to the words of the Apostle in Ephesians 6: "Take the breastplate of faith and the sword of the spirit, which is the word of God." [41] Moreover, two swords are spoken of here because of the Old and the New Testaments. Either that, or by the two swords are understood the sword of the word and the sword of present persecution, concerning which the statement was made of Blessed Mary in Luke 2: "A sword shall pierce your heart because of Him," [42] and in II Kings 13: "A sword shall not recede from your house." [43] These swords ought then to have been enough. And one of them—namely, the sword of persecution—belonged to the apostles passively because it was suffered by them. However, the other, the sword of God's word, was properly theirs because it was to be drawn by them at the appropriate time.

Granting, however, that the two powers of the spiritual and temporal are to be understood in terms of the two swords the apostles possessed, they are still not said to belong to Peter or any other apostle, even though the swords are said to be theirs. For Peter did not touch one of them, namely, the secular sword, because it was not his. He did, indeed, touch the other, the spiritual sword, which the Lord said was his alone, and yet it was not to be drawn by Peter straightaway. Whence the statement was made to him: "Put up your sword into its scabbard." [44] For an ecclesiastical judge certainly ought not to use this sword instantly, but with great deliberation and in circumstances of great necessity for his own spiritual extremity. Otherwise he is to be condemned. Granting, therefore, that those two powers are to be understood mystically by the two swords, this point is in our favor because Peter possessed only one of them as his own, even though there were two. This is why the Lord also said in Matthew 10: "I did not come to bring peace to the world, but a sword," [45] where He says significantly "a sword" and not "swords." And it is said in the person of Christ: "Place your sword on your thigh, etc."; [46] and in Revelation 1, about the Son of Man seated in the midst of the lampstands; [47] and in Apocalypse 19, the comment is made about what is called the word of God, that there issued from his mouth a sharp two-edged sword.[48] Notice, therefore, that he had only one sword from Christ.[49]

Nevertheless, it can be said that the two swords are said there to have existed and to pertain to the apostles, one belonging in itself to the apostles and their successors, which they possessed from Christ, and the other theirs in terms of readiness because it was not repugnant to them and would be theirs with the commission and permission of princes. It can also be said that the aforementioned authority of Bernard [50] is in our favor because he says that both swords belong to the Church, but the material sword is *for* the Church while the spiritual sword is to be exercised *by* the Church. The latter sword is in the hands of the priests, the former in the hands of the soldiers. The material sword, however, must be used well for the assistance of the priest and not by his hand or his command. For he does not have authority to order or compel in this sphere but only to persuade, and that at the emperor's wish.[51]

Chapter 19

Replies to the Sixth Set of Six Arguments

[31] WHEN THE thirty-first argument makes reference to that man from Cremona,[1] I reply: although he throws in many points in support of his position, nevertheless his statements are without doubt so unskilled that they do not seem cogent to me or even worthy of being repeated. However, we shall examine them one by one.

When he says that the Lord ruled by Himself from the beginning of the world until the time of the Flood and that afterward He ruled through Noah, Abraham, Moses, and others, I assert that this position has many defects. First, it supposes that these men were priests. This clearly is false in the case of Noah, since he was neither a priest nor did he perform any of the official tasks of a priest, notwithstanding the fact that he did erect an altar to the Lord. For the acts of erecting an altar to the Lord or praying to Him or calling upon Him are not properly those of a priest, since such acts are not prerogatives of priests only: James 5: "Pray for one another that you be saved." [2] And even if Noah had been a priest, it cannot for that reason be said that he ruled the world through the priesthood, because it is not written that Noah built an altar to the Lord until after he had constructed and commanded the ark.[3] Further, statements about Abraham and Moses show that they were not true priests, since no true sacrifice was offered before that of the true victim, Christ, Who was the first true priest, as follows from chapter 4. Nor were men like Aaron priests in any legal or symbolic manner in respect of dignity and office, although sometimes they were anointed. Nor were sacrifices even performed, although in times of necessity and because of the absence of priests these men did perform some of the actions of priests, as when Moses anointed Aaron, or some such thing. This is why it is said in the Psalms: "Moses and Aaron among the priests, etc." [4] And Anacletus, the second pope, says as much in the letter he wrote to the bishops established in Italy.[5] And even the fact that Abraham is called priest is not relevant, because so too is a person who is more mature not only in age but in wisdom called a priest, in *Decretum* 196, the final chapter.[6]

This argument has a second weakness because, granting that these men were priests, they were still constituted by God to be princes; and therefore they ruled the people as princes rather than as priests. Furthermore, it does not follow that even though the two powers were not distinguished as to subject then, they should exist in one person now. For what was that way then because of the imperfection of the priesthood God later willed to be increasingly more distinct from secular power inasmuch as it achieved greater perfection. Wherefore, as the two powers were distinct in subject in the days of Kings and Judges, so much the more should they be distinct now, as has been said in chapter 10.[7]

[32] The assertion in argument thirty-two that the same person has dominion over the end and over things relating to the end [8] can be seen to be a crude one. This same type of argument might be used to assert that the man who is lord of all horses is thereby lord of all bridles (which exist for the sake of horses). And it is clear to anyone that this does not follow. The argument also errs materially, because it is not true that the pope is lord of spiritual things. For he is only a minister: I Corinthians 4: "Thus man considers us as Christ's ministers and so dispensers of God's mysteries." [9] Moreover, it does not follow that because there is only one lord of spiritual and temporal things there is only one minister. Rather there will be many: I Corinthians 12: "There are divisions of administrations, but only one God, and divisions of works but the same God Who works all things in all things." [10]

Replies to the argument given above concerning ends [chap.

17, *ad* 23] can also be adapted to these texts. In fact, the Cremonan's remark that God gave all things to Peter is frivolous. For He
did not give to Peter [the power] to be their lord, but to be their
teacher and defender against spiritual wolves. Wherefore, Bernard
said to Eugene: "You shall have dominion over wolves, but not over
sheep." [11] And Peter said: "Not as having dominion over those in
your charge but being an example to the flock." [12]

And the Apostle's remark "All things are yours" [13] is not to the
point, because he is not speaking of Peter or of the pope but of all
the faithful, especially the just to whom all things belong insofar as
they relate to some use of cooperation with the good, this being the
way in which all things belong to the just: *Decretum* 23. 7.[14] Or
else he asserts this because, as the Gloss on that text of I Corinthians 12 puts it, "Charity does not seek what is one's own, it makes
everything common so that no one has what is his, yet he has what
is another's to whom it is one in charity." [15]

[33] When argument thirty-three speaks of the sins of emperors on account of which the rule of empire was transferred to
the pope, I reply: this is completely ridiculous. In the first place
because, as Augustine shows in the *City of God* 4,[16] God wills
kingdoms and empires indiscriminately to both good men and bad,
although He wills happiness to the good. And so it is not according to divine law that emperors are to be deprived of their
empires for their sins. Secondly, because not all emperors have
committed the outrages mentioned, the sins of some of them
should not be attributed to other emperors. This is especially so
because they do not succeed to an empire by heredity, but are
elected by the army and through popular support.[17] There is also
a third reason: there have been some popes who were scandalous
and heretical, and who were justly deposed; nevertheless, their
wrongs were not attributed to their truly and duly elected successors. Fourthly, conceding that a guilty emperor can be deprived of
his office, nevertheless nothing of his office in the empire accrues to
the pope as a result of the emperor's crime. For as Augustine says:
"In sinning man justly submits himself to the devil, not however in
the sense that the devil justly has dominion over him." [18] And
this holds particularly with reference to the issue here, for domi-

nation is forbidden to priests, as has been shown above [chap. 8]. Fifthly, what is insinuated at the end of the argument—namely, that what is owed to emperors is so owed from a privilege—is false. For we never hear that this privilege was ever granted by clerics to emperors. Rather, imperial authority is owed them by right, through the action of the people and of the army: *Decretum* 93, "Legimus"; [19] and through the inspiration of God because it is from God: *Decretum* 23. 4, "Quaesitum." [20] And the Commentator says in the *Ethics* 8 that a king exists by the will of the people; but when he is king it is natural that he rule. [21]

[34] When the thirty-fourth argument speaks of the greater power the Church has now through those powers than it had in the beginning, [22] I reply: insofar as the argument appeals to an allegory on this point it has no merit because, as Augustine says in the *Letter to Vincent:* "An allegory does not suffice as proof unless accompanied by a clear authority"; [23] and Dionysius says that mystical theology is not argumentative. [24] Further, the point of the text of Luke 14 [25] concerning the parable of the banquet and the text of the *Psalms* ("Why are the people plotting in vain?") [26] seems—rather than what those men maintain—to convey a moral sense in relation to the persecution of Christ which He now continues in His members through evil men and in His members by the dominion [He will have] over them in the future when all things will be subject to Him in heaven (as the Apostle says in Hebrews 2). [27] However, if the whole is to be explained in terms of the state of the Church Militant in different ages, as they maintain, this still does not support their position. For, as Augustine says in *On the Words of the Lord,* [28] the Lord does not speak as if the Church can now coerce the Jews and Gentiles to the faith, or assert that there are not now in temporal matters things subject by right to kings and princes as was the case in the past. He speaks rather of heretics, who are understood through the term "fences," for those who construct fences make divisions. These are the men who are to be compelled [29] by the Church by law to return. The Church, however, did not do this in the beginning because it lacked the power to do so, insofar as princes and kings were not so favorably disposed to the Church as they are now.

Accordingly, they can act in this way with the support of princes.
And this is how the subject is dealt with in *Decretum 23.* 4 and 6. [30]

[35] Where argument thirty-five refers to [God's] granting
permission for a king only after having been offended,[31] I reply:
the argument has many weaknesses. The Lord established a king
among those people at the same time as the priesthood or before
it, although not with full power [cf. chap. 4]. This can be seen
in the case of Moses and Josuah and their successors who ruled
over that whole people. Wherefore, Moses said, *Numbers* 27, "Let
the Lord God of the spirits of all flesh provide a man who shall be
before this multitude." [32] And it is written concerning individual
judges who lived after Josuah, that the Lord raised up a savior
and that the spirit of God was in them, as follows from Judges 3.[33]
Therefore, they were established by God and were not sent in
judgment of those men, and they were kings in some way inasmuch
as they were individually preeminent over that whole people,
which is the nature of kingship [cf. chap. 1]. This was not, however, a pure rule of kings as distinguished from aristocracy—in
which several men rule according to virtue—or from democracy—
that is, the rule of the people—as will be seen. For still later, in
answer to their petition, He gave them [the right] to have a king
with the fullness of power,[34] although He did not commit to them
[the right of] choice, as the argument asserted. Rather, He reserved the right of choice, as follows from Deuteronomy 17, where
it is said: "You shall constitute as king him whom the Lord, your
God, has chosen." [35] It is also not against kingly dignity that He
granted a king as if offended by their petition, *I Kings,* 8,[36] because
a similar argument could be made concerning the priesthood.
For when Moses said to the Lord, Exodus 4: "Lord, send him
whom You shall send, the Lord said in anger to Moses: Your
brother, Aaron, the Levite, I know to be eloquent: he shall be
your spokesman, etc." [37]

But why, then, did He grant them a king when offended? It
can be asserted that this does not mean that kingly rule was displeasing to Him absolutely as an evil, but that He chose that
people for Himself as unique, Deuteronomy 7,[38] and established
for them first a rule more pure than kingly rule—to wit, a mixed

rule—which indeed was better than a pure kingly rule,[39] particularly for that people. There were two reasons for this: one, because although a rule in which one man is absolutely first according to virtue is better than any other simple rule, as the Philosopher shows in *Politics* 3,[40] nevertheless a mixture of aristocracy and democracy is better than a pure form of rule inasmuch as in a mixed form everyone has some role in ruling. For peace is preserved among the people in this way, and everyone loves and preserves this type of domination, as is stated in *Politics* 2.[41] And this was the type of rule best established by God among those people. It was royal inasmuch as one man was absolutely preeminent over all as an individual, like Moses or Josuah; and it was also something of an aristocracy, which is leadership according to virtue by some of the best leaders, inasmuch as the seventy-two elders were chosen [to serve] under that single man: Deuteronomy 1.[42] And it was also something of a democracy, that is, rule by the people, inasmuch as the seventy-two were elected from all the people and by all the people. And thus it was the best mixture, inasmuch as everyone had something to do with or some role in that rule. And certainly this kind of rule would be the best for the Church, with several men being elected by every province and from every province under one pope. In this way everyone would have some role to play in the rule of the Church.[43]

There was another reason why such a role was better for that people than a pure kingly rule, namely, because although a kingly rule is best in itself if it is not corrupted, nevertheless because of the great power handed over to a king it is easy for a kingship to degenerate into a tyranny, unless there be perfect virtue in the man to whom this kind of power is given.[44] For, as is said in *Ethics* 10, "It is for the virtuous man to bear good fortune well."[45] This perfect virtue, however, is found in few men,[46] and it is particularly scarce among that people insofar as the Jews were cruel and prone to avarice—the very great vices through which one is led into tyranny. Therefore, the Lord did not establish among them a king with such great power, but a judge and a governor with charge over them in the manner just described. For it was in this way that He took greater care of them. Consequently, when He established a king later in answer to their petition as if offended, it was because they were rejecting the other rule which was more useful to them.

Now when reference is made in the same argument to the text of Hosea 8 concerning kings: "They have exercised royal authority, and not from Me"; [47] this has no bearing on the point at issue. For the statement concerns evil kings, and the same thing can be said about evil ecclesiastical authorities, who do not enter the sheep's fold through the door, or who abuse the authority they have been given. And it can be said further that that authority is in our favor, because in Book II to Eugene, Bernard offers the following explanation to those who ask about the authority of the pope and prelates: "It is plain that dominion is forbidden to the apostles. Accordingly, how dare you usurp it either as master of the apostles or as an apostolic lord. Plainly you are prohibited from possessing either one or the other. How else do you think you are exempt from a place among those men of whom the Lord complained, saying: They have exercised authority and not from Me; they established themselves as princes, and I have not known them." [48]

[36] When it is asserted in the thirty-sixth argument that the holdings of priests were exempted by the Pharaoh from tribute and tax,[49] it can be said that this text showed that priests ought to be exempted in respect of personal debts, and also in respect of the dwelling place or manse of the Church, and in respect of things given to them. In this way they are priests and ministers of God for the redemption of souls, and not with reference to the things which by title or sale or otherwise are acquired for the Church. These things are handed over to them as a charge, as is noted in *Decretum 23*, "Tributum," [50] and in the chapter "Secundum canonicam." And it is a favor granted to churches by princes and emperors, as is said in the same text.[51]

Chapter 20
Replies to the Seventh Set of Six Arguments

[37] MOREOVER, to the objection in the thirty-seventh argument concerning bishops summoned by the pope and who remained at the order of the emperor and were reprimanded by the pope because of this, it can be stated, just as John noted with respect to the same text [1] and later in the same question, *Quo ause,*[2] that this is to be understood only of those bishops who were content with a Levitical share.[3] It is understood, however, not to apply to others holding royal articles or other possessions, since such things go along with their particular responsibilities. Rather, such men are held to be obedient to their lords; and the following chapter expressly makes this distinction. But it must be noted, and the point seems very similar, that a monk who is transferred to a bishopric is more directly subject to the archbishop than to his own abbot, and must be more obedient to him. Similarly, a monk transferred to the charge of any parish is held to greater obedience toward the bishop of that region than to his own abbot in matters pertaining to the charge of the parish; the bishop can visit and correct him. Accordingly, a bishop who accepts feudal [4] obligations, especially when this is done with the knowledge and permission of the supreme pontiff, is bound more closely in obedience to his temporal lord than to the supreme pontiff. Indeed, in circumstances where a prince has given him orders in matters pertaining to feudal obligations, he seems to be as far removed from the pope as is the monk from his abbot. Hugh of St. Victor also adjudged

the matter in this fashion in *On the Sacraments* 2. 4, saying that
princes endowing a church cannot transfer dominion to it in such
a way that they themselves retain nothing of dominion. His statement is as follows: "The Church can have lay persons as ministers
through whom it enacts laws and judgments pertaining to temporal
power according to the tenor of laws and the obligations of human
rights. This is in such a way, however, that those who have such
power recognize that they have power from a temporal prince,
and understand that those possessions themselves can never be
removed from kingly power. Rather, if reason and need require,
that power itself owes protection to them, and the possessions owe
it obedience in time of need. For just as kingly power cannot give
protection which belongs to someone else, so too possession, even
that obtained by ecclesiastical persons, cannot negate an obligation owing by rights to a kingly power for protection. For it is
written: 'Render unto Caesar the things that are Caesar's, and to
God the things that are God's.' " [5]

But it is asserted strongly that some men deserve to be deprived of that right should they impede a spiritual good—for example, by impeding bishops from going to the Roman curia even
when they have been called to take part in some spiritual negotia-
tions, or when they or others find it necessary to go there for
dispensation from an irregularity or for some such reason. It is
clear, moreover, that to impede passage in this way is to impede a
spiritual good. Further, such prohibitions of journeys and such
laws against any persons carrying money out of a kingdom [6] can
bring about the collapse of the Roman curia; wherefore the pope
can legitimately complain about and prohibit such things, and
reprimand the forces of any prince who attempts such things.

I reply: to absolutely prohibit anyone from passing or to
impede anyone for whatever reason would be to impede a spiritual
good. But if the prohibition had an exception—for example, were
the prohibition to hold except for a sufficient reason, with the
prince given the authority to grant permission on hearing the
reason—a spiritual good would not be impeded. The prince should
not be considered thereby to have acted unjustly and to be harm-
ing the Church—even if the Roman curia is injured by such pro-

hibitions by not receiving its normal services—unless he has acted for the sole intention of doing damage. For if he acts in this fashion to his own advantage or to the advantage of his own country, this is licit for him even though he causes hardship to others as a consequence, because it is licit for anyone to exercise his own rights.

An argument in support of this view: Someone has a stream rising from its source, which divides and irrigates the gardens of his neighbors with its waters. This man then makes the water rise or run through various parts of his home, and in this way the water is prevented from running into the gardens of his neighbors. Is it not licit for him to do this? The law claims that it is licit, even though something inconvenient happens to others. For the man is making use of what is his by right. So, too, even when the prince acts in this way with the intention of doing harm it is licit in some circumstances for him to do so, namely, if he were to present probable or clear arguments that the pope intended to be his enemy, or that the pope called the prelates to this meeting for the purpose of attempting to arrange something with them against the prince or his kingdom. For it is licit for the prince to repel abuse from the spiritual sword in any way he can, even with the material sword,[7] especially where the abuse of the spiritual sword results in evil to the state whose care devolves on the king. For otherwise he would carry the [material] sword to no purpose.

[38] When argument thirty-eight mentions the possession of prebends,[8] it can be said that that possession can belong to a lay person from custom as well as by written law; for neither of these is more repugnant to a layman than the other. It can also belong by the law of patronage if it were licit customarily, or had been conceded by churches. For *Ethics* 8 speaks of the benefactor from whom actions originate among men, and says that even though there is no obligation in justice, the esteem of one who is possessed of an abundance is obliged by a debt of honor to repay such a man when he can.[9] And this is the basis on which churches that were not initially required by any obligation of justice nevertheless wished, out of a debt of honor, to give something of worth

and utility to the founders and patrons of the churches. They granted something of worth, indeed, in presenting benefices—and this is seen to have been conceded to all patrons in written law— or by conferring those benefices on suitable persons at the stipulation of the clergy. And even though it is not found to be conceded to patrons expressly and generally in written law, it nevertheless was conceded totally and reasonably to certain very distinguished patrons, in order to stimulate further their dedication toward the founding of churches.

And since a practice which is conceded reasonably, but freely and not from any obligation in justice, is transformed by long and prescribed custom into common law, such that Plato says in the *Timaeus* [10] that what is reasonably established at one time cannot be changed by the divine will; accordingly, the aforementioned presentation of ecclesiastical benefices to all patrons is a general obligation, and their possession—by custom—by certain very distinguished men is a special obligation, and one based on law. Therefore, it cannot be taken from these men without injury. In fact, if anyone wished to take it away from them without a clear and sufficient reason, undoubtedly he could not. Possession of a patrimony always holds good, whatever and by whomever may be done against it. For, as has been said above [chapter 6], God did not give Peter or ecclesiastical ministers the power to act indiscriminately, but to act in good faith—and to build and not destroy: II Corinthians, last chapter. [11] For God does not will that anyone's possessions be taken from him unless a sin intervenes. As the Apostle says in Romans 11: "The gifts of God are irrevocable." [12] And it is said in Job 36: "He did not take his eyes from the just man, and he set kings on their thrones for eternity." [13] For it was on account of [their] sins that He made the vessels of the Egyptians to be the spoils of the Hebrews. From the beginning, therefore, and on reasonable grounds, patrons had conceded to them either expressly or, as can be interpreted from long-standing failure to do otherwise, the esteem based on a debt of honor owed to a very distinguished benefactor. A further reason was so that those who had the means might be made more prone to endow churches. Given these facts, there is no doubt that no concession was made by Christ to a pope to enable him to revoke such things, unless there is a clear and serious fault about which a prince has been admonished and found to be incorrigible. This is particularly true since churches receive many benefits from this arrangement.

When it is argued that possession [of prebends] does not belong to a layman because it is spiritual, I reply: [14] it can be said that a thing is not properly called spiritual unless it relates to the Divine Spirit through causality or concomitance. This is the manner, accordingly, in which the ecclesiastical sacraments and also their administration are spiritual; for they contain and cause spiritual grace. Now, an article which has a relation to what is called spiritual is termed an adjunct to the spiritual either through an effect, such as the right to tithe, or through an antecedent, such as the right of patrimony and the possession of prebends. This first kind of thing, which properly speaking is spiritual, does not fall to the layman in any way. Neither does the second kind of article, an adjunct to the spiritual by way of effect. For such an article depends on a spiritual office; and the right to tithe belongs to a person by reason of spiritual offices. Consequently, this right does not belong to a layman any more than a spiritual office belongs to him, although corporeal fruits, which are given the name "tithes," can belong to laymen as a concession from the Church. The third kind of article, however, an adjunct of spiritual office by way of an antecedent (such as the presentation or possession or right of possession) can be acquired by a king as a right for himself, since it is not so dependent on the spiritual; conversely, it can belong to a layman, particularly as a concession or with the permission of the Church and from long and written custom. This would not be repugnant to a king, for if it were, it could not be granted to him by any concession from anyone, just as neither the administration of the sacraments nor the law of tenths can be granted to a layman by any authority whatsoever.

This right is not burdensome for churches. In fact, sometimes it is fruitful, especially when the Church knows and approves of it. Accordingly, when it is said that the burden [to the Church] should not be onerous, I reply: the burden from this situation is

onerous for the patron, on whom the obligation of defense falls.
Indeed, absolutely speaking, it is not onerous at all for the
Church, since she has more to gain than to lose from it.

And when it is said that custom does not prejudice public
law, I reply: since the custom mentioned in many circumstances
is not harmful and is actually beneficial in some, it does not
prejudice public law in genus, although it seems to prejudice it in
species. For it does seem to prejudice bishops, who are deprived
of the possession of benefices owing them by common law.
Churches, nevertheless, sometimes receive an advantage from this
situation in the areas of defense, donation, and foundation. And
hence the right does not prejudice absolutely. Or, as the Philosopher says in *Ethics* 8: "We act in this way as we act with
friends." [15] The ecclesiastic is therefore said to possess the right
not through himself, but through the lay patron to whom the
right was reasonably conceded by him; and this concession is not
revocable except as I have mentioned.

And to what is countered in respect of custom being contrary and harmful to the substance of a contract, I make the
following reply: I say that there is no contract or condition in
these circumstances, because grants to a patron are made absolutely and not under any condition or stipulation, even though an
obligation does follow from possession already enjoyed. Nor is
there anything harmful here, since the right is not extorted from
the churches by violence, but is freely conceded by the church to
the patrons, even though a debt is owing based on an obligation
of honor toward any distinguished benefactor and repayment
should be made to him when it can be so done, as is said in
Ethics 8.[16] Even if, as the argument maintains, the right was contrary to the substance of a contract or debt, it does not therefore
follow that it is not held to be binding in such a case, and that the
grant does not hold. For the point here involves a shameful situation, but not one contrary to the contract. For example: I might
make a contract with you after you have killed a man. Where such
a circumstance exists which involves something contrary to the
substance of the grant, however, the grant or contract is not
binding: for example, if it were the case that I made a contract

with you to procure sterility through the use of a drug or some such thing. In this latter type of situation, a grant made by churches would not hold, and the whole would return to the donors.

When it is stated that the Church "rejoices" in the rights of minors and [when] it considers them to have been infringed, I reply: the mere presence of a minor is not sufficient to require restitution; he must prove that he has been victimized: *Decretum 54*, "Generalis." [17] Certainly the Church cannot act automatically here, since it is clearly the case that this kind of action involves the making of money. Further, great jurists maintain that the Church is appointed [to act] at the last moment of a twenty-six-year period after the injury has been done. In this way the intervention falls within the four-year period deemed the only proper time during which restitution may be made. And the Church cannot act except in that period unless fraud has been proven. On the other hand, other authorities say that restitution can be made up to fifteen years after an injury has been suffered. The Church is to be appointed in the fourteenth year. Still others maintain that restitution can be claimed until the thirtieth year. In this instance the Church [would intervene] on the first day of a person's minority. Further, Godfrey [18] asserts that the [status of the] Church differs from minority in the fact that the Church both prescribes and has prescriptions brought against it, while a minor is always kept unhurt except for the very long prescription, which certainly works against a minor but from which, however, there can be restitution. A prescription against the Church, on the other hand, runs for forty years and there is no restitution from it.

[39] When it is asserted in the thirty-ninth argument that the pope must be perfect in the active life,[19] I reply: from this fact it pertains to him only to dispose of his own property and not that of others, and to preach to others on how to distribute their belongings as the order of charity requires.

[40] When it is argued in the fortieth argument that clerics are more vigorous in reason, I reply: if this is so they ought not therefore to be preeminent in all things but in the greater and better things—namely, in spiritual matters.[20]

[41] Where the forty-first argument asserts that those who speak otherwise do so to seek the favor of princes,[21] I reply: in some cases truth is to be evaded, as Christ evaded the truth concerning Moses's allowing divorce of a wife: Matthew 19.[22] However, it is not licit in any circumstances for anyone to teach contrary to his conscience or to write against the doctrines of religion. And therefore to say that such great men, some of whom were supreme pontiffs, have written against their own consciences to curry the favor of princes or from fear of princes is to commit an affront to heaven. Moreover, it seems more probable that the contrary can be asserted: that those learned men who so unjustifiably extend the authority of the supreme pontiff speak out of fear of or in hope of obtaining favor from the supreme pontiff. For they are ecclesiastical persons who can rather easily be advanced by him, particularly since they assert, although wrongly, that the supreme pontiff freely embraces those who extend his power and represses [23] those who speak out against him. Kings and princes do not do this.

[42] Moreover, when that man from Cremona asserts in the last argument that the men who say the pope does not have power everywhere are to be judged heretics, it must be said that he is imprudent in making this judgment when he tells us that to say such things is to assert that the Church cannot coerce heretics. Now this seems false; for the Church can invoke the secular arm against heretics: *Extra, De hereticis, Ad abolendam,*[24] and the chapter *Vergentis.*[25] Moreover, it can be said that he incurs anathema and is not far from heresy himself if he asserts this position with pertinacity. For the view that the pope has both swords is not found in Sacred Scripture, which is the rule of faith. And the Lord says in Deuteronomy 4: "You shall not make additions to the words I have spoken to you, nor shall you take anything away from them."[26] And it is said in the records of the First Synod of Ephesus that after the creed of the Council of Nicaea had been examined thoroughly, the sacred synod decreed that it was not licit for anyone to produce, compose, or set down another formula of faith than the one which had been defined by the holy fathers who had been gathered at Nicaea by the Holy

Spirit, and that [for so doing] the penalty of anathema was to be incurred.[27] And the same point is reiterated in the records of the Synod of Chalcedon.[28] Further, since the Christian faith is catholic and universal, the supreme pontiff cannot make this a matter of faith without a general council, because a pope cannot destroy statutes of a council: *Decretum* 19, Anastasius." [29] For although a council cannot impose a law on a pope: *Extra, De electione, Significati,*[30] and *Decretum* 35. 9 "Veniam," [31] this is not to be understood to apply to things which are matters of faith, insofar as the world is larger than the city, and the pope in council is greater than the pope alone: *Decretum* 93, "Legimus." [32]

Chapter 21

Concerning the Donation of Constantine and the Power the Pope Possesses through It

HAVING SEEN what powers ecclesiastical ministers possess from the fact that they are the vicars of Christ, one must now see what powers the supreme pontiffs possess as a result of the Donation of the emperor Constantine the Great.[1] For it is said that he gave the western imperial power and the imperial symbols, such as his palace and crown and other things of this kind, to Sylvester and his successors. Accordingly, some are of the opinion that the supreme pontiff is emperor and lord of the world by reason of this Donation, and that he can install and remove kings just as the emperor can [2] —particularly when the imperial power is vacant [3]—and that appeals can be directed to him in the same way as to the emperor.

Now in order to present these points more adequately, it is
necessary first to set down the pertinent facts concerning this Donation and the transfer of the imperial power which are written in the
chronicles and ancient histories. This will allow one to see more
clearly what the lord pope can do by virtue of the Donation, particularly what he can do in relation to the king of France.

Accordingly, as noted in the *Chronicles* of Hugh of Florence,[4]
in the book *On Cosmography*,[5] in the *Epistle of Constantine to the
Bishops* [6] and in Constantine's will,[7] one must realize that Constantine himself made a gift of only one specific province, Italy, and
certain other territories; France was not included.[8] Constantine also
transferred the imperial power to the Greeks, and built a new Rome
there.[9] Regarding other points asserted concerning the transfer of
the imperial power from the Greeks to the Germans in the person
of Charlemagne as carried out by the Romans and the pope,[10] it
must be understood that according to the aforementioned chronicles no such transfer was made.[11] Rather, the imperial power remained with the Greeks in fact, and with the westerners in name.
Either that or a division [of the empire] was made, with two men
being designated emperor, to wit, one man in Rome and the other
in Constantinople, inasmuch as the Romans are said to have withdrawn from the imperial power of the Greeks [12] for three reasons:
because of state defense, which the Romans received from Charlemagne and which the emperor Constantine was neglecting; because
they were provoked by the action of the empress Irene, who hid
her own son, Constantine, and his sons as well, in order to rule
alone; because they declared themselves in favor of the imperial
power of the victorious Charles, being dissatisfied with the transfer
of the imperial power from themselves to the Greeks, which had
been carried out by Constantine. It is apparent from these facts,
then, that the pope has no power in the kingdom of France based
on this Donation and transfer.

Four reasons can be offered in support of this conclusion: [1]
First, the Donation had reference only to a specific territory in which
France was not included; and no transfer was made to the Germans
of the whole imperial power, or of authority over the world as a

whole. This last point follows from the fact that there continued to be emperors among the Greeks after the transfer, which was not really a transfer of the imperial power at all but rather a division.

[2] Secondly, the Donation had no significance for the four reasons stated in the *Gloss of Civil Law*,[13] and as legal experts commonly maintain. These reasons are [a] first, that in virtue of his office an emperor is always called august, since it is his role always to enlarge the imperial authority and not diminish it. Hence, this Donation does not seem to have been valid, particularly since it was so great and immense, although it would have been valid if it had been done differently with respect to repayment and with the provision of some means for governing. This argument is found in *De tutoribus, Cum plures* and below,[14] and there is nothing contrary to this point in the law asserting that the measure of a donation to the Church is size, a point found in *Authentica, De rebus ecclesiae non alienandis; Sancimus*.[15] For that law is to be understood to refer to Constantine's giving from Caesar's patrimony possessions he held before he was emperor, and not to his giving from the patrimony of the state treasury, which the emperor ought always to keep, and from which he cannot make grants except in moderation and for certain reasons. This point is made in *Authentica, Quomodo oporteat episcopos et cleros, coll. II*.[16] Either that or it is not to be understood in the sense of a prince giving something to the Church, but in the sense of his making an exchange for something ecclesiastical. In this instance there is no difficulty as long as the prince's property is greater than and not commensurate with what he receives from the Church.

[b] Secondly, the emperor is administrator of the imperial power and the state, as maintained in the laws taken from the code of Hostiensis: *Instituta, De constitutione principium*, the first law.[17] But if the emperor is administrator of the imperial power, the Donation is worthless, as maintained in *Instituta, Pro emptore 1. Qui. fundum, Si tutor*.[18]

[c] Thirdly, there is a law regulating this kind of donation: *De donatione inter virum et uxorem, 1. Donationes*.[19] Moreover, a law made by one man can be revoked by his successor, since equals

do not possess imperial power equally: *Instituta, De arbitriis, 1. Nam et magistratus.*[20] The aforesaid Donation, accordingly, was not valid.

[d] Fourthly, his successor can give away another portion on the same basis as that on which a person can give away a first portion; and in this way the imperial power would be diminished and despoiled of its goods.[21] But this is unfitting, because it is proper for the imperial power to encompass a large territory. This argument is found in *Instituta, De fundamentis domorum, 1. Scilicet,*[22] and in *Authentica, Ut judices suffraganei, Cogitatio, coll. II.*[23] And on these grounds jurists assert that the Donation was not valid.

In fact, the view that the Donation was displeasing to God can be taken from the argument found in the *Life of Pope Sylvester,*[24] to the effect that at the time of the Donation angels' voices were heard in the heavens saying: "Today poison has been poured into the Church." Again, St. Jerome [25] says of Constantine that from his day to the present there was spoliation of churches and discord in the whole world. Jerome also says of him that he later turned to such cruelty that he killed his own son, Crispus, and his wife, Fausta.[26] Also he was baptized late in life by Eusebius, bishop of Nicomedia, and thus was baptized twice; and what is more, dogma declined into Arianism in his day.[27] Many trustworthy writers of chronicles who are worthy of belief say the same thing in their chronicles. Moreover, the position of some men who wish to argue that Jerome's remarks should be understood as applying to Constantine's son can be shown to be false, because St. Jerome was sufficiently explicit that he was speaking about Constantine. He does state, however, that spoliation of churches did not begin under Constantine, although there was a great persecution of the Church during his reign.[28] The chronicles also assert that Constantine alone, and not his son, had a wife named Fausta. Also, it can be determined that this particular Constantine was not known to Eusebius, bishop of Nicomedia; it was another Constantine who died and was buried in his church. Jerome and others, then, attribute wicked deeds to Constantine the Great, even though his piety resulted in his being returned to the enjoyment of a higher reputation by St. Gregory in the Register.[29] And the Greeks, too, conceived a devotion for him because of his having founded Constantinople in their territory.

[3] Thirdly, it appears that from this Donation the pope has no authority over the king of France, even granting that the Donation was valid and was a general donation of the whole imperial power. For even though the Gauls became subject to the Romans in the time of Octavius Augustus as a result of certain events, these people were not Franks. Different histories record that, after the fall of Troy, twelve thousand Trojans under the leadership of Athenoras—for which reason they were first called Athenoridians—reached parts of Pannonia, near the Melotidan Marshes, where they built the city of Sycambria. They continued to be hostile to the Roman Empire and they remained there until the time of the emperor Valentinian, by whom they were driven out of the district for their refusal to pay tribute to the Romans according to the custom accepted by other peoples. They left this territory under their leaders—Marcominus, Surmonis, and Ginnibaldus—and settled near the banks of the Rhine in the territory of Germany and Alemania; the same Valentinian later unsuccessfully tried repeatedly to conquer them. He gave them the name "Franks," that is, fierce ones. From that time on the power of the Franks developed so greatly that they subjugated the whole of Germany and Gaul as far as the summit of the Pyrenees and beyond. They settled in Gaul, and named it France; and they were subject neither to the Romans nor to anyone else.[30]

[4] Fourthly, conceding that the Donation of Constantine was valid and involved the gift of the whole imperial power, and conceding that the Franks at that time were subject to the imperial power—points we do not concede—even at that the pope has no power over the king of France, since the pope is not emperor. Even if it were conceded that the pope was emperor, the Franks had declared themselves opposed to the emperor even in those days. For saintly kings have exercised authority over the kingdom of France for a very long time and in good faith, as is proven from the fact that St. Louis, who was canonized[31] by the Church in recognition of his evident merits, held this position. And in canonizing him the Church approved this state of affairs, whatever certain theologians

say, since the appropriation of things and the subjection of men are accomplished through human law. According to Augustine,[32] human laws can for a sufficient reason determine that what is mine be common property or someone else's, can make what is mine cease to be mine, and can transfer ownership. It was on this basis, too, that imperial laws determined something could be transferred by means of prescription after a long period of time, and that ownership could be transferred for the sake of common use or in dislike of neglect, and in favor of the good faith of the person holding possession, and so that cases not stretch out and be prolonged indefinitely, and so that a person not hold what belongs to someone else, but only what is his own, made his own indeed by a legitimate prescription. Granting, therefore, that the kingdom of France at one time was made subject to the Roman Empire, the subjection was prescribed.

This is also shown from the *Chronicles* of Sigebert,[33] and from other chronicles as well. For it is written there that Charlemagne brought the whole of Italy back under the rule of the king of the Franks. The *History of the Romans*[34] also relates that long ago there was an imperial authority among the Franks, and yet it stated that Italy is not now subject to the Franks, a situation which can arise only through some prescription of time having significance in such a case.[35]

It also appears from what has been said that the position of some jurists[36] concerning the prescription of jurisdiction over subjects has no value. They assert that only the subjection owing to barons by their inferiors, and not that owing to an emperor, can be by way of prescription, although subjection to a superior remains nonetheless. The reason alleged for this position is that it is not fitting for several persons to possess authority, since several persons dissent easily among themselves. Rather, a single person should be ruler of the whole world. Consequently, the value of a prescription ought not to be maintained. But this argument is of little worth, as can be seen from the statements in chapter 3 above. For it is true that several persons easily disagree about one thing, and that therefore the rule of kings is better than aristocratic rule, as said above in chapter 1. However, it is better for several men to be rulers of the whole world than for one man to rule it. This last point is also clear from the fact that the world certainly did not enjoy such great peace in the period when emperors ruled as it had both before and after, but brother killed brother and mother killed son, and conversely, and other horrible crimes were committed throughout the world, and the worst types of quarrels took place, the particular details of which need not be recounted here.

Their contention that a prescription cannot be made against the imperial power of the Romans is also surprising, since before the kingship of the Romans there were other imperial powers, such as that of the Babylonians which began with Ninus [37] in the time of Abraham, and the Carthaginian Empire begun under the leader, Cola, in the time of Judges, and the Macedonian or Greek Empire begun by Alexander at the time of Maccabees; and any one of these, as was the Roman Empire, was established by God.

If, therefore, there is no impediment to the Greeks' holding imperial authority from God, and if the Romans made a prescription against the Greeks and tried to usurp the imperial authority by expelling the Greeks, why cannot some men also make a prescription against the imperial authority of the Romans and throw off their dominion over them, particularly when they did not subject themselves to the Romans voluntarily but were subjected by the violence of the Romans? This is what is written about the Gauls: that the Franks earlier never came voluntarily to subject themselves to the Romans but were always rebellious to the extent that it was possible for them to be. Sometimes they even defeated the Romans while at other times the Romans defeated them. If, then, the Romans took their power of dominion by force, why cannot their dominion also justly be taken from them by force, or prescription also be made against them?

Now, if someone says that it was according to God's will that other imperial powers cease to exist and the imperial power of the Romans expands, why can it not be said on the same basis that the Roman Empire ought to cease at God's will, and that those who were previously in some way subject to the Romans ought no longer to be subject, if they do not so wish and if they are able to break away? In fact, Scripture seems to make the point rather clearly, with reference to the imperial power of the Romans, that it more than any other empire ought to collapse. For it is written in Numbers 24, in the prophecy of Balaam: "They shall come from Italy in triremes and conquer the Assyrians, and spread destruction among the Hebrews; and in the end they too shall perish." [38] The master of the *Histories* comments on this as follows: "Just as he foretold the rule of the Romans, so too did he foretell their destruction at the end of time." [39] Similarly, commenting on the text of Daniel, which mentions the vision of the fourth beast which trampled things under its feet,[40] the Gloss says there was nothing stronger than the kingship of the Romans, and that in the end there will be nothing weaker or more fragile than it.[41]

Chapter 22
Whether in Matters of This Kind It Is Licit to Dispute with and Pass Judgment on the Pope

IT SEEMS THAT one should ask now whether it is reprehensible to judge the deeds of a pope, inasmuch as some say that this is to touch a mountain and commit an affront to heaven.[1] They also claim this as the reason Dioscorus was condemned forever by a general council,[2] because he reprimanded and wished to pass judgment on Pope Leo.

Now on this point it is necessary to consider that action and judgment against a pope can be understood in four ways: to wit, in relation to his status, his power, his abuse of power and his personal defects. I say that it is licit to express doubts and to take action concerning the pope's status, concerning the issue, namely, of whether a man is or is not pope, since a doubt can arise about this from a defect in the election. Even when the form of election is clear, a mistake may occur in the election of a pope just as in the election of any other ecclesiastical prelate. The election may also be set aside because of a personal defect, insofar as sometimes there may be a person in the office who must be removed: for example, if the pope were a woman or a heretic. There have been such persons, and this is the reason why they are not listed in the catalogue of popes. And to the extent that it is necessary to investigate the truth of these matters, so much the more dangerous would it be not to know the truth about them. It is to be noted, moreover, that very careful observation should be kept on opportunities for the commission of faults and on persons exhibiting faults, so that the faults of deception and pride not be tolerated in such persons. Indeed, if after careful investigation by learned men and by those whose business it is to carry out an investigation something illegitimate with respect to status is discovered about the person or the election of a pope, there can be no concealing it. Rather, he must be admonished to yield his office; and if he refuses, he can be charged, a general council can be convened, and he can be called before that council. In fact, to prevent the sacraments of the Church from being profaned, the man ought to be removed from office forcibly when he proves to be obstinate in such a case, and an appeal can be made to the secular arm if necessary.

This is what is written in the *Chronicles of the Romans* [3] concerning Benedict IX and Cadelus, bishop of Ostea, Constantine II and certain others; they were fittingly deposed from office by the intervention of the secular arm. To the question but who is to judge him a heretic? I reply: if the man has said anything contrary to what is contained in the deposit of faith otherwise approved by the Church and maintains this view by explicit affirmation, he can be said already to have been judged, since he who does not believe has already been judged.

Now concerning the power of the lord pope—to wit, the issue of what he can and cannot do—I believe it is not reprehensible to inquire about the truth of such a matter, since ignorance is dangerous and there is no certitude on some matters; as for example whether the pope can dispense a bigamist, or whether he can dispense from a solemn vow of continence, since one pope is found to have dispensed in fact and another has said he cannot do so: *Extra, De ingredientibus monasterium.*[4] And there is an indefinite number of uncertain points concerning the power of the pope about which it is useful to raise questions, and also to judge with humility, according as there seems to anyone to be reasons for such attitudes.

Regarding abuse of the pope's power and personal defects—whether, namely, he confers prebends for the common needs of the Church or for his own private good, and whether he is chaste and sober or sinful—without doubt it is not licit to judge [of such matters] unless there is some clear and manifest evidence against the person. Rather, one must always interpret and accept things in the best light, even if *prima facie* something of an evil character occurs. And it is even less licit to judge a pope than to judge anyone else. Even if something intrinsically evil such as incontinence or homicide or something forbidden by law is done, the pope cannot be judged by anyone else in the manner of an authority, with the other person charging him or excommunicating him. For the pope has no superior. This is why Dioscorus was condemned forever by a general council, for having excommunicated Pope Leo, as we read in *Decretum* 21.[5]

Some men also assert that the pope is not to be judged even in the manner of a simple judgment, because if we are to interpret the murder of Samson,[6] which was intrinsically evil, as done at divine instigation, so much the more ought we to interpret every deed of the most holy father as a good. And even if any papal act is deceitful or intrinsically evil, we must consider the act to have been performed at divine instigation, by whose command and order the Holy Church is ruled, rather than as the act of an individual person. St. Augustine, however, replied adequately [to this view] in Book I of the *City of God*.[7] For he says that we interpret Samson's murder as an act done at the instigation of God, Who worked miracles through Samson himself.

Therefore, I say that the pope can be judged for his own actions; he can be prevailed upon, and he can be reprimanded by anyone when he manifestly errs: for example, by depriving churches

of their own rights, by dispersing the Lord's flock, or by scandalizing the Church by any of his deeds. And if this is not done by right
of office, nevertheless it is done through the zeal of charity, which
imposes no penalty but exhorts him with reverence, for the affection
owed to any person ought not to be less for a pope simply because
of the higher status to which he has been raised. Consequently, just
as the pope is not held in any less affection in charity by reason of
the status to which he has been raised, the converse is also the case,
according to Augustine, as long as he retains his authority. For
everyone is bound to fraternal correction of any fault through the
zeal of charity and the consequences entailed in his own act. And
whatever is binding from the effect of charity does not bind the
pope in any lesser way, although he is bound with humility and
reverence. Accordingly, Galatians 2,[8] when Peter came to Antioch,
Paul opposed him to his face because he deserved censure. And
no one speaking of this incident says anything about touching a
mountain or committing an affront to heaven. For when a pope
clearly makes a mistake, he is not heaven; nor is an affront per-
petrated against heaven, that is, against him when he is corrected.
Rather, this is done for his own good. Furthermore, no one should
fear that this kind of action will cause scandal for the pope, because
the risk of scandal does not injure mature men but only weaklings.
Accordingly, fear of scandal to the pope on this account holds the
pope to be a weakling, and less perfect than any other man whom
someone dares to correct as a wrongdoer. Therefore, the men who
declare such things about the most holy father as that he is vindic-
tive and that he bears down heavily on every man who passes any
kind of judgment on his actions truly commit an affront to heaven.
These views are not to be held, since the pope is not a weakling
but a mature man, and more mature than other men.

But what if the pope declares that he considers a certain man
who maintains a position about which opinions differ among learned
men to be a heretic, and makes this declaration without a general
council: as, for instance, if he considers heretical every man who
asserts that the king of France or any such person is not subject to
the pope in temporal matters?[9] I reply: statements made indiscriminately by the pope must always be interpreted in as sensible a man-

ner as possible. Hence, his spoken words ought not to be taken as
meaning that appeals can be made to him, or that the pope is able
to interfere in matters relating to what is yours and mine. For this
would clearly be contrary to Scripture and common doctrine [chap-
ter 13]. This view would be a kind of novelty, something the pope
would bring forward only after very mature consideration, and after
having previously called a general council, and after having discussion of it carried on everywhere by learned men. Accordingly, the
pope's statements must be taken in a sensible manner, to wit, as applying to a crime where, for example, a question of sin is raised.
Or else the statement should be understood as having reference to
the forum of conscience, as mentioned above, until he makes his
meaning on the matter clear. And if finally he does make his meaning clear in so novel and injurious a sense that he must be opposed,
he still ought to be tolerated patiently as long as possible, without
danger to justice and truth. As the text of Matthew 5 says: "Whoever torments you, go a thousand paces with him, and two thousand
more."[10] And recourse ought to be had to God, Who holds the
heart of a pope in His hand just as He does the heart of a king,
and Who can incline him in whatever way He wishes, and influence
him and remove the pope from his throne just as He can a king.[11]

However, if there is danger to the state's good order because,
to wit, the people are being led into a wrong opinion, and there is
danger of rebellion, and the pope is unjustifiably influencing the
people through an abuse of the spiritual sword, and where there is
also no hope[12] of his ceasing otherwise, I think the Church ought
to be mobilized against the pope in this case, and should act against
him. In fact, a prince has the power to repel the violence of the
pope's sword with his own sword, used in moderation. And in so
doing a prince would not act against the pope insofar as he is pope,
but against his own enemy and an enemy of the state. So too the
Jew, Ehud, who killed King Eglon of Moab with a spear he had
strapped to his thigh because Eglon was pressing the people of
God into heavy servitude,[13] is not reputed to have killed a ruler but
an evil man and an enemy. To act in this way, indeed, is not to act
against the Church but for it. This is how the people, encouraged
by a commendable zeal for the faith, deprived Constantine of his

eyes and deposed him, for he was a scandal to the Church. In this way also, Emperor Henry went to Rome and by imperial and canonical censure deposed Benedict IX and two others, who were scandalizing the Church with their disputes, and constituted Clement II pope of the Roman church, as we read in the *Chronicles of the Romans.*[14]

Chapter 23
Foolish Arguments Employed by Some Who Contend that the Pope Cannot Resign

NOW BECAUSE I seem to have submitted earlier that the pope can resign and be deposed, and while still living can cease to be pope, one must see the arguments employed by those who assert that the pope cannot resign voluntarily, and that he cannot be deposed solely by the authority of lesser prelates, just as arguments in favor of the two positions clearly distinguished in the beginning of this treatise are set down above in a particular chapter [11]. For there are many arguments leading to both conclusions.

[1] Accordingly, these men's first argument is that the pope cannot resign because papal authority is from God alone.[1] Moreover, things which are from God or are committed to someone from another higher source cannot be removed by anyone of lower authority. Therefore, the papal dignity which is committed by God cannot be removed by anyone lesser than God.

[2] A second argument is that no one can transfer any

authority or power he cannot confer. But no one except God can confer papal authority. Therefore, neither can anyone take it away—which, however, is what would happen if the pope could resign.

[3] A third argument is taken from the decree *Inter corporalia*,[2] which expressly indicates that deposition, transfer, and absolution of bishops are reserved to the pope alone, and only insofar as he is God—that is, God's vicar. Therefore, because papal dignity excels all dignities, removal of a pope from office can be done only by a person superior to the pope—namely, God. There seems to be no reason why God would wish that bishops could be removed only by the superior pope acting as God, while the pope could be removed by persons inferior to himself. It seems, rather, that only He Who is superior to the pope can on His own authority remove a pope.

[4] A fourth argument is that the highest created power cannot be removed by any created power. But the papal power is the highest created power; therefore, etc.

[5] A fifth argument is that neither the pope nor the entire universe of creatures can make a high priest to be a high priest. Much less, therefore, can either make a pope cease to be pope.

[6] A sixth argument is that the pope is pope only by divine law, and not by the law of any creature or the law of all creatures taken together. Therefore, it seems that his power as pope cannot be removed in any way. The fact that the pope agrees and submits himself freely to the law establishes that he cannot be made to be not a pope by any creature or by all creatures taken together.

[7] A seventh argument is that no one can void any person's oath unless he be someone who is himself above the oath. The papal oath, however, transcends all others, because the pope swears to take charge of the universal Church and of the Lord's flock, and to render account for it. Accordingly, he can be absolved from this obligation by God alone. For no one can absolve himself from an obligation he has to a superior; only the superior can absolve him.

[8] An eighth argument is that no one seems to be able to

absolve himself from sin. Accordingly, neither can this be done with respect to papal power, which would be the case if the pope could resign voluntarily.

[9] A ninth argument is that papal obligation does not seem capable of removal except through a power higher than the papal power. But since there is no greater power except that of God, therefore, etc.

[10] A tenth argument is that no ecclesiastical dignity can be removed after legitimate confirmation [except] by a power superior to it. But the pope has no power higher than his except God's; therefore, etc.

[11] An eleventh argument is that the Apostle wishes Christ's priesthood to exist forever because Christ lives forever.[3] In no way, therefore, can the life of the high priest exist unless the high priesthood exists. But this would be false if the pope can resign.

These are the arguments I have been able to see in support of the view that the pope cannot resign or be deposed.

Chapter 24
The Pope Can Resign

NOW ONE needs to show in many ways—to wit, by the use of examples,[1] authorities and arguments—that the pope can resign and also that he can be deposed against his will.

An example of resignation can be seen in the case of St. Clement, who is said in the *Acts of the Roman Pontiffs*[2] to have resigned, and to have reaccepted the papal throne after Linus and Cletus. Accordingly, Clement held office immediately after Peter, and on his resignation Linus and Cletus took the throne. And again after them Clement took it back; and in accepting it then he became the fourth in succession after St. Peter. This example, however, can be challenged to the extent that we find in Aymo's *Memory of Christian Things* [3] and in several other histories the assertion that Linus and Cletus did not reign as popes but as coadjutors of the pope, to whom in his own lifetime St. Peter handed over the dispensation of ecclesiastical matters, while busying himself with prayer and preaching only. This is the reason why the aforementioned Linus and Cletus deserved to be placed in the list of popes, insofar as such great authority had been granted to them. Accordingly, then, as far as these writers are concerned, Clement did not resign, but held office immediately after Peter up to the time of Anacletus or Evaristus. I think it more true, however, that Clement was earlier, and that therefore he truly wished to resign, because Clement was ordained by Peter while Peter was still alive, as Peter himself wrote to St. James, bishop of Jerusalem.

Another example is the case of Marcellinus, who lived at the time of Diocletian. This man resigned, as the Ordinary Gloss asserts: 7. 1, "Non autem"; [4] and *Decretum 21,* "Nunc autem" states that he deposed himself. [5] Now his resignation was a kind of deposition because, as Huguccio says in the *Deeds of the Roman Pontiffs,* [6] he was the very one to pass sentence on himself, saying: I, Marcellinus, judge myself condemned and deposed for the crime of idolatry, which unhappily I have committed. I also anathematize whoever hands my body over for burial.

Another example is the case of Pope Cyriacus, who is said to have been martyred with Ursula and the eleven thousand virgins. For it is written of him that on a certain night it was revealed to him that he would receive the palm of martyrdom with those virgins. Then he gathered the clergy and cardinals together, having summoned them all and particularly the cardinals, and before them all he renounced his dignity and office. However, this Cyriacus is not listed in the catalogue of popes because he was thought to have resigned the papal office for the sake of the delights of the virgins rather than out of piety. [7]

Authorities among learned men also are agreed that the pope can resign and be deposed. Accordingly, the Ordinary Gloss 7. 1, "Non autem,"[8] raises in a formal way the question of whether a pope can resign, and answers in the affirmative, giving as a reason that Marcellinus and also Clement did resign. Huguccio also raises the same question in the same place, saying: "But what about the resignation of a pope? Can he resign because he wishes to enter the religious life, or is ill or elderly?" His answer is that certainly he can resign; and he offers as a reason the fact that Marcellinus and Clement resigned. Similarly, Huguccio raises the same question in *Decretum* 21, "Nunc autem,"[9] and answers that he believes the answer is yes, if it is expedient and if at any time [the pope] has committed a fault.

Arguments for this position can be adduced also from the notion of final cause; for no one is elected pope except for the common good of the Church and the Lord's flock. Indeed, it is to promote this purpose that he governs. If, therefore, he found himself to be or was found to be totally inept and useless after he had taken office, or an impediment such as insanity or something similar interfered, he ought to seek a release from his office from the people[10] or from the assembly of cardinals,[11] who act in place of the whole clergy and the whole people in such a case. And he is bound to yield his office whether or not he obtains permission. For if otherwise, and the person who presides uselessly or for evil and confusion in the Church and the damnation of his own soul cannot resign, what was instituted out of charity militates against charity. It is generally true in fact that no obligation made voluntarily can prejudice either charity or an obligation by which anyone is bound to be solicitous for the salvation of his own soul. So, too, a religious who has taken vows to follow a certain rule can leave it freely, if it seems suitable for him and for his soul to adopt a stricter rule, whether or not permission has been sought for and obtained from his superior: *Decretum* 19. 2, "Duae sunt leges."[12] And there is no reason for restricting in public law what is carried on in private law. Therefore, if weakness of soul or ineptitude or scandal to the Church or disturbance to the Church or division among the Lord's flock comes under investigation, and the pope raises divisions and excites scandals and does not stop when admonished to do so, he can even be compelled to yield: *Extra, De renunciatione, Quidem cedendi* and *Cum in postulatione.*[13]

Therefore, it is not unreasonable to assert that the pope can be deposed and can resign when invited to and prevailed upon by the people, as St. Cyriacus did, and that in such cases even someone who is unwilling can by popular agreement be deposed and compelled to resign. This is so because, like every other prelate, the pope himself does not hold office on his own account but for the people, this being the purpose for which he governs. Accordingly, agreement of the people is a more operative factor in this case for deposing an unwilling man if he is seen to be completely ineffective and for electing another than is the man's own willingness to resign, with the people willing the same.

Nevertheless, in the case of a deposition by the people of someone who does not wish it or is unwilling to be deposed, action must be taken with greater care than is needed for a voluntary yielding or resignation. All that is needed for a resignation is to allege a reason before the college of cardinals, which represents the whole Church in such circumstances. It is fitting for a deposition, however, that it be carried out by a general council, as is proved in *Decretum* 21, "Nunc autem," [14] where it is asserted that a general council was called to depose Marcellinus.

I believe, however, that the college of cardinals would be absolutely sufficient for a deposition of this kind, because insofar as their consensus makes a pope to occupy his position in the Church, similarly it seems that it can depose him. And if indeed there were a reasonable and sufficient cause, they would depose him meritoriously. If, on the other hand, there is not a sufficient reason, then they do wrong. But to say that what has been adduced here does not hold in the case of a pope because he has no superior but God is not correct, as will be proven in the replies to the arguments.

Chapter 25

Replies to the Foregoing Arguments

[1] TO THE FIRST ARGUMENT, therefore, which asserts that the papacy is from God alone, I reply: it must be said that papal power can be considered in two ways. In the first way in itself; and in this way it is from God alone, because only God can give men the power to loose or bind in heaven what is loosed or bound on earth. Papal power, however, can be considered in another way, as it exists in this or that particular person. And this is solely from God insofar as we attribute all our works to God: Isaiah 26: "All our works You work in us, O Lord." [1] For it is He who works all things in all things, and wills and perfects. [2]

But the things which are from God in this manner do not exclude our operation, as we are cooperators with God. For just as every work of ours is attributed to God alone if we act well, so too is it ours if we are imperfect in the task. Therefore, although the papal authority is from God alone in itself, nevertheless it is in this or that person through human cooperation, to wit, through consensus of the elected and the electing. Accordingly, it can cease in this or that individual person through a human consensus. In the same way the rational soul exists in the created world through God alone, even though its existence in a particular body involves the cooperation of nature to dispose and organize a body; and consequently the rational soul can cease in a particular body because, for example, the natural heat consumes so much moisture that the body is not suitable for a rational soul.

[2] To the second argument, which maintains that God alone can confer papal authority and therefore He alone can remove it, I reply: what has been said in answer to the first argument can be said here too. Another example can be added as well. For God alone gives grace; and yet it is necessary for man to cooperate with it, because according to Augustine [3] He who made you will not justify you without you. Therefore, man can remove grace from himself through his own action.

[3] To the third argument, invoking the decree *Inter corporalia*,[4] where deposition, transfer, and resignation of bishops are reserved to the pope alone, I reply: this argument favors the conclusion that the pope can resign his office without the authority of his superior, rather than that he cannot. For a requirement among things in this world is that the same elements by which they are constituted are what in contrary fashion destroy them.[5] Hence, the relationship between a prelate and the Church can be dissolved when there is dissension between the person elected and the electors, the elements through whose consent the relationship is established. Accordingly, any bishop who finds himself weak and inept and useless in the care and rule over his church can adduce a reason before the people or his own chapter [6] and can resign, unless the action is forbidden to him by his superior, to whom it is specifically reserved by bishops and archbishops through the decree *Inter corporalia*.[7] And since the prohibition found with respect to lesser bishops is not found to apply to the pope, the pope therefore can resign and be deposed without the authority of any superior. For in matters which occur according to the requirements of fact and of cause, anything is licit which is not forbidden. However, in those matters which occur with certain conditions as to fact and cause, nothing is licit which is not consented to. For example, giving orders concerning churches, which pertains to the pope as head of the Church, is beyond the jurisdiction of lower bishops. Wherefore, this power is not licit for any one of them unless specifically consigned to him. Therefore, there is no similarity between the pope, from whom there is nothing reserved to a superior and who is not forbidden to resign,

and the lower clergy to whom this is forbidden and from whom some things are reserved to a superior.

Nevertheless, one can offer a different reply to this argument and certain others, and assert that where a clear and reasonable cause appears, just as where there is a clear defect, the consent and authority of God to renounce and depose are supposed, just as divine agreement is supposed in his confirmation.

However, we must consider that someone can bolster the aforesaid argument from the decree as follows. It is said there that the spiritual bond between bishop and church is stronger than the carnal bond between man and wife. If, therefore, the carnal bond between a man and his wife cannot be dissolved by any human power or authority or by the intervening consent of anyone, neither can the spiritual bond between pope and church. For in the episcopacy marriage is contracted in election, ratified in confirmation, and consummated in consecration.

I reply: the spiritual bond is said to be stronger than the carnal bond because it is higher in dignity, not because it is longer lasting. For even after a bishop's consecration the spiritual marriage can be dissolved: by transfer, as is asserted in *Decretum* 7. 1, "Mutationes," [8] and the chapter, "Pastoralis"; [9] by deposition: *Decretum* 50, "Postquam"; [10] and by yielding: *Extra, De resignatione*, [11] in many places. But this is not the case with a carnal marriage. On the one hand, therefore, a spiritual bond is called stronger than the carnal because it imposes more burdens and is more stringent than a carnal bond, not because it is more indissoluble. For a prelate should have greater concern for his church as a common good than a man for his wife, since she is a particular good. On the other hand, a spiritual bond is said to be stronger because in itself it is stronger then the carnal.

Nonetheless, what is carnal is more durable, because, for example, married persons cannot be separated as long as they live, a view most powerfully held in Christ's law. He ordained this in the Gospel, saying: "What God has joined together, let no man separate." [12] Wherefore, the Apostle says in I Corinthians 7: "It is not I but the Lord who commands a wife not to leave her hus-

band. And if she does, let her remain unmarried, or be reconciled
to her husband." [13] The reason, moreover, for God ordering carnal
marriage not to be dissolved is that, although sometimes this can
result in a particular good, such dissolution would produce a
common evil, since men thereby would be encouraged to leave
their wives. The contrary, however, is the case in a spiritual marriage. For if a person cannot resign or be deposed and someone
else elected, even though he is useless and giving scandal, this
would be a common evil; for it would result in benefit to the particular person who is in authority. Therefore, such a thing is not
prohibited. Rather, if the reason is understood why the legislator prohibits a carnal marriage from being dissolved, one already
knows that a spiritual marriage should be dissolved when it appears clearly to be prejudical to the common good.

[4] To the fourth argument, which seems particularly to
prove that the pope cannot be deposed against his will because
the papacy is the highest created power, I reply: some would say
here that the argument concludes to the truth because, although
a pope can resign, he cannot be deposed against his will unless he
is a heretic; for as a heretic he can be considered dead, and a
person considered to be in this state cannot be the leader of the
Christians. They show this through an appeal to what is asserted
in *Decretum* 21, "Nunc autem," [14] where it is said that no one
can properly be subjected to limitations placed on him by persons
inferior to him in dignity or in the order of judicial ranks. And the
same text speaks of Pope Marcellinus, and asserts that none of the
bishops dared to prefer charges against him, but said frequently
to him: "Judge your cause not by our judgment, but from your
own mouth." [15] And again they said: "Do not listen to our judgment, but keep your case in your own grasp"; and again they said:
"You shall condemn yourself out of your own mouth." This is why
we find it said in stories about him that he deposed himself, and
afterward was reelected by the people [chapter 24]. I do not
understand this position; for even though he presides over the
Church, if he can resign without the Church wishing him to, as has
been said of St. Cyriacus, why can he not be deposed by the
Church against his will?

Further, in the special case of a bishop of the church at no time exercising his office while of sound mind, or doing so only occasionally, he can be deposed if he has declined a request to resign, and he should be deposed, and someone else should be elected: *Decretum* 7. 1, "Qualiter", and "Quamvis triste"; [16] and John commenting on those texts; [17] and *Extra, De renunciatione, Quidam cedendi*. [18] Similarly, therefore, the college of cardinals can act in place of the whole Church to depose an unwilling pope.

Again, we read in *Decretum* 40, "Si papa": He who would judge all is to be judged by none, unless he be observed to be deviating from the faith. [19] And the Gloss on this text says that if he be observed to be wandering into any other crime and does not correct himself when warned to do so, and scandalizes the Church and is incorrigible, then he can be called to account; [20] for such obstinacy is tantamount to heresy.

Again, if someone who has lapsed into heresy can be deposed because he is considered as being dead, why can he not be treated similarly if he lapses into some other vice from which he does not prove to be corrigible? For such a man is held to be the same as a dead man and is considered to be nothing, according to the view of Augustine, who declares that sin is nothing and men are nothing when they commit sin. [21] Another reason that someone else can be ordained in a case where a man who is required to do so refuses to resign is the issue of revolt. For wickedness already is seen to be committed here.

Indeed, when it is said about Marcellinus that they did not dare to condemn him, I reply: this was because he was under pressure from Diocletian, and because he repented and wished to be corrected, and because nothing was proved against him except insofar as he confessed it voluntarily through his own mouth; and therefore he was judged from his own mouth.

Indeed, when it is said at the beginning of the argument that the papacy is the highest created power, and thus cannot be taken away, I reply: although it be the highest created power in a person, nevertheless equal or greater power exists in the college [of cardinals] or in the whole Church. [22] Or it can be asserted that a pope can be deposed by the college, or rather by divine authority in a general council, the consensus of which is supposed and presumed to be able to depose a man when there is clear evidence of scandal and incorrigibility on the part of the man holding office.

[5] To the fifth argument, where it is said that it cannot happen that the chief high priest ceases to be chief high priest just as it cannot happen that a high priest ceases to be a high priest, I reply as follows: there is no parallel here. For the words "priest", "high priest" do not designate anything but what relates to order —to wit, the priestly character or the power based on that character. They designate this in different ways, however. For the character imprinted on the priesthood is a quasi-imperfect one, and on it is based the power of hearing confessions, but not the power of creating another priest similar to himself in the power of hearing confessions. The perfection of the character, however, is conferred on a bishop; and on it is based the perfect power by which he can make someone else a priest. And so the bishop is like a mature man, while the simple priest is like a boy.

The bishop, moreover, is not just any priest, but a great man and a protector of the Church, because through ordination he can, as it were, produce other priests like himself. Now an archbishop, patriarch or primate, and pope do not by virtue of their titles possess anything more in relation to an increase or greater perfection of the power or authority than the priesthood and episcopacy. They are given these titles only from the designation which their level of jurisdiction has in comparison with the episcopacy: the archbishop, indeed, has jurisdiction in his province, the primate in his country, and the pope in the entire Church. Now, since the power of orders is indelible and its perfection is indelible insofar as it is founded on the character and the perfection of the character, no power can make a priest cease to be a priest, or a bishop cease to be bishop. Jurisdiction, however, can be abolished and removed, just as it can be increased or diminished. When jurisdiction is removed, then, the pope ceases to be pope, and the chief priest ceases to be chief priest, although he does not cease to be a high priest.

[6] To the sixth argument, which asserts that the pope is not

pope except through divine law and not through the law of any creature or even of all creatures, and that the fact he submits himself freely to the law shows that he cannot cease to be pope through the action of any or every creature, I reply: this argument rests on a twofold base. One is the fact that the pope is pope through divine law, which is immutable, and therefore he cannot cease to be pope. The other is that he subjects himself freely to the law, and that it is continued in him.

As for the first base, one can reply that notwithstanding the fact that the pope is pope through divine law, which is immutable, he can still cease to be pope. For although divine law is immutable formally and in itself—for example, the law that lower things are brought back to God through higher things, and thus lower prelates are led to God through the pope—nevertheless, it is mutable materially, to wit, in this man or that, as Celestine or Boniface. This is bcause a creature cooperates with it, as has been said above [*ad* 2]. Whence, it is according to divine law that there be a pope over all men, and this cannot be otherwise. But that this or that man be pope is a mutable condition, because the consent of the electors and of the person elected cooperate in this situation.

As to the second base, one can reply that the pope submits himself freely to the law of the Church, which is to be perpetuated in matters relating to the issue of orders, because he can always perform the things pertaining to spiritual marriage—that is, ordain. For if the pope ordains someone, that person is ordained. But as for those things which relate to jurisdiction, he does not freely subject himself to the Church in perpetuity and immutably according to the law; for jurisdiction can be removed. Moreover, there can be reasons why those things which are from ordination cannot be taken away while those pertaining to jurisdiction can, because the things pertaining to jurisdiction are not from above nature, not above the work of arranging, not above the work of man. For it is not above human arrangement that men rule over men, even though it is in a certain way natural [see chapter 1]. Moreover, what is not prohibited in such cases is conceded, just as a thing is destroyed through the same causes as those through which it is constructed when they relate to one another in contrary fashion. And, therefore, just as jurisdiction is given by the consent of men, so too is it removed by consent to the opposite.

Now, the things relating to ordination are above nature, above the work of arranging and of things; hence the character or spiritual power for the pronouncement of these words is imprinted on the soul. Wherefore, the character of such words is imprinted whenever the power is expressly conferred. But because there is nothing expressly established about it being removed in any way whatsoever, the impression of conferral of the character on which the powers of ordination is based is indelible. Therefore, the fact that the pope subjects himself freely to the law means a continuation of those elements involved in orders that relate to the priesthood and the episcopacy in which the character and the perfection of the character are imprinted. But it does not mean a continuation of power in respect of the things that relate to the papacy or the high priesthood, since the papacy and the high priesthood only add jurisdiction, and jurisdiction can be renounced.

[7] To the seventh argument, concerning the oath a pope takes, I reply: the pope's oath to take universal charge of the Lord's flock must be understood to apply to him as long as he is in office, that is, as long as he is pope. For this is how those who become rulers of secular states swear to keep the statutes of the states, and to keep those states in good condition. All such oaths are to be understood as lasting for as long as their office lasts. An oath by which anyone would swear permanently to remain in office or in the papacy, and simply and absolutely to take charge of a people for all time, would be illicit; for it could militate against the common good, inasmuch as he might find himself inadequate, and the common good would lanquish and die.

[8] To the eighth argument, that no one can absolve himself from sin, I reply: the cases are not the same. For to absolve oneself from sin is to ascend while to absolve oneself from the papacy is to descend. Moreover, the argument is not valid that, if someone cannot ascend, neither can he descend. It can also be argued that a man absolved himself from sin in contrition, and that if he is bound to confess afterward to another person by whom he

is absolved, this is only because of a precept of the Lord: James 5: "Confess your sins to one another"; [23] and in Luke 7: The Lord directed the lepers,[24] through whom we are to understand sinners, to show themselves to the priests.

[9] To the ninth argument, that papal obligation cannot be taken away except through a higher obligation, the same reply can be made as was made to that other argument: [25] the obligations of pope are not unconditional; the condition is, to wit, the time during which the man holds office.

[10] To the tenth argument, that no ecclesiastical dignity can be taken away after legitimate conferral by a superior, I reply: it is clear that this is to be understood concerning a dignity confirmed by a superior. However, a pope's ascent to office has no confirmation by a superior; and therefore his descent from this office is a surrender of it without a superior.

[11] To the eleventh argument, about the eternal priesthood of Christ, a reply follows from what already has been said. For the priesthood of Christ was eternal because Christ lived forever by virtue of His offering. And I concede that the pope's priesthood endures in this way as long as he lives; for he possesses an indelible character, and will be a priest forever, and will always be able to offer sacrifice at the altar. But it is not necessary for a man's pontificate to last as long as he lives. The pope can give it up or be deposed for sufficient reason, since the office of pope designates a jurisdiction beyond the episcopacy and the priesthood which is mutable. And the pope would not be pope without this jurisdiction.

Thus ends the treatise on kingly and papal power written by Master John of Paris, of the Order of Friars Preachers.

Notes

GENERAL INTRODUCTION

1. Walter Ullmann, *The Growth of Papal Government in the Middle Ages, a Study in the Ideological Relation of Clerical to Lay Power*, 2d ed. (London: Methuen, 1964).

2. Irenaeus employed the term *principalitas* in respect of the Church. See Ullmann, *Papal Government*, pp. 4, 5.

3. See P. Battifol, "Papa, sedes apostolica, apostolatus," *Rivista di archeologia cristiana* 2 (1925):99–116; H. Rahner, "Navicula Petri," *Zeitschrift für katholische Theologie* 69 (1949):28–29.

4. No question in medieval political history has been more controversial than this conception of Christendom as a unitary politico-ecclesiastical society within one church. Among recent articles on the subject are Alfons M. Stickler, "Concerning the Political Theories of the Mediaeval Canonists," *Traditio.* 7 (1949–51):450 ff; Gerhart Ladner, "The Concepts of *ecclesia* and *christianitas* and the Relation to the Idea of Papal *plenitudo potestatis* from Gregory VII to Boniface VIII," *Miscellanea historicae pontificae* 18 (Rome, 1954): 49–77. See also E. Gilson, *Les Métamorphoses de la cité de Dieu* (Louvain, 1952).

5. A careful biographical study of John of Paris can be found in Jean Leclercq, *Jean de Paris et l'écclesiologie du XIIIè siècle* (Paris, 1942), pp. 6–25; and a more recent account of John's career is found in F. J. Roensch, *Early Thomistic School* (Dubuque: Priory Press, 1964), pp. 98–104; 142–48. See also Marc Griesbach, "John of Paris as a Representative of Thomistic Political Philosophy," in *An Etienne Gilson Tribute*, ed. Charles J. O'Neil (Milwaukee: Marquette University Press, 1959), pp. 33 ff.

6. Of the twenty extant manuscripts of the work, its attribution to John is made explicitly in fifteen of them: see Leclercq, *Jean de Paris*, p. 6, note 1. For information on the catalogue data, see *ibid.* note 3.

7. Cf. *Histoire littéraire de la France* (Paris, 1896), 25:244–47; Leclercq, *Jean de Paris*, p. 7.

8. Although this designation has led earlier to speculation that its basis was pathological, Leclercq is quite specific that "Quidort" was John's family name: Leclercq, *Jean de Paris*, p. 7, note 3.

9. Cf. P. Glorieux, "Un Memoire justificatif de Bernard de Trilia," *Revue des*

sciences philosophiques et théologiques 17 (1928):407–13; "Le mémoire justificatif de Bernard de Trilia," *Revue des sciences philosophiques et théologiques* 19 (1930):473.

10. The text of John's *correctorium* was edited by J. P. Muller, *Le corruptorium correctorii "circa" de Jean Quidort de Paris,* Studia Anselmiana 9 (Rome, 1941).

11. John's doctrine maintained that in transsubstantiation the consecrated bread becomes the body of Christ by assumption of Christ's humanity rather than by conversion.

12. Etienne Gilson, *History of Christian Philosophy in the Middle Ages* (New York: Random House, 1955), pp. 413–14.

13. The classic presentation of the great dispute is found in G. Degard, *Philippe le Bel et le saint siège de 1285 à 1304,* 2 vols. (Paris, 1936). See also J. Rivière, *Le Problème de l'église et de l'état au temps de Philippe le Bel* (Paris, 1926); C. T. Wood, ed., *Philip the Fair and Boniface VIII* (New York, 1967). See p. 121.

14. Leclercq, *Jean de Paris,* p. 14. This dating places the composition of the treatise between the two estates-general called by Philip to deal with his controversy with Boniface. It is perhaps not without interest that John's own views on the primacy of a general council over papal authority antedate the explicit efforts of the latter of these two meetings to summon Boniface before a general church council to review the legitimacy of his election to the papacy.

15. *Extravagantes* 8, "De majoritate et obedientia," in *Corpus iuris canonici,* ed. A. Friedberg (1879; reprint, Graz, 1959), 2:1245. English translations of the bull are readily available in several volumes of documents and readings from medieval history, among which is *Church and State through the Centuries,* ed. Sidney Z. Ehler and John Morrall (Westminster, Md.: Newman Press, 1954), pp. 90–92.

16. *Cf. The Cambridge Medieval History,* vol. 6, *Decline of Empire and Papacy* (Cambridge: University Press, 1968), pp. 405–11.

17. H. Denifle and E. Chatelain, *Chartularium universitatis parisiensis,* 4 vols. (Paris, 1889–1897), 2:101, note 634.

18. P. Feret, "La Faculté de théologie de Paris et ses docteurs les plus célèbres," *Moyen Age* 3 (Paris, 1896):374; Maurice de Wulf, *Histoire de la philosophie médiévale* (Louvain, 1925), 2:43; R. Scholz, *Die Publizistik zur Zeit Philipps des Schönen* (Stuttgart, 1903; reprint, Editons RODOPI, Amsterdam, 1969), p. 29. *Cf.* Leclercq, *Jean de Paris,* p. 21, note 3.

19. R. Holtmann, *Wilhelm von Nogaret* (Frieburg in Breisgau, 1898), p. 220; Leclercq, *Jean de Paris,* p. 21, note 6.

20. A modern edition of this work exists: Aegidius Romanus, *De ecclesiastica potestate,* ed. Richard Scholz (1929; reprint, Aalen, 1961).

21. See p. xxiii.

22. See p. xxv.

23. James of Viterbo, *De regimine christiano,* ed. H. X. Arquillière (Paris, 1926); Henry of Cremona, "De potestate papae," in R. Scholz, *Die Publizistik,* pp. 459–71; *Non ponant laici* in *ibid.,* pp. 471–86; *Determinatio compendiosa de jurisdictione imperii,* ed. M. Krammer (Berlin, 1909).

24. Aegidius of Rome, "De renuntiatione papae," in *Biblioteca maxima pontificia,* ed. J. T. Rocaberti (Rome, 1698–99), vol. 2.

25. Godfrey of Fontaines, "Quodlibet XIII," 5, in *Les Quodlibets treize de Godefroid de Fontaines,* ed. J. Hoffmanns, Les Philosophes belges (Louvain, Editions de l'Institut supérieur de philosophie, 1935), 5:224–28.

26. M. Grabmann, *Die Lehre Hl. Thomas von Aquin der Kirche als Gotteswerk* (Regensburg, 1903).

27. Leclercq, *Jean de Paris,* p. 35.

28. "Quaestio in utramque partem," in *Monarchia s. romani imperii,* ed. Melchoir Goldast (Hanover, 1614; reprint, Graz, 1960), 2:95–107; "Quaestio de potestate papae 'Rex pacificus,' " in *Histoire de différend d'entre le pape Boniface VIII et Philippe le Bel,* ed. P. Bupuy (Paris, 1655), pp. 663–83.

29. "Disputatio inter militem et clericum," in *Monarchia s. romani imperii,* 1. 13–18.

30. H. Finke, *Aus den Tagen Bonifaz VIII,* pp. 100–16, cited in Leclercq, *Jean de Paris,* p. 38, note 2.

31. Ullmann, *Papal Government,* p. 382.

32. Dante Aligheri, *Le opere di Dante Aligheri,* ed. E. Moore, Vol. "De monarchia" (Oxford, 1924), pp. 339–76; William of Ockham, *Breviloquium de potestate papae,* ed. L. Baudry (Paris, 1937); "Dialogus," in *Monarchia s. romani imperii* 2. 398–976; Marsilius of Padua, *Defensor pacis,* ed. C. W. Previté-Orton (Cambridge: University Press, 1928); Alan Gewirth, tr. *Marsilius of Padua, the Defender of Peace,* vol. 2, *The Defensor pacis* (New York: Columbia University Press, 1956).

33. "Novellae constitutiones," 6, pr., in *Corpus iuris civilis* (Berlin, 1895), 3:36.

34. Ullmann, *Papal Government, passim.*

35. *Cf.* the efforts of Henry IV, in his struggle with Pope Gregory VII, to develop the concept of *rex-sacerdos.* See Ullmann, *Papal Government,* pp. 352 ff.

36. Hugh of St. Victor, "De sacramentis christianae fidei," *Patrologia latina cursus completus,* ed. J.-P. Migne (Paris, 1862), vol. 176.

37. Honorius of Canterbury is cited as a source for Hugh by Ullmann, *Papal Government,* p. 440.

38. *Cf.* John Courtney Murray, "Contemporary Orientations of Catholic Thought on Church and State in the Light of History," *Theological Studies* 10 (1949): 177 ff; and the necessary correctives in the important article of Marc F. Griesbach, cited in note 5, above.

39. Alan Gewirth, *Marsilius of Padua, the Defender of Peace,* vol. 1, *Marsilius*

of *Padua and Medieval Political Philosophy* (New York: Columbia University Press, 1951), p. 33.

40. Leclercq, *Jean de Paris*, pp. 151 ff.

41. One of Dante's teachers, Remy of Florence, was a transmitter of Quidort's thoughts: Leclercq, *Jean de Paris*, p. 169, note 1. Remy's connection with John, however, is not reflected in Dante.

42. Peter's statements have come down both through a summary of them and his own reply made by Cardinal Pierre Bertrand, found in Durand de Maillanes, *Libertez de l'église gallicane* (Lyon, 1771), 3:444–98.

43. In *codicem Justiniani* 3. 1, "Cunctos populos" (Venice, 1586), cited in Leclercq, *Jean de Paris*, p. 153, note 1.

44. Peter of Palud, *In II sententiarum Petri Lombardi expositio*, ms. Vat. lat. 1075, fol. 80r, cited in Leclercq, *Jean de Paris*, p. 153, note 2.

45. Guillaume, *De causa immediata ecclesiasticae potestatis* 4. 1 (Paris, 1506), cited in Leclercq, *Jean de Paris*, p. 153, note 4; William of Ockham, "Defensorium de paupertate Christi contra errores Joannis XXII," in *Appendix ad fasciculum rerum expetendarum*, ed. J. Brown (London, 1690); *Breviloquium de potestate papae*, pp. 136–37, 139. Raoul of Presle, "De potestate pontificali et imperiali seu regia," in *Monarchia s. romani imperii* 1:39–57.

46. Nicholas of Clamanges, *Le Traité de la ruine de l'église de Nicolas de Clamanges* 1, ed. A. Colville (Paris, 1936), pp. 112–15; Peter of Aily, *De ecclesiae et cardinalium auctoritate* 3, ed. Ellies du Pen, in *Gersonii Opera* (Paris, 1706) 1, col. 914–17, pp. 896–99.

47. John Gerson, *De potestate ecclesiastica* 4–5 (Paris, 1606), 1:115–18; *Tractatus de statibus ecclesiasticis* 1:186–95. *Cf.* Leclercq, *Jean de Paris*, p. 155, note 2.

48. Jacques du Paradis, *De septem statibus ecclesiae* (Paris, 1449), cited in Leclercq, *Jean de Paris*, p. 155, note 3; Denis le Chartreux, "De auctoritate summi pontificis et generalis concilii," 3. 8, *Opera minora* (Tournai, 1908), 4:625, cited in Leclercq, *Jean de Paris*, p. 155, note 4.

49. Cardinal Turrecremata, *Summa de ecclesia*, 2. 89 (Salamanca, 1560), p. 332; 2. 96, p. 397; 2. 113, p. 403; J. A. Delfino, *De ecclesia* (Venice, 1552) 2:204v–205.

50. Jacques Almain, "Libellus de auctoritate ecclesiae," 2, ed. W. Richer, in *Vindiciae doctrinae majorum scholae parisiensis* (Cologne, 1683) 4:29; "De potestate ecclesiastica et laica," 1. 2, *ed. cit.*, 4. 81, cited in Leclercq, *Jean de Paris*, p. 156, note 4; "Joannis Majoris disputatio ex sententiarum IV libris" 24, in *Vindiciae doctrinae majorum scholae Parisiensis* 4. 247.

51. Bellarmine, *De romano pontifice* 5. 1 (Venice, 1721) 1:433.

52. Aubert le Mire, *Auctorium de scriptoribus ecclesiasticis*, part 405 (Hamburg, 1718), p. 74; Oudin, *De scriptoribus ecclesiasticis* (Leipzig, 1722), 3:637; *Bibliothèque historique de la France* (Paris, 1768), 1:475; Bulaeus, *Historica universitatis parisiensis* (Paris, 1668), 4:70, 267; see Leclercq, *Jean de Paris*,

p. 157, notes 6 (for Boulay) and 7 (for Victoria); Molina, *De justitia et jure* 2. 21 (Cologne, 1733) 1. 60. 12; 28. 1. 73.

53. Cited in Bouchel, *Decreta ecclesiae gallicanae* (Paris, 1609), p. 739; *cf.* Leclercq, *Jean de Paris*, p. 158, note 2.

54. Cardinal du Perron, "Harangue au tiers état sur le sujet du serment," *Oeuvres* (Paris, 1622), pp. 613–14.

55. Jean Savaron, *Erreurs et impostures de l'examen de la souveraineté de vois* (Paris, 1616), pp. 68–70, 74.

56. Cited in Leclercq, *Jean de Paris*, p. 159, note 2.

57. Boussuet, "Defensio declarationis cleri gallicani" 1. 3. 25, in *Oeuvres* (Paris, 1865), 21:465–66.

58. Cited in Leclercq, *Jean de Paris*, p. 159, note 6.

59. *Tractatus de libertatibus ecclesiae gallicanae* (Liège, 1684), pp. 189, 613.

60. F. Pena, *De temporali regno Christi*, cited in Leclercq, *Jean de Paris*, p. 159, note 8.

61. Marca, cited in Leclercq, *Jean de Paris*, p. 159.

62. The most recent controversy involving an interpretation of John's political theory has concerned itself with his faithfulness to the doctrines of St. Thomas Aquinas. Dom Leclercq designated him a "faithful disciple" of Saint Thomas: Leclercq, *Jean de Paris*, p. 85; and this view was concurred in by John Courtney Murray, who went on to contend that Quidort's doctrine in the *De potestate* could point the way to a contemporary resolution of the church-state issue: John Courtney Murray, "Contemporary Orientations." Griesbach, on the other hand, takes a more qualified view about John's thomism in a carefully nuanced argument that in no way lessens the judgment of Murray on the contemporary value of John's position: Griesbach, "John of Paris."

PROLOGUE

1. The controversy over the right of mendicant friars to hear confessions and preach was addressed by Boniface VIII in the bull *Super cathedram* of February 18, 1300, a document John must have had in mind when he chose this contemporary ecclesiastical problem to illustrate the virtues of the *via media* approach to such problems. Boniface's resolution of the controversy in favor of the mendicants was shortly qualified by restrictions imposed on the mendicants' powers to confess by his successor, Benedict XI, in the bull *Inter cunctos* of 1304. Quidort himself took part in the controversy, which erupted in 1304, over this latter papal document. See Leclercq, *Jean de Paris*, p. 8.

2. Boethius, "Liber de persona et duabus naturis," prooemium, (*PL* 64. 1341). John is greatly indebted, in the formulation of his position in this first paragraph, to Thomas Aquinas, *Contra impugnantes dei cultum et religionem* 3. 70–77, especially 73–75 (ed. Raymond M. Spiazzi [Turin, 1958], p. 24).

3. The Waldensians, adjudged heretical for their views, were along with the

Albigensians one of the greatest sources of disturbance to the twelfth- and early-thirteenth-century Church. Founded about 1176 by Peter Waldo, a wealthy banker from Lyons, they were violently opposed to the clergy and advocated a return to the simplicity of the Apostolic Church and elimination of organizational and bureaucratic structures in the Church. See Philip Hughes, *A History of the Church,* 3 vols. (New York: Sheed and Ward, 1948) 2:336–38.

4. John deals with the Donation of Constantine at length in chapter 21.

5. Matt. 6:19. Note: References for biblical citations are from the King James version. The translation is rendered directly from John's text, which was based on the Vulgate text.

6. I Tim. 6:8, 9.

7. Matt. 6:24.

8. Matt. 6:31.

9. Matt. 6:26.

10. Matt. 10:9.

11. Luke 14:33.

12. Acts 3:6; See Moneta of Cremona, *Adversus Catharros et Valdenses,* 5. 5. 7 (Rome, 1743), pp. 446–48.

13. Matt. 2:3; *cf.* chap. 8.

14. John later specifies only one of these *moderni,* Henry of Cremona; see chap. 11, *arg.* 31,32,33,34,42. See also Leclercq's careful analysis of these "modern" theocratic advocates: Jean Leclercq, *Jean de Paris et l'ecclesiologie du XIIIè siècle* (Paris, 1942), pp. 29–33, and especially Leclercq's comment that although he never refers directly to Aegidius of Rome's work, *De ecclesiastica potestate,* this is the single most useful source for John's enumeration of his opponents' views.

15. Although John refers here to the papalist argument that the pope stands in the place of Christ (*loco Christi*), it is clear that the argument he has in mind is that which designates the pope as "vicar of Christ" (*vicarius Christi*). John is perfectly aware that this had been one of the cornerstones of the papalist claims since Innocent III had formally incorporated it within the canonists' armory. See Walter Ullmann, *The Growth of Papal Government in the Middle Ages, a Study in the Ideological Relation of Clerical to Lay Power,* 2d ed. (London: Methuen, 1964), p. 428, note 4.
Its use as a title exclusively applicable to the pope came to be adopted as a result of its employment by St. Bernard: *cf.* Bernard of Clairvaux, "Epistola CCLI," (*PL* 182. 451); "De consideratione" 2. 8. 6, *Sancti Bernardi Opera,* ed. J. Leclercq (Rome, 1961), 3:424; 4. 7. 23, *ibid.,* 3:426.
The general character of the argument, though not the term *vicarius Christi,* is found as far back as Pope Gelasius and Pope Leo I. John himself frequently employs the term when referring to the pope; he uses it in the following paragraph. He accepts the term, but accepts also the necessity of denying temporal authority to the "vicar of Christ." (Chaps. 8, 12, 13, *passim.*) John was well

aware of the need to dismiss the papalist claims resting on the notion of the pope as "vicar of Christ." See Ullmann's application of this necessity to his assessment of the anonymous antipapalist *York Tracts* and the twelfth-century *Liber de unitate ecclesiae conservandi:* Ullmann, *Papal Government*, pp. 394–404.

16. *Decretalium d. Gregorii papae IX* 4, "Per venerabilem," *Corpus iuris canonici* 2. 714. John returns to and deals at length with the papalist position summarized here in chap. 13. See also chap. 10.

17. Vigilantius was an early-fifth-century parish priest in Gaul whose views on the cult of martyrs were considered heretical by St. Jerome. None of Vigilantius' own writings are extant, and his doctrines are known only in the incomplete expression given them by Jerome. See below, note 20.

18. Augustine, "De agone christiano" 12 (*PL* 40. 297).

19. Jovinian, an ex-monk and man of the world, maintained that since baptism guaranteed salvation, mortification of the flesh was absurd. He was excommunicated by Pope Siricius (384–398), and drew written criticisms of his views from Sts. Ambrose and Jerome. See following note.

20. Jerome, "Adversus Vigilantium liber" 1 (*PL* 23. 355). For the argument about ownership being repugnant to the pope by reason of his state and John's response, see Thomas Aquinas, *Contra pestiferum doctrinam retrahentium homines a religionis ingressu*, 1. 735–36, (ed. Raymond M. Spiazzi [Turin, 1961], pp. 159–60.)

21. *Glossa interlinearis in I Petrum* 2:13 (Anvers, 1634), 6:1319.

22. John Chrysostom, "Opus imperfectum in Mattheum, Homilia XXXVIII" (*PG* 56. 841); cited in Thomas Aquinas, *Catena aurea in Mattheum*, 21:12. See chap. 9.

23. For John, the general right of clerics to have dominion or jurisdiction over temporal things is restricted to the right, enjoyed by any man, to possess one's own private property—that is, the right based on his own expenditure of labor or money. The only exception to this general principle is stated immediately: *viz.* some type of specific concession or permission granted to a cleric by a temporal ruler. See chaps. 6, 7, 12.

24. This disclaimer indicates John's wish to be considered an orthodox Christian. There is no need to raise the issue of whether or not he sees his own position as heterodox, as has been suggested in respect of the more extreme antipapalist position of Marsilius of Padua. See Alan Gewirth, *Marsilius of Padua, the Defender of Peace*, vol. 1, *Marsilius of Padua and Mediaeval Political Philosophy* (New York: Columbia University Press, 1951), pp. 82–84.

CHAPTER 1

1. The term I have chosen to translate *regnum* is "kingship" rather than the more general term "state," although it is clear that John designates the basic unit of political society as a *regnum*. In fact, he concedes that there can be

other types of political entity than monarchies, and even his notion of monarchy admits the possibility of other sources of authority within it than the king alone; he speaks frequently of the consent of the people. See chaps. 10, 15, *ad* 9, 17, *ad* 21, 19, *ad* 33.

For John, however, kingship—one-man rule by a king—is the best form of temporal authority; and his position in discussing the legitimacy of the exercise of temporal authority by a cleric is stated consistently in terms of the contrast between the basic type of authority in temporal matters, kingship, and the basic type of authority in spiritual matters, priesthood. For qualifications and reservations on the one-man character of both these types of authority see the remaining citations for this chapter and those for chapter 24.

2. This definition of kingship (or state) is basically Aristotelian, although the definition is not found in so many words in Aristotle; *cf.* Aristotle, *Politics* 1. 2. 1252b27. The definition in its Aristotelian derivation was common to many medieval political thinkers, especially those who followed Aristotle in describing temporal authority and political society as natural to man: *Cf.* Thomas Aquinas, *De regimine principum* 1. 1; Ptolemy of Lucca, *De regimine principum* 4. 2; Aegidius of Rome, *De regimine principum* 1. 1; James of Viterbo, *De regimine christiano* 2; Englebert of Admont, *Liber de ortu, progressu et fine romano imperii* 13; Dante, *De monarchia* 1. 5; Augustinus Triumphus, *Summa de ecclesiastica potestate* 1. 6; Marsilius of Padua, *Defensor pacis* 1. 4. 1; William of Ockham, *Dialogus,* 3. 2. 2. 5.

3. Aristotle, *Politics,* 1. 2. 1252b33. John's characterization of the kingly state as a "perfect community" is, again, typically medieval and can be seen frequently in this period: *Cf.* Thomas Aquinas, *De regimine principum* 1. 1; Aegidius of Rome, *De regimine principum* 3. 1. 1; Englebert of Admont, *Liber de ortu, progressu et fine romani imperii* 15; James of Viterbo, *De regimine christiano* 1. 1; Dante, *De monarchia* 1. 3. 5. See also, note 6 below; chap. 19, *ad* 35, especially note 49.

The emphasis is on the state viewed from the side of its purpose, end, or final cause as well as its perfection seen from the point of view of completeness. See Aristotle, *Politics* 1. 2. 1252b35. The teleological character of John's definition, while typically medieval, must meet the kind of reservation that can be brought against this method of defining a political society. See Gewirth, *Marsilius of Padua* vol. 2, *Defensor pacis* (1956), pp. xxxviii; li. On the general use of the *Politics* as a source for medieval political theories, see G. von Hertling, "Zur Geschichte der aristotelischen Politik im Mittelalter," *Historische Beitrage zur Geschichte der Philosophie* (Kempten and Munich, 1914), pp. 20–32; M. Grabmann, "Studien uber den Einfluss der aristotelischen Philosophie auf die mittelalterlichen Theorien uber das Verhaltnis von Kirche und Staat," *Sitzungsberichte der Bayerischen Akademie der Wissenschaften*, Phil.-hist. Abt no. 2, (1934); M. Grabmann, "Die mittelalterlichen Kommentare zur Politick des Aristoteles," *Ibid.* vol. 2, no. 10 (1941); G. Lagarde, *La Naissance de l'esprit laique au déclin du moyen âge*, 3d ed. (Louvain, Editions de l'Institut supérieur de philosophie, 1956).

4. Aristotle, *Politics* 3. 7. 1279a5–10. For similar insistence on the end of political society as the common good, see Thomas Aquinas, *De regimine prin-*

cipum 1. 1; Aegidius of Rome, *De regimine principum,* 3. 2. 2; Dante, *De monarchia* 1. 12; James of Viterbo, *De regimine christiano* 2. 2; John of Jandun, *Questiones in duodecim libros metaphysicae* 1. 18; William of Ockham, *Dialogus* 3. 1. 2. 6; *Octo quaestiones de potestate papae* 3. 4. Contrast Marsilius of Padua, *Defensor pacis* 1. 9. 5, 6, 7, 9.

5. For the distinctions among kingship, aristocracy and polity see Aristotle, *Politics* 3. 7.

6. Ezek. 34:23. This use of a scriptural text to support the Aristotelian preference for one-man rule illustrates the reaction of many medieval users of the Aristotelian *Politics* to the Philosopher's reluctance to favor a single political authority in a state. Aristotle himself says that this type of rule would be "best" if a single man could be found who was preeminent in virtue. Logically, it would seem, such a person ought to rule, and all other men ought to pay him a willing obedience. However, in practice Aristotle himself despaired of finding such a paragon of virtue, and favored a mixed polity as the best type of government or political society (*Politics* 3. 15–17). Typically, medieval Aristotelians simply ignored Aristotle's practical reservations about finding this maximally virtuous leader, accepted his statements extolling such a single man as the natural embodiment of authority, and suppressed any reference to Aristotle's own declared preference for the mixed polity. John follows such a procedure here, and bolsters the argument in favor of one-man rule by an appeal to scriptural authorities. Later, however, he makes some interesting and important references to the benefits of a mixed polity, and even extends the Aristotelian preference for such a system to the Church. See chap. 19 (*ad* 35), especially note 49.

7. Aristotle, *Politics* 1. 2. 1253a2. The view that man is by nature a political animal is to be found also in Thomas Aquinas, *De regimine principum* 1. 1; Ptolemy of Lucca, *De regimine principum* 4. 2; Aegidius of Rome, *De regimine principum* 3. 1. 4; James of Viterbo, *De regimine christiano,* 1. 1; Dante, *Il convivio,* 4. 4.
A little later on in this same chapter John repeats this principle, adding "social" to the list of natural qualities: "Man is naturally a civil or political and social animal."

8. Aristotle, *Politics,* 1. 2. 1252b15–1253a15. On the point of the relationship between speech and man's social nature as perfected in a community see Thomas Aquinas, *De regimine principum* 1. 1; Ptolemy of Lucca, *De regimine principum* 4. 3; Aegidius of Rome, *De regimine principum,* 2. 1. 1; 3. 1. 4; Marsilius of Padua, *Defensor pacis* 2. 22. 15; G. Lagarde, "Une adaptation de la Politique d'Aristote au XIVè siècle," *Revue historique de droit français et étranger* 4th series, vol. 11 (1932):236–37.

9. In this instance I have translated *regnum* as "kingdom," implying some quality of territorial extent as well as a form of political authority (see chapter 21). John does not mention here any form of political authority of larger territorial extent than a kingdom. In the present context this is consistent with his description of the ascending order of perfection among communities, from household to village to kingdom, the last-mentioned being perfect because

all-providing in terms of its members' needs. In chapter 3, however, John specifically rejects any theory of universal political authority. Note his use of *regnum* here too to designate a territorially limited state. Later, he makes reference to an emperor as a temporal ruler having no superior (chapter 10) and also refers on one occasion to the emperor as having "universal and ubiquitous jurisdiction over temporal affairs" (chap. 13).

10. The analogy between one-man rule in a state, the single common power of soul in organisms, and unity in the governance of the universe is also found in Thomas Aquinas, *De regimine principum*, 1. 2; Ptolemy of Lucca, *De regimine principum* 3. 1; Aegidius of Rome, *De regimine principum*, 3. 2. 3; Dante, *De monarchia* 1. 8; James of Viterbo, *De regimine christiano* 2. 5; Marsilius of Padua, *Defensor pacis*, 1. 17, 8, 9.

11. Proverbs 11:14. *Cf.* Thomas Aquinas, *In I politicorum* 1. 31.

12. Kingship is the preferred form of government among all medieval Aristotelians, all of whom tend to view the state from the standpoint of virtues which the ideal king should attempt to foster, and which he himself might personify. See Thomas Aquinas, *De regimine principum* 1; Ptolemy of Lucca, *De regimine principum* 3. 12; Aegidius of Rome, *De regimine principum,* 1. 1. 3; 1. 2. 7; 1. 3. 4; Englebert of Admont, *De ortu, progressu et fine romani imperii* 2. 14, 15; James of Viterbo, *De regimine christiano,* 2. 2, 6, 8; Augustinus Triumphus, *Summa de ecclesiastica potestate,* 44. 1; John of Jandun, *Questiones in duodecim libros metaphysicae,* 1. 1. 18; 1. 2. 11.

13. John's ideal of peace and order as promoted through unity of political authority in the state is the traditional one expressed by medieval political theorists. See John of Salisbury, *Policraticus,* 5. 22 ff; Thomas Aquinas, *In decem libros ethicorum Aristotelis ad Nicomachum expositio,* Lect. 8, n. 474; *Summa theologiae,* 2–2. 183. 2, *ad* 3; *De regimine principum,* 1. 12; Ptolemy of Lucca, *De regimine principum,* 4. 23; Aegidius of Rome, *De regimine principum,* 1. 2. 11; Marsilius of Padua, *Defensor pacis,* 1. 2. 3; 1. 19. 2.

14. Aristotle, *Politics,* 3. 7. 1279b6–10. See also chap. 19, *ad* 35.

15. Aristotle, *Politics* 1. 5. 1254a35. See above note 10.

16. Aristotle, *Politics,* 1. 2. 1253a7.

17. Orosius, *Historiarum,* 1. 1 (*PL* 31, 669).

18. Cicero, *De inventione* 1. 2, ed. & transl. H. M. Hubbell (Cambridge, Mass., 1949), p. 6.

19. Aristotle, *Politics,* 1. 2. 1253a28–9.

20. Cicero, *De inventione* 1. 2, p. 6.

21. John has used the term "law of nations" (*ius gentium*) earlier in this chapter, but this is the first effort he makes at its definition. The "law of nations" is that body of written legislation common to all political societies which embodies basic principles of the "natural law." The ideology is completely derivative from Thomas Aquinas: *Summa theologiae,* 1–2, 95. 4. John's canonist opponents, for the most part, had a completely different notion of "na-

tural law": *cf.* Walter Ullmann, *Medieval Papalism, the Political Theories of the Medieval Canonists* (London, Methuen, 1949), pp. 38 ff.

CHAPTER 2

1. While the point is implicit in John's earlier remarks about the proper end of a political society, this is his first explicit comment about the "moral" character of a state's purpose. The purpose of a state, and of its authority, is to make men good, to achieve virtue for its citizens. Again the concept is Aristotelian, and again it is a typically medieval one: Aristotle, *Politics* 3. 9. 1280b1 ff; 6. 13. 1332a4 ff; *Nicomachean Ethics* 2. 4. 1105a29 ff. See also Thomas Aquinas, *Summa theologiae*, 1–2. 96. 2; 1–2. 100. 9; *De regimine principum* 1. 14, 15; Ptolemy of Lucca, *De regimine principum* 3. 3; 4. 24; Godfrey of Fontaines, *Quodlibeta* 1. 6; James of Viterbo, *De regimine christiano* 2. 4; Englebert of Admont, *De ortu, progressu et fine romani imperii*, 7. 8; Durand of St. Pourçain, *De origine et usu jurisdictionum* 2; Alexander of St. Elpidius, *Tractatus de ecclesiastica potestate* 2. 3. 1; John of Jandun, *Questiones in duodecim libros metaphysicae* 1. 1, 18; 2. 11.

2. Here John transcends the Aristotelian framework of argument and basis for his position, adding to the Aristotelian concept of the natural for man the Christian element of the "supernatural." See also Thomas Aquinas, *Summa theologiae* 1. 2. 1–5, esp. 5. 3 and 5. 5.

3. John repeats, in the supernatural order, the same argument, linking unity of end to unity of personal agent to achieve this end, that he employed in advocating a one-man rule in a political society in the previous chapter.

4. Romans 6:23.

5. Reference to God, more specifically to Christ, as "king" has many and long-standing precedents, and was made quite universally by both papalist and anti-papalist commentators. The issue, of course, was to specify what was meant by designating Christ as king. See also, Walter Ullmann, *The Growth of Papal Government in the Middle Ages, a Study in the Ideological Relation of Clerical to Lay Power*, 2d ed. (London: Methuen, 1964), pp. 26 ff.

6. Jeremiah 23:5.

7. Hebrews 5:1. John has now specifically designated Christ as king and priest. This double designation, which John frequently employs, is traditional and reflects the frame of reference normally employed by the papalists. John's acceptance of the terminology, while almost unavoidable, shows again his tendency to turn away from radical rejection of the traditional framework of expression. It is the papalists' interpretation of these traditional formulae to which he takes exception. See chap. 8 and Ullmann, *Papal Government*, pp. 26 ff.

8. This, too, is the traditional concept of the sacraments of the Church: they are means, given to the Church by Christ, to assist men in achieving salvation. *Cf.* the traditional medieval description of the sacraments in Thomas Aquinas,

Summa theologiae 3. 60, esp. 60. 4; *In IV Sententiarium,* 1. 1. 1; Peter Lombard, *Sententiae* 4. 1.

9. Romans 1:20.

10. On this definition of priest *cf.* Thomas Aquinas, *Summa theologiae,* Suppl. 34. 1.

11. Hebrews 5: 1.

12. John's formula definition of priesthood finds echoes in other sections of the treatise: chap. 12; chap. 19, *ad* 35. See also the purely rationalistic and empirical basis for formulating a definition of the priesthood, its nature and function in Marsilius of Padua, *Defensor pacis,* 1. 5. 10–13; and Alan Gewirth, *Marsilius of Padua, the Defender of Peace,* vol. 1, *Marsilius of Padua and Medieval Political Philosophy* (New York: Columbia University Press, 1951), pp. 43, 83–84; 108–115; 119–125.

CHAPTER 3

1. II Cor. 13:10.

2. The distinction John draws between the power of bishops and the power of ordinary priests on the issues of consecration and jurisdiction is crucial for any doctrine of hierarchical structure in the Christian Church. John argues that bishops, like all priests, have the power to consecrate the bread and wine into the Body and Blood of Christ. All ordained priests, simple priests and bishops (and pope) alike, possess this power to an equal degree. Bishops (and by inference the pope as well), however, have additional powers as "higher and perfect ministers," and these are not possessed by ordinary priests: the power to confer the priesthood on another man and the power to exercise jurisdiction over other priests. The specific character of this episcopal (and papal) power of jurisdiction is the crux of the issue. John's view that the priest receives his jurisdiction from the bishop is traditional: *cf.* Thomas Aquinas, *Summa theologiae,* Suppl., 40. 4. In point of fact, the first half of John's chapter follows closely the contents of Thomas Aquinas, *Summa contra gentiles,* 4. 76 and *In IV Sent.,* 13. 1. 1. *resp.* 2, *ad* 2.

3. Pseudo-Dionysius, "De ecclesiastica hierarchia," 4. 3 (*PG* 3. 506). John's reference to the Pseudo-Dionysius marks the introduction of a major authority for the traditional medieval conceptions of unity and order applied to the formulation of political theory. It is the base for all arguments and procedures employed by the papalists in their development of a universalist theologico-political theory subsuming all political authority under the spiritual authority of the papacy, and was also a normal part of the intellectual framework of many antipapalist descriptions of papal authority. *Cf.* Boniface VIII, *Unam sanctam,* and the commentary on this attributed to Aegidius of Rome, edited by P. de Lapparent, in *Archives d'histoire littéraire et doctrinale du moyen âge* 18 (1940–42):127–45; Aegidius of Rome, *De ecclesiastica potestate* 1. 4; Augustinus Triumphus, *Summa de ecclesiastica potestate* 44. 1; Alexander of St. Elpidius, *Tractatus ecclesiastica potestate* 2. 6. 4; James of Viterbo, *De*

regimine christiano 2. 2. 5; Francis of Mayron, *Quaestio de subjectione* 1. 10.

4. The term Church Militant is pseudo-Dionysian in origin, although the notion of the Church and of Christians as "militant" goes back as far as St. Paul. The argument for universal papal authority based on the concept of "one head" is treated again in chap. 18, *ad* 29. The conception of the parallel between Church Militant and Church Triumphant was a strong basis for the papalist position: see Walter Ullmann, *Medieval Papalism, the Political Theories of the Medieval Canonists* (London: Methuen, 1949), pp. 159–60.

5. The Church Triumphant is the pseudo-Dionysian correlative of the Church Militant (see Pseudo-Dionysius, "De ecclesiastica hierarchia," 4. 3 [*PG* 3. 506]), and this term has had a lengthy history. The Church Triumphant is the heavenly kingdom, in the literal sense. In heaven Christ rules supreme. Again, however, the possibilities for interpreting the terminology in such a way as to emphasize some form of ecclesiastical "triumph" over the whole universe of the temporal world are clearly present, and they did not go unnoticed by the papalists. See Ullmann, *Medieval Papalism*, pp. 77 ff.

6. Rev. 21:3.

7. Hosea 1:11.

8. John 10:16.

9. John is prepared to accept the view that the unity and supremacy of papal authority derived directly from Christ, in virtue of the commission to Peter. He does not find it necessary to limit papal authority by ascribing its origin to any other than a divine source, as Marsilius of Padua does in introducing the element of popular consent. See Marsilius of Padua, *Defensor pacis,* 1. 13. 7 ff.; 1. 15. 2; 1. 18. 3; 1. 15. 4, 9; Gewirth, *Marsilius of Padua,* 1:167 ff.

10. John 21:17.

11. Luke 22:32. The argument in this chapter parallels Humbert of Rome, "Opus tripartitum," 2. 14, in *Appendix ad fasciculum rerum expetendarum* (London, 1690), 2:209.

12. For John, all men and by extension all ecclesiastics are ordered to one supreme spiritual authority according to "divine ordinance." They are ordered to political authority not by explicit law but by "natural inclination." This natural inclination toward political society, however, does not extend to a single person's being the supreme political authority, any more than a universal political society is imposed by divine law. Accordingly, the character of political authority is multiform, less rigidly specified than spiritual authority. This point is crucial for John's development of the distinction between the two spheres, temporal and spiritual. It is also the starting point for his rejection of a universal or world state, a point of great interest in this treatise which is not easily reconcilable with John's emphasis in chapter 1 on the value of a unified type of political authority. Dante, too, asserts that the Church was caused by divine ordinance and not by nature, while the state proceeds from the natural law: Dante, *De monarchia,* 3. 14.

13. The argument that differences of climate and other circumstances justify

a diversity of forms of political authority and society is not peculiar to John: cf. Englebert of Admont, *De ortu, progressu et fine romani imperii* 16; Dante, *De monarchia* 1. 14. John, however, is more explicit than earlier medieval theorists in the arguments he advances against a single world state, and anticipates Marsilius of Padua in his seemingly complete lack of interest in the issue of imperial political authority. John does not mention the issue of empire here as a possible form of temporal authority, although in chapters 3 and 13 he does comment very briefly on it. See Walter Ullmann, *The Growth of Papal Government in the Middle Ages, a Study in the Ideological Relation of Clerical to Lay Power,* 2d ed. (London: Methuen, 1964), p. 457, note 2.

14. The distinction between the spiritual "sword" as verbal and the temporal "sword" as manual is Bernardine in origin: John's application of it in terms of limiting the extent of a single state's territorial jurisdiction is not. Quidort echoes here the famous retort of Pierre de Flotte to Boniface VIII: the pope is concerned with a mystical body and thus works only with words; the king, however, must govern in the proper sense of that term and hence his power is manual. See Ullmann, *Papal Government,* p. 457.

15. See chap. 7. This emphasis on private property is one that John finds very useful in his limitation of ecclesiastical authority; he employs it several times: chaps. 6, 7, 12.

16. See chap. 3.

17. Aristotle, *Nicomachean Ethics* 2. 6. 1106b1.

18. *Cf.* Thomas Aquinas, *In II ethicorum Nicomachum* 7. 325–26. John's reference to Averroes as a critic of world government is paralleled later (ch. 19, *ad* 33) by his use of the commentator in support of the value of popular consent for the exercise of political authority.

19. Aristotle, *Politics* 1. 2. 1253a1.

20. Augustine, *De civitate dei* 4. 15; see also 3–15. John's appeal to the authority of St. Augustine in favor of a territorial limit to the perfect state is found also in Engelbert of Admont, *De ortu, progressu et fine romani imperii* 16.

21. Augustine, *De civitate dei* 4. 15.

22. *Decretum magistri Gratiani* 7, "In apibus," *Corpus iuris canonici* 1. 582.

CHAPTER 4

1. The issue of whether kingship or priesthood came first in time is important for John insofar as a standard papalist claim was that the priesthood was prior to kingship in history. See Hugh of St. Victor, *De sacramentis* 2. 2. 7 (*PL* 176. 420). Curiously enough, John's position that temporal authority existed historically before spiritual authority was asserted by the canonist, Huguccio, before the opposite position became a dominant feature of the papalist argument: Huguccio, *Summa decretorum* 96. 6, quoted in Walter Ullmann, *Medieval*

Papalism, the Political Theories of the Medieval Canonists (London: Methuen), p. 144; *cf. ibid.,* p. 151.

2. Augustine, *De civitate dei* 16. 17.

3. Dante, employing the same basic source of information as John for the history of the foundations of early kingdoms, insists that Ninus was the first man to aspire to world domination, something Dante viewed with much greater equanimity than did John: Dante, *De monarchia* 2. 8. *Cf.* Augustine, *De civitate dei* 16. 17.

4. John's source for this account of early world history is either Orosius, *Historiarum adversum paganos libri VII* 1. 4, or Augustine, *De civitate dei,* 16. 17.

5. For the view that Christ was the first "true" priest inasmuch as He possessed the complete fullness of the priesthood (*tota sacerdotii plenitudo*) see Thomas Aquinas, *Summa theologiae* 3. 63. 6. *Cf.* chap. 19, *ad* 31.

6. Deut. 32:17.

7. Heb. 10:1.

8. Reference to Melchisedech as both "king and priest" was standard in papalist texts. See Gen. 14:18; Ps. 109:4; Heb. 7:1–2, 10, 11, 15, 21. It was apparently introduced into papal literature by Leo I, in Epistle 156. 3–5; and may be found in the texts of Gelasius and Isidore. It was given its classic medieval thrust by Innocent III and his followers. See Walter Ullmann, *The Growth of Papal Government in the Middle Ages, a Study in the Ideological Relation of Clerical to Lay Power,* 2d ed. (London: Methuen, 1964), pp. 13, 23–24, 25 (note 2), 29, 317 (note 2), 397–98.

9. Heb. 7–9.

10. Methodius is referred to by John from mention made of him by Peter the Eater, *Historia scholastica, Genesis XLI,* (PL 198. 1091).

11. John is careful to point out that his reference to the fact that the Old Testament kings were anointed is not intended to indicate that temporal rulers require anointing in order to exercise their authority. The anointing of these early figures, in his view, indicated their status as prefiguring and symbolizing a spiritual, not a temporal, role: *viz.* the role of Christ in relation to His people. See chap. 18, *ad* 26. There can be no doubt that this role of Christ toward His people was not a temporal one. See also chap. 8.

12. Peter the Eater, *Historia scholastica, Genesis XLVI,* (PL 198, 1094).

13. Gen. 12:2.

CHAPTER 5

1. The concept of priority in dignity of the priesthood over kingship also became current through Hugh of St. Victor, *De sacramentis* 2. 2. 7, a text with which John is clearly familiar. (See chap. 4.) It was with Hugh that the concept of a universal Church as a fully autonomous entity having governing

principles of its own reached full maturity. See Walter Ullmann, *The Growth of Papal Government in the Middle Ages; a Study in the Ideological Relation of Clerical to Lay Power,* 2d ed. (London: Methuen, 1964), pp. 437–42.

2. The argument involving the ordering of ends to one another, with the ultimate end the most perfect, was another favorite tool in the construction of the papalist edifice. The implication taken and insisted upon by the papalists was that the temporal ruler, whose end or purpose was subordinate to that of the spiritual ruler, was therefore himself fully subordinate to the spiritual authority. It was the responsibility of the temporal ruler, then, to subordinate himself in all things to the higher ruler; and in this way the autonomy of temporal or secular rule is destroyed. See Aegidius of Rome, *De ecclesiastica potestate* 3. 4; Durandus of St. Pourçain, *De jurisdictione ecclesiastica* 3; Ullmann, *Papal Government,* pp. 445–46; *Medieval Papalism, the Political Theories of the Medieval Canonists* (London: Methuen, 1949) pp. 85–86. See also chap. 11, *arg.* 23, chap. 27, *ad* 23.

3. *Decretum* 96, "Duo sunt quippe," 1. 339. See also chap. 10.

4. "Decretales" 33, "Solite benignitatis," in *Corpus iuris canonici* 2. 198. The sun and moon argument is also taken from Gregory VII, and like the gold and lead analogy it had become a standard item in the papalist armory. See Gregory VII, *Register* 7. 25, "to the Conqueror," p. 505. The biblical reference is quoted from Ambrosius, that is, "De dignitate sacerdotali" 2 (*PL* 17. 569–70). This comparison was used later by Thomas à Becket: see D. Knowles, *Episcopal Colleagues of Archbishop Thomas Becket* (Cambridge: University Press, 1951), p. 147; Ullmann, *Papal Government,* pp. 282–83. John repeats the argument in its papalist context, chap. 11, *arg.* 4.

5. Hugh of St. Victor, "De sacramentis" 2. 2. 4 (*PL* 176, 418).

6. Bernard of Clairvaux, *De consideratione* 1. 6. 7, p. 402. The allusion here is to Luke 5:23, and the basis for Bernard's position is I Cor. 6:4. John himself refers frequently to this Bernardine position: See chaps. 6, 8, 10, 11, *arg.* 30.

7. It is at this point that John begins his effort to fracture the monolithic structure of the papalist argument based on unity and hierarchy. For John, in addition to the principle of unity and hierarchy, it is necessary to accept the principle of diversity in hierarchy, or dual hierarchy under a single head, Christ, insofar as Christ possessed two natures, divine (spiritual) and human (temporal). See below, chap. 13, note 10.

8. John argues that the spiritual order's superiority in dignity over the temporal does not require that temporal authority be derived from the spiritual. He employs other arguments to make the same point about the necessity of distinguishing temporal from spiritual authority: to argue that temporal authority is derived from the spiritual absolutely is to destroy the integrity of political authority, which must be held to be intrinsically distinct from the spiritual power: chap. 17, *ad* 24. See also Dante, *De monarchia* 3. 16; *Quaestio in utramque partem,* 5; *Quaestio de potestate papae,* pp. 670–678; they parallel the distinction between the divine and the human natures in Christ: chap. 19, *ad* 32. See also *Disputatio inter militem et clericum,* pp. 13–14; *Quaestio*

in utramque partem 5, pp. 103, 104; Dante, *De monarchia* 3. 12; they parallel the orders of the theodogical and the moral virtues, each of which has its own integrity and dignity: chap. 18, *ad* 27.

The papalists, for their part, accepted the distinction but interpreted it to mean that the only powers it denied to the pope were those supernatural powers over the whole of creation which belong to God alone: *cf.* Aegidius of Rome, *De ecclesiastica potestate* 3. 9; James of Viterbo, *De regimine christiano* 2. 9; Alexander of St. Elpidius, *Tractatus de ecclesiastica potestate* 1. 4.

9. The view that secular and spiritual authority both derive from a single, supreme source, God, and not from one another can be found in the Justinian Code, in a passage that has been said to be a kind of common denominator of both papalist and antipapalist doctrines: "Novella VI," *Codex Justiniani,* 1. 4. 34. See Ullmann, *Medieval Papalism,* p. 139. A similar idea is to be found in the old canon law. See *Decretum* 23, "Quesitum est," 1. 924. The famous Gelasian text also can be taken in this sense: Gelasius, *Epistola XII,* 2, p. 351. See Ullmann, *Papal Government,* pp. 19–26.

10. John hangs the basis for differentiating and separating the spheres of spiritual and temporal authority on the intention of the single source for these two orders of authority. They are to be distinguished according to what God intended when He established both. John becomes more precise about this divine intention later (chap. 13). This is not to say, however, that for John the differentiation between the orders of the spiritual and the temporal rests on a pure divine voluntarism; for while he does assert that the order of the spiritual authority rests on "divine law," he is quite explicit that the order of temporal political authority is based on nature and derives from the natural law as inclination (chaps. 1 and 3). It also seems fair to say that his conception of divine law is coordinated with his thomistically inspired doctrine of natural law, and as such relates ultimately to the Divine Intellect rather than the Divine Will. See Thomas Aquinas, *Summa theologiae* 1–2. 90. 1; 91. 1–4.

See Dante, *De monarchia* 3. 14. On twelfth-century advocates of the lay thesis see Ullman, *Papal Government,* p. 403 *Cf.* Henry's efforts to assert the duality of the two spheres: Ullmann, *Papal Government,* pp. 345 ff.

11. *Decretum* "Nos si inconpetenter," 1. 496.

12. For John priority in dignity of the priesthood is a characteristic only of the Christian priesthood. Jewish and Gentile priests are for him not true priests, and subordinate to kings even in dignity.

13. Valerian Maximus, *Factorum dictorumque memorabilium* 1. 1, ed. C. Kempf (Leipzig, 1888), p. 5, note 9. This passage is the only one in John's treatise that contains complimentary remarks about the Roman Empire; these remarks have no significance in respect of the political hegemony or propriety of the Roman Empire. Later, John repudiates arguments extolling the value of the Roman Empire, and cites Scripture as containing at least the suggestion that God willed its collapse (chap. 21). See Thomas Aquinas, *De regimine principum* 1. 14.

14. This is the first specific reference to the kingdom of France. Later John

refers to it again in terms of the issue of the exercise of papal jurisdiction over the king of France (chap. 21).

15. Caesar, *The Gallic War* 6. 13, ed. & transl. H. J. Edwards (Cambridge, Mass.: Harvard U. Press, 1946). *Cf.* Thomas Aquinas, *De regimine principum* 1. 14.

CHAPTER 6

1. John introduces a third element for measuring the priority of priesthood and kingship, thus expanding the Victorine frame of reference in a way that makes it possible to disagree most strongly with Hugh. See also chaps. 4 and 5.

2. There are two classes of things about which John raises the issue of papal control: (1) external ecclesiastical goods (*bona exteriora ecclesiastica*)—material possessions belonging to clerics or in some way relating to the material possessions of churches; he also uses the term *temporalia* to designate temporal goods belonging to ecclesiastics or the Church in some way; (2) "the goods of laymen" (*bona laicorum*)—material possessions belonging to laymen. Material goods, then, whether relating to priests or laymen are "external goods." "Internal goods" are spiritual goods.

3. In chapter 8 John distinguishes dominion from jurisdiction, the latter of which he defines.

4. I have not found any instance of a papalist arguemnt employing precisely the terminology *causalitate praecedere,* although the idea is common enough. See chaps. 11 (*arg.* 17, 18, 20, 23, 32); Walter Ullmann, *The Growth of Papal Government in the Middle Ages, a Study in the Ideological Relation of Clerical to Lay Power,* 2d ed. (London: Methuen, 1964), pp. 277–89; 413 ff.

5. John makes use of this concept of private property rights in his rejection of papal authority over temporal goods. See below, this chapter, and chaps. 7 and 12. See also Thomas Aquinas, *Summa theologiae,* 2–2. 66. 2. John's treatment of his problem parallels Godfrey of Fontaines, *Quodlibet* 13. 5, pp. 224–28. There is some question about whether the reference here to the church at Chartres is not in actuality to that of Châlons instead. See Leclercq, *Jean de Paris,* p. 14, note 5.

6. The "right of use" is distinguished from the "right of possession" or dominion: *cf.* Thomas Aquinas, *Summa theologiae,* 2–2, 66. 2.

7. This notion of proportional right of use related to a person's status is also a common feature of the doctrine of material goods John is presenting. It is often referred to as "distributive justice" to distinguish it from "simple justice." The distinction originated with Aristotle, *Nicomachean Ethics* 5. 5, 1132b21 ff; and was developed by Thomas Aquinas, *Summa theologiae* 2–2, 61. 1–2.

8. This formula is the one John employs to describe most succinctly the character of papal authority in respect of all goods: the pope is "universal dispenser" (*universalis dispensator*). The reference here is only to ecclesiastical

goods, spiritual and temporal, but in chapter 7 John extends the notion to cover all goods later.

9. This was the designation—lord (*dominus*)—applied by the papalists to describe the pope's relation to all goods. See Aegidius of Rome, *De ecclesiastica potestate* 2. 4; James of Viterbo, *De regimine christiano* 2. 8; William of Cremona, *Reprobatio errorum*, pp. 18–21.

10. *Decretum* 12, "Augusto sedis," 1. 687. John admits the possibility that the pope may decide to appropriate particular goods to an individual ecclesiastic. But this must be done within the general framework of what the pope may legitimately do with ecclesiastical goods. Thus a limit exists concerning what the pope can do even with respect to ecclesiastical goods, and it is not the pope himself who determines this limit. The only exception Quidort admits to this general principle relates to a case of urgent necessity for the Church, over which the pope is admitted to have ultimate jurisdiction. But even here, properly speaking, such an action falls within the legitimate limits of papal authority, and thus is not a genuine exception. See chap. 7.

11. John does not deny the plenitude of power (*plenitudo potestatis*) to the pope. He interprets it to signify jurisdiction, not dominion, over material goods; and as such it is subject to the conditions of jurisdiction legitimate for a "dispenser" rather than an owner.

12. Augustine, "Epistola 185" 9 (*PL* 33. 809).

13. I Cor. 4:1. John, in the preceding argument, has been following Thomas Aquinas, *Summa theologiae* 2–2. 185. 7–8.

14. Bernard of Clairvaux, *De consideratione* 2. 6. 10, p. 417.

15. "Liber sextus decretalium" 7, "Quoniam aliqui," in *Corpus iuris canonici* 2. 971.

16. *Ibid.* It is interesting to see John making such extensive use of texts from Pope Nicholas I to support his own position; for Nicholas was one of the strongest advocates of the plenitude of papal power, and texts of his contain some of the most pungent expressions of this claim. See Ullmann, *Papal Government*, pp. 190–209.

17. John's rejection of the papalist claims based on the concept of the pope as *vicarius Christi* begins here. See chap. 1.

18. This distinction between Christ as God and Christ as man as a basis for dismissing the papalist claim is used frequently by John. See chaps. 8, 9. The same position can be found in the anonymous tracts: *Disputatio inter clericum et militem*, pp. 13–14; *Quaestio in utramque partem* 5, p. 104; *Quaestio de potestate papae*, pp. 68–69.

19. The two preceding paragraphs parallel Godfrey of Fontaines, *Quodlibet 8*, pp. 224–25.

20. II Cor. 13:10; II Cor. 10:8.

21. This emphasis on the necessity for the pope to make restitution for any misuse or misappropriation of goods is an important facet of John's position

that the pope enjoys no papal authority over material goods. See above and chaps. 7, 12, and Prologue.

22. John discusses the issue of papal deposition at greater length elsewhere (chaps. 22–25).

23. *Decretum* 40, "Si papa suae" 1. 146.

24. *Glossa ordinaria decreti* 40. 6 (Lyon, 1618), p. 194.

25. *Decretum* 21, "Nunc autem" 1. 71. John's final position on this matter is that a general council is not necessary for papal deposition, and that it can be achieved by action of the college of cardinals (chap. 24).

26. The pope cannot act contrary to the law. Neither can a king nor any temporal or ecclesiastical power. This conception of limiting a ruler's authority within the specified limits of the law was commonly mentioned among those medieval political thinkers influenced by Aristotle. See Thomas Aquinas, *In VIII libros politicorum Aristotelis commentarium* 1, 10; Ptolemy of Lucca, *De regimine principum* 3. 20; 4. 1, 18; Aegidius of Rome, *De regimine principum* 3. 2. 2; 2. 1. 14; Engelbert of Admont, *De ortu, progressu et fine romani imperii* 16; Marsilius of Padua, *Defensor pacis* 1. 10. 2; 1. 14. 10; 1. 15. 7; 1. 10. 1. Cf. R. W. and G. J. A. Carlyle, *A History of Mediaeval Political Theory in the West*, 2d ed., vol. 3 (New York: Barnes and Noble, 1936), pp. 30–40; 52–59; 125–146.

27. Rom. 11:29.

28. Gen. 6:7.

29. Ex. 12:36.

30. Job 36:7.

CHAPTER 7

1. For John, neither prince nor pope can infringe upon the right of private property. He does admit, however, that this right is not an absolute one: the rights of the community—the common good—have precedence over the individual's property rights as the "needs of use of the country [*patria*] require." But this is a specification of the nature of the right of private property, not a rejection of the right itself.

2. In detailing his position concerning circumstances of extreme necessity for the Church, John is consistent in retaining the principle that papal action in such circumstances must conform to specifications relating to the nature of the events themselves, rather than being based on any plentitude of power possessed by the pope for application to material goods.

3. What John understands by ecclesiastical censure (*censura ecclesiastica*) is clarified in chap. 13. For the preceding paragraphs see Godfrey of Fontaines, *Quodlibet* 13. 5, pp. 227–29.

4. John provides for the possibility that the papacy may encourage the free granting of material goods to the pope. The pope cannot require that persons

cede things to him; but he can encourage them to do so by granting spiritual benefits (indulgences) to them in return for their material generosity. Later he also contends that it is legitimate for churches to grant the possession of prebends to laymen in return for their generosity to the Church (chap. 20, *ad* 38).

CHAPTER 8

1. Ecclus. 1:8.

2. Jer. 23:5.

3. I Peter 2:9.

4. The position that all the faithful are *viri ecclesiastici* and priests was frequently asserted by both papalist and antipapalist writers: cf. Thomas Aquinas, *De regimine principum* 1. 14; James of Viterbo, *De regimine christiano* 2. 3; Alvarius Pelagius, *De planctu ecclesiae*, 1. 51; Alexander of St. Elpidius, *Tractatus de ecclesiastica potestate*, 1. 2; Marsilius of Padua, *Defensor pacis* 2. 2. 3.

5. *Glossa interlinearis in I Petri* 2. 5 (Anvers, 1634), 5:1318.

6. Rev. 5:10.

7. John Damascene, "De fide orthodoxa" 3. 20 (*PG* 94. 1082). This argument can be found in Thomas Aquinas, *Catena in evangelium Johannis* 28. 10, p. 564b.

8. John 18:36.

9. *Glossa ordinaria in Joannem* 18: 36 (Anvers, 1634) 5:1293.

10. *Ibid.*

11. Leo I, "Sermo XXXII," 2 (*PL* 54. 235).

12. Micah 5:2.

13. John Chrysostom, "Opus imperfectum in Mattheum, Homilia II" (*PG* 56. 640).

14. Eusebius, "Historia ecclesiastica" 1. 3 (*PG* 20. 74).

15. Dan. 7:14.

16. Luke 12:14–15.

17. Bernard of Clairvaux, *De consideratione*, 1. 6. 7, pp. 401–2. Of course John is aware that Bernard, whom he quotes here in support of an antipapalist view, was himself an outspoken advocate of the doctrine of the plenitude of papal power: See Walter Ullmann, *The Growth of Papal Government in the Middle Ages; a Study in the Ideological Relation of Clerical to Lay Power*, 2d ed. (London: Methuen, 1964) pp. 426 ff.

18. *Ibid.*

19. Matt. 22:21.

20. Jerome, "In Mattheum" 2. 22 (*PL* 26. 169).

21. Hilary of Poitiers, "In Mattheum," 2. 22 (*PL* 9. 1045).

22. Matt. 17:27.

23. *Decretum* 23, "Tributum," 1. 961.

24. John 13:16.

25. Matt. 10:24. John's marshalling of texts in refutation of the position that the pope as *vicarius Christi* has jurisdiction over material goods by virtue of Christ's human nature is impressive. He cites canonical texts fourteen times, the New Testament four times, John Chrysostom and Bernard of Clairvaux twice each, and offers one text each from St. John Damascene, Leo I, Eusebius, St. Jerome, and Urban IV.

CHAPTER 9

1. This argument from Matt. 21:12 was in common use by the papalist writers. See the Prologue, especially note 23, and below, note 14. It is interesting that Marsilius of Padua employs a technique similar to that of John. Marsilius lists scriptural texts in support of the contention that jurisdiction over temporal goods (Marsilius terms it "coercive rulership") belongs to clerics. He also lists many of the same texts as those cited by John: Marsilius of Padua, *Defensor pacis* 2. 3. 5.

2. *Decretum*, 3, "Ex multis temporibus" 1. 415.

3. Matt. 21:13.

4. Matt. 21:2–3; see also Marsilius of Padua, *Defensor pacis* 2. 3. 5.

5. Matt. 8:32; see also Marsilius of Padua, *Defensor pacis* 2. 3. 4.

6. Matt. 28:18; see also Marsilius of Padua, *Defensor pacis* 2. 3. 3.

7. Thomas Aquinas, *Catena aurea in Matthaeum* 28:18. p. 424b.

8. Ps. 2:8. Marsilius of Padua refuses to consider any Old Testament texts, on the grounds that Christians possess a New Law, and are bound not at all by the Old: Marsilius of Padua, *Defensor pacis* 2. 9. 10; 2. 3. 9.

9. The distinction between Christ as God and Christ as man, as already noted, need not receive the explication John gives it here. See chap. 6, note 18.

10. *Decretum* 10, "Quoniam idem," 1. 21.

11. *Glossa ordinaria decreti* 69, "De consecratione" (Lyon, 1618), p. 1962.

12. *Decretum* 2, "Sacerdos," 1. 1350.

13. *Novellae* 6, pr.; 3. 36.

14. John Chrysostom, "Opus imperfectum in Matthaeum, Homilia XXXVIII," (*PG* 56. 841), cited in Thomas Aquinas, *Catena aurea in Matthaeum*, 21:12, 1. 305a. See also the Prologue.

15. *Glossa ordinaria in Matthaeum* 21:2 (Anvers, 1634) 5:324.

16. Matt. 28:18.

17. Jerome, as quoted in Thomas Aquinas, *Catena aurea in Matthaeum,* 28:1, 424a.

18. Remigius of Auxerre as quoted in Thomas Aquinas, *ibid.*

19. Thomas Aquinas, *Expositio in Psalmum* 2.

20. *Glossa interlinearis in Psalmum* 2: 3. 464.

21. Ps. 2:9.

22. *Glossa interlinearis, ibid.* This distinction between rule over wrongs and rule over possessions is found in Bernard of Clairvaux, *De consideratione* 1. 6. 7, p. 402. See also chaps. 10 and 13.

CHAPTER 10

1. The seriousness with which John considers the issue of the papalist claims based on the notion of the vicariate of Christ is seen in his continued investigation of the point, even in the *dato non concesso* form. This chapter is the lengthiest in Quidort's treatise. See also chap. 11, *arg.* 6; and John's reply in chap. 14, *ad* 6.

2. Medieval arguments in favor of dualism of autonomous spheres of spiritual and temporal power can be said to begin seriously with the efforts of Henry IV of Germany to counter the claim of Gregory VII: See Walter Ullmann, *The Growth of Papal Government in the Middle Ages, a Study in the Ideological Relation of Clerical to Lay Power,* 2d ed. (London: Methuen, 1964), pp. 347 ff.

3. This is John's first theoretical reference to "emperor." He does not often mention the role of emperor as supreme political authority. See chaps. 18, *ad* 28 and 13.

4. Eph. 5:23; *cf.* I Cor. 12:27. The Pauline analogy, in which the Church is seen as an organic body with Christ as its head, had been used extensively by the papalists to bolster their position, beginning with Leo I, "Epistola CLVI," 3–5 (*PL* 16. 1079); see also Gelasius, *Epistola I,* 23, p. 299; Isidore of Seville, "Quaestiones in veterum testamentum" in Esdram. 1. 2 (*PL* 83. 423); the rejection of the organic view of the Church in "Liber de unitate ecclesiae conservanda" 2. 3 (*MGH, Ld L.,* 2. 214).

5. Ambrose as cited in *Glossa ordinaria in Ephesianos* 1 (Anvers, 1634) 6. 532. *Cf.* Thomas Aquinas, *Summa theologiae* 3. 13. 2, *ad* 1.

6. This is a good example of John's use of abstract, philosophical principles to bolster his case for the division of powers between pope and king (or emperor). The three principles involved are all more or less Aristotelian.

7. See Thomas Aquinas, *Summa theologiae* 3. 64. 3 and 4.

8. *Ibid.*

9. Richard of St. Victor, "De potestate ligendi et solvendi" 24 (*PL* 196. 1176).

10. As far as it goes, this argument in its negative form is not without merit, even though it is a typical example of the various and complicated efforts made by medieval writers to determine the nature and extent of papal power by appeal to and exegesis of scriptural texts. In general, this form of argument was almost as barren of merit as it was ingenious. See chap. 28, *ad* 30.

11. Aristotle, *History of Animals*, 4. 11. 537b22 ff.

12. John cannot mean that kingly and sacerdotal powers were *always* separated in the Old Testament, for in chapter 4 he concedes that Melchisedech embodied both powers.

13. See chap. 17, *ad* 23.

14. Aristotle, *Politics* 6. 5. 1320a30 ff.

15. Bar. 3:24.

16. Matt. 21:13.

17. Rom. 13:4.

18. Aristotle, *Politics* 1. 1. 1252b2.

19. Aristotle, *Politics* 1. 1. 1252b4. The argument in this paragraph follows Thomas Aquinas, *In I Politicorum* 1. 20–21.

20. Rom. 12:5–6.

21. I Cor. 12:17–21.

22. This justification for the reality of temporal authority (and no one, not even the most extreme advocate of papalist supremacy, ever denied completely the legitimacy of temporal authority) goes back to the Gelasian text: Gelasius, *Epistola XII; Epistola XIV*, 22, p. 375. See also II Tim. 2:4, a text John himself cites immediately below. An echo of this reappears in John's use of the famous text of St. Bernard on papal power. See chap. 18, *ad* 29.

23. II Tim. 2:4.

24. *Decretum* 10, "Quoniam idem," 1. 21.

25. *Decretum* 96, "Cum ad verum," I. 339.

26. Matt. 20:25.

27. Matt. 18:18.

28. *Decretum* 21, "In novo testamento," 1. 69.

29. John here contests a basic feature of the papalist argument, *viz.*, the view that Peter was not merely "the first" to receive apostolic powers from Christ, but that all power was given to him directly by Christ as a personal commission, and that Peter in turn delegated power to the other apostles. See also Prologue, note 16.

30. This reference to common law (*ius commune*) is a curious one. John employs the term in chapter 13 as part of a quotation from a canonical text, and it is not clear just what he has in mind by it. If by "common law" he meant canonical legislation, it was not the case that the existing canons em-

phasized unambiguously anything concerning only a territorial difference between papal and episcopal jurisdiction.

31. Matt. 20:25.

32. Bernard of Clairvaux, *De consideratione* 2. 6. 11, p. 418; *cf.* Rom. 4:2.

33. *Ibid.*

34. *Ibid.*, p. 419.

35. *Ibid.*, p. 402.

36. *Ibid.*

37. *Decretum* 10, "Quoniam," 1. 21.

38. *Decretum* 96, "Cum ad verum," 1. 339.

39. *Decretum* 96, "Duo sunt quippe," 1. 340.

40. The canons certainly do not all assert this, nor do even those just cited by John. For example, the Gelasian *duo quippe* text does not contain or even warrant the interpretation John is giving these texts. The clearest demarcation between the two spheres as both coming directly from God is to be found in the Justinian *Novella* text, to which John makes no reference here but cites later on in the paragraph (see note 48). Huguccio, Innocent's teacher, was the most noted canonist to have taught that both pope and emperor receive their authority to rule mankind directly from God. It is a curious fact that Huguccio himself did not refer this position to the Justinian authority but to Gratian's statement: Huguccio, *Summa* 97, quoted in Walter Ullmann, *Medieval Papalism, the Political Theories of the Medieval Canonists* (London: Methuen, 1949), p. 142. It is likely that John had Gratian in mind, and curious that he makes no reference here to Huguccio, to whom he does refer three times in his consideration of papal resignation and deposition (see chap. 24). These later references to Huguccio seem to be taken from citations to him made by Aegidius of Rome.

41. *Decretum* 23, "Quesitum est," 1. 924.

42. *Decretum* 96, "Si imperator," 1, 341.

43. *Decretum* 93, "Legimus," 1. 327.

44. *Decretales* 28, "Si duobus," 2. 412.

45. *Decretales* 17, "Causam," 2. 712. The issue of papal authority to adjudicate legitimacy is treated more extensively in chapter 15, *ad* 10.

46. *Decretales* 7, "Verum quoniam," 2. 250.

47. *Decretales* 5, "Ceterum quia," 2. 240.

48. *Novellae* 6, pr.; 3. 36.

49. *Decretum* 28, "Magnum quidem," 1. 634.

50. Rom. 13:1.

51. I Peter 2:18.

52. *Decretum* 28, "Magnum quidem," 1. 634. John's use of canonical texts to bolster his own position is an impressive demonstration of his knowledge of the canonical literature. It is also a good indication of the diversified character of this body of authorities as it relates to the problem of papal supremacy. It was futile for anyone to argue that the canons all spoke with one voice on this issue. Nor is this surprising, given their collection character. A more reasonable approach to the value of the canons on such an issue is that of Dante, who refused to consider any of them as holding much authority: Dante, *De monarchia* 3. 3. John, however, does not take such an attitude expressly. His marshalling of canonical texts in favor of his own position is some indication of his willingness to employ them as authorities. Elsewhere he does offer a reservation on the value of the authority of individual papal pronouncements which might also be considered applicable to the canons: chap. 10 below; chap. 14, *ad* 6. Dante also argues that the canonists, by and large, were ignorant of theology and philosophy: Dante, *De monarchia,* 3. 13.

53. On the special case of papal temporal authority *cf.* Prologue.

54. *Decretales* 7, "Vergentis," 2. 782: Hostiensis, *Apparatus* 5. 7. 9. See Henry of Cremona, *Summa super titulos decretalium* 4, "Qui filii," (Lyon, 1558), fol. 314, note 9.

55. *Cf.* John's extensive treatment of the Donation of Constantine in chap. 21.

56. *Decretum* 96, "Constantinus," 1. 342.

57. Rom. 13:4, 6.

58. *Glossa ordinaria in Romanos* 13: 6. 166.

59. John's explicit reference to France is instructive, although not well specified here. See chaps. 5 and 21.

60. The reference to a king's popular election is repeated in chaps. 15, *ad* 9, 17, *ad* 21, 19, *ad* 33; 24. The view that kingly authority rests in some way on popular consent was commonly held in this period. See James of Viterbo, *De regimine christiano* 2. 3; Alexander of St. Elpidius, *Tractatus de ecclesiastica potestate* 2. 8; William of Ockham, *Breviloquium de potestate papae* 4. 3, pp. 107–8. Unlike Marsilius of Padua, however—at least in Discourse I of the *Defensor pacis*—John and such other thirteenth-century thinkers as Thomas Aquinas do not seem to make it a *sine qua non* of legitimate government, even though Quidort mentions it here as one of the two essential ingredients for the exercise of temporal authority. See Alan Gewirth, *Marsilius of Padua, the Defender of Peace,* vol. 1, *Marsilius of Padua and Medieval Political Philosophy* (New York: Columbia University Press, 1951), p. 33.

61. I Peter 2:13.

62. *Glossa interlinearis in I Petrum* 2. 6. 1319.

63. Rom. 13:1.

64. Leclercq notes that this reference to Ambrose is not found in the *Glossa ordinaria:* Leclercq, *Jean de Paris,* p. 199, note 6. Nor have I found it elsewhere.

65. *Cf.* John's earlier argument showing the greater need for a hierarchical structure in the Church than in civil society: chap. 3; and see also chap. 18, *ad* 29.

66. John's view that ecclesiastical office in some way derives from the choice of the people and their consent is an extraordinary position, although it seems in the context here to be almost a casual remark. He repeats it in chap. 13 and extends it in chaps. 19, *ad* 35, 24, 25, *ad* 3. But he does not develop the notion in any complete way. It was developed in considerable detail by Marsilius of Padua: "I wish to show that after the time of the apostles . . . and especially now when the community of believers have become perfected, the immediate efficient cause of the assignment or appointment of a prelate (whether of a major one, called the "bishop," or of the minor one, called "curate priest," and likewise of the other minor ones) is or ought to be the entire multitude of believers of that place through their election or expressed will, . . ." *Defensor pacis* 2. 17. 8, in Gewirth, tr. *Marsilius of Padua,* vol. 2, *Defensor pacis* (1956), p. 258.

67. Matt. 10:1–33; Luke 10:1–6.

68. John 20:22.

69. *Decretum* 21, "In novo testamento," 1. 69. See above, note 29.

70. Gal. 1:1.

71. Gal. 1:12.

72. Gal. 1:17–18.

73. Aristotle, *On Sleeping and Waking* 1. 454a8.

74. Bernard of Clairvaux, *De consideratione* 4. 3. 7, p. 454.

75. Chap. 18, *ad* 30.

76. This is not quite what Bernard had in mind.

77. I Cor. 6:4.

78. The identification of "contemptibles" with laymen had its origin in the Pauline text cited directly above. It was furthered and promoted by all canonists following Gratian's explicit insistence on interpreting the Pauline term *contemptibiles* as "*id est, laici,*" *Decretum* 11, "Clericum," 1. 641. This conception had a particular value for the papalist, who used it to justify his insistence that temporal matters were unworthy of the attention of ecclesiastical authorities. Such an attitude had the twofold advantage of extending some functional role to temporal rulers (*laici*), while at the same time making perfectly clear the relatively inferior role these persons played. The whole burden of Bernard's advice to his protegé, Eugene, was that temporal affairs were unworthy of the pope's attention; and this argument was repeated over and over among the canonists. See Ullmann, *Medieval Papalism,* p. 88.

79. *Glossa interlinearis in I corinthianos* 6. 6. 238.

80. This interpretation, while gratuitous from the point of view of the Pauline text, is not unnaturally consistent with John's position.

81. Hugh of St. Victor, "De sacramentis" 2. 2. 7 (*PL* 176. 420). See chap. 20, *ad* 37.

CHAPTER 11

1. John's list of 42 arguments in favor of the papalist position is not exhaustive, although it is extensive. In his edition of Aegidius of Rome's *De ecclesiastica potestate,* Scholz has compiled a list of more than 200 scriptural texts employed by the advocates of the plentitude of papal power in their ingenious efforts to bolster their views by appeals to divine authority: Aegidius of Rome, *De ecclesiastica potestate,* ed. R. Scholz, Index IV. For Aegidius' own list of scriptural authorities see *De ecclesiastica potestate* 1. 5; 2. 5, pp. 14–15, 55. Leclercq makes an important comment on John's use of these opposing arguments: that Quidort has taken them from the writings of the "modern" or contemporary papalists, who stress the literal meaning of such texts and often isolate the arguments themselves from their scriptural or canonical contexts for the purpose of giving them an extreme interpretation, while for his part, John frequently has countered these writings by simply relocating them in their proper context: Jean Leclercq, *Jean de Paris et l'écclesiologie du XIIIè siècle* (Paris, 1942), p. 33.

2. Jer. 1:10; *Decretales* 6, "Solitae," 2. 198.

3. Matt. 16:19; 23:18.

4. I Cor. 6:3.

5. *Glossa ordinaria in I corinthianos,* 6: 6. 638.

6. Gen. 1:16. See chap. 5. This argument is derived from Gregory VII, *Register,* 7. 25, "to the Conqueror," p. 505. See Walter Ullmann, *The Growth of Papal Government in the Middle Ages; a Study in the Ideological Relation of Clerical to Lay Power,* 2d ed. (London: Methuen, 1964), 282.

7. *Decretum* 15, "Alius," 1. 756.

8. *Decretum* 22, "Omnes," 1. 73.

9. *Decretum* 63, "Tibi domino," 1. 246.

10. *Decretum* 15, "Alius," 1. 756.

11. *Decretales* 6, "Venerabilem," 2. 80. Dante cites this papalist argument: Dante, *De monarchia* 3. 11.

12. *Decretales* 17, "Per venerabilem," 2. 714.

13. *Decretales* 2, "Licet," 2. 250.

14. *Decretum* 15, "Alius," 1. 756; "Quia presulatus," 1. 419.

15. The view that the pope exercises universal jurisdiction *ratione peccati* is a particularly vexing one to handle, and had a lengthy history. A fundamental claim of the canonists involved the principle that all crimes were spiritual crimes, and as such fell properly within the jurisdiction of the ecclesiastical authority: See Walter Ullmann, *Medieval Papalism, the Political Theories of*

the Medieval Canonists (London: Methuen, 1949), p. 103. It is derived from the Aristotelian concept of final end or final cause: Aristotle, *Metaphysics* 1. 3, 983b1. See chap. 12, note 17 and below, *arg.* 23.

16. A "base matter" (*foedum*) was one involving lay (contemptible) affairs.

17. Matt. 18:15.

18. Matt. 18:17.

19. *Decretales* 2, "Novit ille," 2. 242.

20. Deut. 17:8.

21. *Decretales* 17, "Per venerabilem," 2. 714.

22. James of Viterbo, *De regimine christiano,* pp. 165, 234.

23. Thomas Aquinas, *Summa theologiae* 1. 115. 3.

24. Aristotle, *The Soul* 2. 1. 412a20. Ullmann notes the curious fact that while this text is the obvious source for this notion that the soul is superior to and rules the body, and that this Aristotelian work was current in western Europe in the early thirteenth century, very few medieval users of the principle refer to *The Soul* as its source, and almost all who do are antipapalist: Ullmann, *Medieval Papalism,* p. 110.

25. Hugh of St. Victor, "De sacramentis" 2. 2. 4 (*PL* 176. 418).

26. I Cor. 2:15.

27. The term "royal priesthood" (*sacerdotium regale*) has a lengthy history in this controversy, and goes back to the First Epistle of Peter: I Peter 2:9. See also chap. 8.

28. Hugh of St. Victor, "De sacramentis" 2. 2. 4 (*PL* 176. 418).

29. Augustine, *De civitate dei* 2. 21.

30. Rom. 13:1. John's position here is not quite that of the Pauline text cited.

31. The argument from the concept of hierarchy amplifies this notion of the mediating function of the spiritual in respect of the temporal: see the following argument.

32. I Cor. 12:27. This is John's first explicit use of the Pauline term "mystical body" of Christ to designate the Church, although he has employed the head and body metaphor earlier, in chap. 10.

33. Bernard of Clairvaux, *De consideratione* 4. 3. 7, p. 454. John has cited a part of this text earlier in favor of his own antipapalist doctrine: chaps. 5, 6, 8, 10. Dante also cites the "two swords" argument of the papalists: Dante, *De monarchia* 3. 9.

34. Henry of Cremona. Henry is the only contemporary John mentions by name. Just why this is so is not clear, although it seems that Quidort's criticism of Henry indicates clearly their mutual involvement in the confrontation between the papacy and Philip the Fair. They were, of course, on different sides. See Leclercq, *Jean de Paris,* p. 32.

35. *Decretum* 94, "Dominus noster," 1. 329.

36. Ps. 99:6.

37. Henry of Cremona, *De potestate papae*, p. 465.

38. I Cor. 3:22–23.

39. *Glossa interlinearis in I corinthianos* 6. 224.

40. *Decretum* 11, "Privilegium," 1. 660.

41. Luke 14:16–25.

42. *Decretum* 23, "Displicet," 1. 919.

43. Ps. 2:1.

44. Ps. 2:9, 10, 11.

45. I have been unable to find the use of this rather striking argument among papalist sources.

46. Any of the preceding arguments could be given as a reference insofar as they all conclude that the spiritual power can in some way employ physical force in temporal matters.

47. Deut. 17:14.

48. I Sam. 8:7.

49. Hos. 8:4.

50. Gen. 47:20–22. This argument in favor of the papalist position is an old one. It can be found in Thomas Aquinas, *Summa theologiae* 3. 48, attributed to Alexander of Hales; in Ptolemy of Lucca, *De regimine principum* 16; but according to Scholz, Quidort probably found it in the contemporary source of the Memoir of the Cistercians to Boniface VIII of 1299: See R. Scholz, *Die Publizistik zur Zeit Philipps des Schönen* (Stuttgart, 1903; reprint, Amsterdam, 1969), p. 244, note 65.

51. *Decretum* 22, "Tributum," 1. 961.

52. This is the only explicit reference John makes to contemporary conditions.

53. *Decretum* 22, "Reprehensibile," 1. 958.

54. This distinction between the active life and the contemplative life is found in Aristotle, *Metaphysics* 2. 1. 993b21. Its direct application to the distinction between temporal affairs and spiritual matters, however, is not and is fatuous at best. *Cf.* Thomas Aquinas, *Summa theologiae* 1. 18. 2, *ad* 2.

55. This argument seems to be a loose variant of the Aristotelian notion of natural superiority in intellect among different persons used as the basis for a doctrine of natural slavery. See Aristotle, *Politics* 1. 1. 1252a30–32; 1. 5, 1254b15 ff. There was considerable agreement among medieval thinkers on this concept: see Thomas Aquinas, *Summa contra gentiles* 3. 81; *Summa theologiae*, 1–2. 94. 5, *ad* 3; 2–2. 57. 3, *ad* 2; Ptolemy of Lucca, *De regimine principum* 2. 10; 4. 18; Godfrey of Fontaines, *Quaestiones quodlibetales* 8. 16;

Aegidius of Rome, *De regimine principum* 1. 2. 7; 2. 3. 13–14; John of Jandun, *Questiones in metaphysicam* 1. 22; 12. 22; Augustine Triumphus, *Summa de ecclesiastica potestate* 23. 6; 23. 3; William of Ockham, *Dialogus* 3. 2. 2, 3; Dante, *De monarchia* 1. 7; 1. 3, to justify the supremacy of the Roman Empire. Among his contemporaries only John seems to have had reservations about this principle: see chap. 20, *ad* 40. Leclercq confesses himself unable to identify the source of this argument: Leclercq, *Jean de Paris*, p. 33.

CHAPTER 12

1. *Glossa ordinaria in Lucem* 5. 825.

2. John's definition of priesthood here is fuller than the one to which he refers, but not substantially different.

3. Thomas Aquinas, *Summa theologiae*, 1. 78. 4.

4. Aristotle, *On Sleeping and Waking*, 1. 454a8. See also chap. 10.

5. Hugh of St. Victor, "Summa sententiarum," (*PL* 176. 319).

6. Peter Lombard, *Sententiae*, 4. 1. 2–4 (Quarrachi, 1916), 2:745.

7. John again makes use of the concept of the value of private property or jurisdiction. See also chaps. 4 and 7.

8. John correlates these *six* powers to his own just completed list of *five* by lumping together the first two in the new listing with the first of the previous set. See below.

9. Luke 22:19.

10. This is John's first use of the classic term "the power of the keys (*potestas clavium*). Note his immediate circumscription of it as "spiritual" jurisdiction in the forum of conscience, the "internal" forum.

11. Matt. 16:19.

12. Matt. 18:18.

13. John 20:22–23.

14. See below, and note 6.

15. Matt. 10:7.

16. Matt. 28:19.

17. The standard position of papalist writers was that the need to correct sin was the actual basis for the existence of all political authority, that in fact the basis for any temporal power was the necessity to control and punish the sinful character of men. According to this same tradition, the pope exercises universal jurisdiction on the same basis—*ratione peccati*. See chap. 11, *arg*. 12. This concept of the state owing its legitimacy to the existence of sin in the world is Augustinian, and seems to run counter to the Aristotelian conception of the state as a natural development embodying man's natural inclinations. See also Augustine, *De civitate dei*, 19. 15; Alan Gewirth, *Marsilius of Padua*,

the Defender of Peace, vol. 1, Marsilius of Padua and Medieval Political Philosophy (New York: Columbia University Press, 1951), pp. 85 ff.; chap. 1.

18. John specifies by way of example the type of sin against which the apostolic authority of correction can be applied: to scandals within the Church. However, he is not precise about the type of sin, if any, against which this authority cannot be applied.

19. Matt. 18:15–17.

20. Glossa interlinearis in Matthaeum 18. 5. 306.

21. Matt. 18:18.

22. Matt. 18:17.

23. Glossa interlinearis, ibid.

24. John 21:16.

25. John accepts that the power of determining the proper ecclesiastical jurisdiction for individual ministers of the Church was a commission given directly to Peter alone by Christ. This is a far cry, however, from the plentitudo potestatis claimed by the papalists as derived from the Petrine commisison. See chap. 10.

26. I have been unable to locate an advocate of this view.

27. Theophylis is cited from Thomas Aquinas, Catena aurea in Joannem, 21: 3. 2. 590a.

28. Ibid.

29. John 21:16.

30. Thomas Aquinas, Catena aurea in Joannem, 21:16. 2. 598a.

31. Matt. 10:7.

32. Matt. 10:8.

33. Glossa interlinearis in Matthaeum 10. 5. 190.

34. Matt. 10:9.

35. Glossa interlinearis in Matthaeum 10. 5. 191.

36. Matt. 10:10.

37. Glossa interlinearis in Matthaeum 10. 5. 192.

38. Matt. 10:10.

39. Glossa ordinaria in Matthaeum 10. 5. 178.

40. Ibid.

41. Matt. 28:20.

42. Luke 10:4.

CHAPTER 13

1. John makes two items correlatives: ecclesiastics do not possess either dominion or jurisdiction over temporal affairs; and temporal rulers are not subject to them in temporal affairs.

2. John is laying the groundwork for later statements in this chapter regarding the "accidental" or "indirect" power over laymen's goods, which he concedes to ecclesiastics.

3. John 20:22.

4. John Chrysostom, as cited in Thomas Aquinas, *Catena aurea in Joannem* 20. 3. 2. 538a.

5. Coercion, for John, clearly implies the physical ability to apply some kind of material (which includes financial) punishment. Dante has a position comparable to John's treatment: Dante, *De monarchia* 3. 8.

6. I Tim. 2:7.

7. Bernard of Clairvaux, *De consideratione* 2. 6. 10, p. 418.

8. Bernard of Clairvaux, *De consideratione* 4. 3. 6, p. 453.

9. I Peter 5:3.

10. Interestingly, John's first reference to the indirect power ecclesiastics have over laymen is related to their legitimate and authoritative activities of teaching and giving moral advice. They can persuade men of what is morally right and wrong.

11. Matt. 18:17.

12. *Ibid.*

13. John declares that it is proper for an ecclesiastic to make the judgment as to whether or not a given type of act, *viz.*, usury, is sinful; determination of the moral value, or lack of it, of an act falls within the sphere of the spiritual. This kind of judgment relates to an act which is a "sin or error of opinion." That is, the act being judged is seemingly an abstraction, a category or type of activity; and as such it is obviously spiritual. See chap. 15, *ad* 12.

14. The second type of sin—the sin of using or spending what belongs to another—is an overt act; it is an act given physical expression. Such an action falls within the jurisdiction of a temporal judge. John is thus maintaining the distinction between the spiritual and the material or temporal in a most explicit way. The spiritual authority judges spiritual acts—and judges them as to whether or not they should be performed; the secular or poltical authority judges actions physically performed.

15. Augustine, *Confessions* 3. 8.

16. *Decretum* 7, "Quo iure," 1. 13.

17. John's use of the term "sin" (*poena*) is unfortunate, since it may seem to

imply the exercise of moral judgment by the secular judge. It is clear from what he says, however, that the function of exercising moral judgment inheres in the spiritual authority, while the secular judge has jurisdiction over physical acts. This apparently airtight compartmentalization is not without difficulties: cf. *Introduction,* pp. xxxiv–vi.

18. In the Prologue and in chapter 10, John has suggested what such other basis might be.

19. Bernard of Clairvaux, *De consideratione* 1. 6. 7, p. 402. Bernard's term is *crimina,* not *corda.* See chapter 9, note 22.

20. Matt. 18:16.

21. Thomas Aquinas, *Catena aurea in Matthaeum* 18:16. 1. 273b.

22. *Decretum* 96, "Duo sunt," 1. 340.

23. *Glossa ordinaria decreti* 96, "Duo sunt," p. 468.

24. *Decretales* 17, "Lator praesentium," 2. 711. A standard papalist argument was just the reverse: that inheritances were subject to papal approval: cf. James of Viterbo, *De regimine christiano* 2. 8; Aegidius of Rome, *De ecclesiastica potestate* 3. 5; Alvarus Pelagius, *De planctu ecclesiae* 1. 66; Alanus, *Compilatio prima, de Judeis et Saracenis,* c. Judei, 5, cited in Walter Ullmann, *Medieval Papalism, the Political Theories of the Medieval Canonists* (London: Methuen, 1949), pp. 99–100, esp. p. 99, note 2.

25. *Decretales* 17, "Causam," 2. 712.

26. *Decretales* 1, "Novit ille," 2. 242.

27. *Decretales* 28, "Si duobus," 2. 412.

28. This was a standard response on the part of papalists to inconvenient papal texts.

29. Aristotle, *Nicomachean Ethics* 4. 7. 1127a30–35.

30. Augustine, "Sermo CLXXXI," (*PL* 31. 981).

31. Augustine, "In Joannem, XLIII," (*PL* 35. 1712).

32. Gregory the Great, "Moralium," 26. 5. (*PL* 76, 351).

33. The terms John first employs to designate what has been described as his doctrine of indirect power are power exercised "conditionally and accidentally" (*sub conditione et per accidens*).

34. Chaps. 12, 13, 15, *ad* 12.

35. For John, excommunication is the "ultimate" penalty a spiritual authority can impose. However, he does not shrink from the consequences in the political sphere of imposing this spiritual penalty. See Alan Gewirth, *Marsilius of Padua* vol. 2, *Defensor pacis* (New York: Columbia University Press, 1956), p. li, especially note 16.

36. For John the deposition of an incorrigibly heretical prince is carried out "by the people," even when the pope excommunicates all the faithful who refuse to withdraw their obedience from the sinful ruler.

37. John insists that a ruler's crime must be "ecclesiastical" to warrant even a conditional or accidental action on the part of a spiritual authority resulting in the ruler's deposition. One can only deduce the meaning of "ecclesiastical crime" in this context, since John does not define it in any precise way. Such a deduction, however, leads to the conclusion that, for John, an ecclesiastical crime (he also employs the term "derelict in spiritual matters") is any act about which the judgment can be made that this kind of action is morally wrong. He instances "matters of faith, marriage, and things of this kind, the jurisdiction of which pertains to ecclesiastical judgment," and specifically distinguishes between "sin" and "crimes of commerce": chaps. 15, *ad* 12 and above, notes 13, 14. See also Thomas Aquinas, *De regimine principum* 1. 14; Dante, *De monarchia* 3. 16.

38. John's reference to the role of the cardinals is imprecise. Later he formulates a more specific role for them in relationship to the papacy: chap. 24. See also the position of Aegidius of Rome mentioned in the following note.

39. John argues that the pope can be "deposed by the people." This parallels his earlier comment that bishops and priests exercise jurisdiction by consent of the people: chap. 10. See also chaps. 19, *ad* 35, 24, 25, *ad* 3. Aegidius of Rome asserted that "the consent of man" was involved in some way in the exercise of papal authority: Aegidius of Rome, *De renuntiatione papae* 16; see also 5, 11, 24. But as Gewirth points out, Aegidius meant by this that it was the cardinals who elected the pope, see *De renuntiatione papae* 23, and that Carlyle was in error in maintaining that for Aegidius "the authority of the ruler was derived from the people," Robert W. and A. J. Carlyle, *Political Theory in the West*, 2d ed., vol. 5 (New York: Barnes and Noble, 1936), 469; Gewirth, *Marsilius of Padua, the Defender of Peace*, vol. 1, *Marsilius of Padua and Medieval Political Philosophy* (1951), p. 281, note 74.

40. Chap. 10. The attribution of universal and ubiquitous jurisdiction to both pope and emperor is convenient for the sweep of John's argument, as it involves the comparison between the rulers of the two spheres—spiritual and temporal authority: see chap. 3. He immediately reverts to the term "king," although the role of the emperor is discussed a little later. See chap. 10.

41. John seems to be trying to formulate a role for the barons and peers of the kingdom in relation to the king. In chapter 10 he noted that the king's authority rested on the consent of the people. Now he attributes the right of deposition of a monarch to his barons and peers, and in chapter 14, *ad* 5 suggests that the nobles also exercise a right of election. Ptolemy of Lucca held that the imperial ruler was elected by the seven German princes, or by the army of senators: Ptolemy of Lucca, *De regimine principum* 3. 19, 20. Augustinus Triumphus held that the emperor was elected by the German princes, but only with papal authority: Augustinus Triumphus, *Summa de ecclesiastica potestate* 35. 1, 2.

42. Rom. 13:4.

43. *Glossa ordinaria in Romanos* 13. 6, 166.

44. The *Decretum* text cited immediately quotes Jerome on Jer. 22.

45. *Decretum* 23, "Regum est," 1. 937.

46. Vincent of Beauvais, *Speculum historiale*, p. 1011.

47. John accepts the fact of the *privilegium fori*, the privilege of clerics to be judged only in ecclesiastical courts; but the basis for the privilege in his opinion is a special concession from a temporal ruler. The claim for clergy to be judged only by their ecclesiastical superiors and not by political authority was an ancient one: see Gelasius, *Epistola* 2. 8; Gergory II, text found in E. Caspar, "Papst Gregor II und der Bilderstreit," in *Zeitschrift fur Kirchen geschichte* 52 (1933): 86, lines 425 ff; John VIII, "Epistola CLV," (*MGH, Epistolae* 7. 129. 1. 26). Its biblical foundation was Matt. 10:24 and Luke 6:40. Marsilius of Padua was not so well disposed to such a privileged position for the clergy: Marsilius of Padua, *Defensor pacis* 2. 8. 7. See also chap. 14, *ad* 5.

48. Vincent of Beauvais, *Speculum historiale*, p. 525.

49. Ps. 105:15.

50. I Sam. 10:1, 16:13; II Sam. 2:4, 5:3; I Kings 1:39; 19:16.

51. II Sam. 1:16.

52. John specifies here the role of the cardinals: they "represent the whole clergy."

53. For John, the secular authorities have no option but to act on behalf of the Church in deposing an evil and incorrigible pope. It is interesting to note, however, the difference in terminology and his earlier description of how the Church reacts to a request from the nobility for assistance in deposing a king: "The Church can admonish . . . and proceed against." Apparently, however, it need not do so. John is not completely balanced in his attribution of rights and obligations to the two spheres.

54. Bernard of Clairvaux, *De consideratione* 3. 4. 17, pp. 445.

55. *Decretum* 96, "Cum ad rerum," 1. 339.

56. *Decretum* 23, "Principes seculi," 1. 936.

57. Vincent of Beauvais, *Speculum historiale*, pp. 958, 992–93.

58. II Kings, 12:7–15.

59. Matt. 18:17.

60. *Glossa interlinearis in Matthaeum*, 18. 5. 306.

61. Matt. 18:18.

62. *Glossa interlinearis, ibid.*

63. John Chrysostom, as cited in Thomas Aquinas, *Catena aurea in Matthaeum* 18. 16. 1. 273a–b.

64. I Cor. 5:11.

65. Titus 3:10–11.

CHAPTER 14

1. Jer. 1:10.

2. *Glossa ordinaria in Jeremiam*, 1. 4. 569.

3. Augustine, *De civitate dei* 17. 20.

4. Matt. 4:8–10.

5. Heb. 11:33.

6. Prov. 16:32.

7. Ps. 2:6.

8. Matt. 26:39.

9. Ps. 2:9.

10. *Glossa ordinaria in psalmos*, 2.

11. *Glossa interlinearis in psalmos*, 2.

12. I Cor. 3:9.

13. Jer. 1:1.

14. Jer. 1:9.

15. Bernard of Clairvaux, *De consideratione* 2. 6. 13, p. 420.

16. Bernard of Clairvaux, *De consideratione* 4. 4. 6, p. 453.

17. Matt. 16:19.

18. John Chrysostom, as cited in *Glossa ordinaria in Matthaeum* 16: 5. 282; Rabanus Maurus, "Commentarium in Matthaeum," 16 (PL 107. 992).

19. Jerome, as cited in *Glossa ordinaria in Matthaeum* 16: 5. 281.

20. Richard of St. Victor, "De potestate ligandi et solvendi" 2 (*PL* 196. 1167).

21. I Cor. 6:3.

22. Ambrose, as cited in *Glossa ordinaria in I corinthianos* 6. 238.

23. See Thomas Aquinas, *Expositio in I corinthianos* 6. 1. 268 ff.

24. Gen. 1:16.

25. Pseudo-Dionysius, "Epistola IX," (*PG* 3. 1106). See chapter 27, *ad* 30; chapter 19, *ad* 34.

26. I concur in Leclercq's judgment that this reference is not to be found in Isidore's *Commentary on Genesis* 1:16 or in the *Glossa ordinaria*. Nor have I found it elsewhere.

27. Dante was another antipapalist who grappled with this favorite papalist argument. He, too, begins with the insistence that the argument is mystical, and hence of little value since mystical doctrine is not argumentative. He also gets entangled in pseudo-science; for while he does not assert, as does John,

that the moon has its own "proper power to cool and moisten," he does insist that the moon's movement arises from its own power, and that it is the source of some of its own light: Dante, *De monarchia* 3. 5. Elsewhere Dante refers to two suns to evade this argument as a basis for subordinating the emperor to the pope: *Purgatorio* 16. 107 ff.

28. On this historical incident see Walter Ullmann, *The Growth of Papal Government in the Middle Ages; a Study in the Ideological Relation of Clerical to Lay Power*, 2d ed. (London: Methuen, 1964), p. 53; for reference to papalist interpretation of the event see Ullmann, *Medieval Papalism, the Political Theories of the Medieval Canonists* (London: Methuen, 1949), pp. 149, 177–80.

29. *Glossa ordinaria decreti* 3. 15. 6, p. 1083.

30. Vincent of Beauvais, *Speculum historiale*, p. 953.

31. *Ibid.*

32. *Ibid.*

33. See chapter 13 and *Glossa ordinaria decreti*, 3. 15. 6, p. 1083.

34. Vincent of Beauvais, *Speculum historiale*, p. 896.

35. Sozomenus, a fifth-century ecclesiastical historian, probably took his account of this anecdote from Rufinus (see following note). The story itself is, of course, an intriguing one for purveyors of a theory of temporal power as legitimately applicable to spiritual authorities. An earlier account of Constantine's action at the Council of Nicaea is found in John of Salisbury, *Policraticus, the Statesman's Book of John of Salisbury* 4. 3, tr. J. Dickinson (New York: Russell & Russell, 1963), pp. 9–10.

36. Rufinus, "Historia ecclesiastica" 1. 2 (*PL* 21. 468–69). See Vincent of Beauvais, *Speculum historiale*, p. 527. Gregory I was the first to cite this story from the ecclesiastical history of Rufinus: see Ullmann, *Papal Government*, p. 39.

37. Hugh of Florence, as cited in Vincent of Beauvais, *Speculum historiale*, p. 525.

38. Constantine's will is not extant, and there is no substantial evidence that it ever has existed.

39. Vincent of Beauvais, *Speculum historiale*, p. 525.

40. *Decretum* 96, "Constantinus," 1. 343.

41. Vincent of Beauvais, *Speculum historiale*, p. 273.

42. Vincent of Beauvais, *Speculum historiale*, p. 993.

43. This is Nicholas I, one of the most trenchant formulators of papalist formulae. See chap. 6, note 16. See also *Quaestio in utramque partem*, p. 105, regarding the first half of John's reply here.

44. John's skepticism in regard to the value of a single unsupported papal statement in defense of papal claims is a refreshing change from his marshalling of canonical authorities on his own behalf.

45. Matt. 18:18.

46. *Glossa ordinaria in Matthaeum* 18:18.

47. Matt. 16:19.

48. Matt. 10: *passim.*

49. Maximus Confessor, "Sermo in Epiphania" 11 (*PL* 57. 285).

CHAPTER 15

1. Otto was crowned by Pope John XII on February 2, 962, and immediately confirmed the Carolingian donation to the papacy.

2. There is no notion in John's conception of empire here that it has universal extent. See his comments on the limited extent of the Roman Empire, and on the limited time period for its hegemony, in chapter 20.

3. This was always the ultimate test for papalist claims to universal authority; and it was shirked by them, even though, following Gregory VII, they distinguished between excommunication and deposition of a temporal ruler. Deposition simply gave expression to the delinquent's incapacity to rule, and was a direct consequence of excommunication. The many papal documents decreeing excommunication of kings, princes, etc. and the release of their subjects from obedience to them are gathered in G. B. Pallieri and G. Vismara, *Acta pontificia juris gentium* (Milan, 1946), pp. 52 ff.

4. Chap. 14, *ad* 5.

5. The argument that the popes transferred the imperial power from Constantinople to Rome hangs on the significance of the coronation of Charlemagne by Pope Leo III in 800. This incident, or at least an interpretation of it, and the Donation of Constantine were the two major historical examples used by the papalists to support their position. Innocent III was the first canonist to take full advantage of this papal translation of the empire from the east to the west in the person of Charlemagne. See Walter Ullmann, *Medieval Papalism, the Political Theories of the Medieval Canonists* (London: Methuen, 1949) pp. 168–69. John's response to this difficulty is repeated in chap. 21. Dante was another who argued against this papalist claim. He insisted that usurpation of a right does not destroy the right, implying that Adrian usurped an imperial right in the transfer, and goes on to note that otherwise the Church would be shown to be dependent on the empire, since Otto restored Pope Leo and deposed Benedict: Dante, *De monarchia* 3. 11.

6. Chap. 15, *ad* 8.

7. John is not entirely happy with the idea that the imperial power was divided; he does not assert it categorically as a fact but "as if" (*quasi*) it had been done. He exhibits the same uncertainty again: chap. 21.

8. John is again explicit about the function of popular choice in the establishment of temporal authority, but whether or not it is an essential condition of the legitimacy of temporal power is never made explicit. John, however,

does assert that the people do this by right (*de iure*). Immediately he speaks of the army as making an emperor, and of the people establishing the position of king (temporal monarch), whereupon that man's army elevates his status to that of imperial power. Many of John's contemporaries held views which in some way appeared to advocate popular consent in some form. Some maintained, following St. Augustine, that the exercise of sovereignty by the people depended on whether they were virtuous and moderate or depraved: see Augustine, *De libero arbitrio* 1. 6. 4; Thomas Aquinas, *Summa theologiae*, 1–2. 97. 1; James of Viterbo, *De regimine christiano*, 2. 8; Ptolemy of Lucca, *De regimine principum* 3. 6. Thomas Aquinas also held that while election was the best form of government it was not the only legitimate form: *Summa theologiae* 1–2. 105. 1; and this seems as close as any of these doctrines get to that of Quidort: see chap. 19, *ad* 33.

9. Cited in Vincent of Beauvais, *Speculum historiale*, p. 961.

10. *Ibid.*

11. *Ibid.*

12. John reiterates the view that initially any disposition of temporal authority and goods is the right of the temporal ruler: in this case, Constantine. The limitations on Constantine as a temporal ruler as applied to his "donation" are examined later: chap. 21.

13. This is the most general statement regarding the universality of papal authority over temporal affairs. John immediately restricts it territorially.

14. That is, the papal states.

15. John the Teuton, in *Glossa ordinaria decretalium* 17, "Petrus diaconus," (Lyon, 1618), p. 1549.

16. *Decretales* 2, "Licet," 2. 250.

17. *Glossa ordinaria decretalium* 2, "Licet," p. 1237.

18. The issue of the pope's right or authority to legitimate persons is a classic example of the complexity of the problem of church-state relations, especially in the Middle Ages: Ullmann, *Medieval Papalism*, pp. 105 ff.

19. Release of a subject from an oath of allegiance was simply another power said to be possessed by the pope and exemplifying the plenitude of that power. The historical case to which the papalists normally referred in this connection was that of Pope Zacharias's action in respect of Childeric: see chap. 11 *arg.* 5, and John's reply, chap. 25, *ad* 5. John deals with this argument in the same fashion in which he replied to Argument 5. See *Quaestio in utramque partem*, p. 106.

20. John's atttitude toward arguments based on fact is already known: see chap. 14, *ad* 5. On the facts of this incident see L. Halphen, *Charlemagne et l'empire carolingien*, 2d ed. (Paris, 1949), pp. 21 ff.

21. Regarding the barons' functions in respect of an unsuitable king, see chap. 13.

22. While John is not explicit here about the meaning of "a sufficient and clear reason" for the pope to absolve a vassal from the bonds of a feudal oath to his lord, he seems to be offering a wide latitude to the papacy for intervention in political affairs. Obviously, if John is to admit any instance of papal intervention of this kind, he must accept the legitimacy of such papal action, and it can be argued that his insistence that the cause for intervention must be "sufficient" is something of a limit. It would have been more helpful, however, for Quidort to be more precise about the conditions under which such papal intervention is *not* legitimate.

23. I Cor. 3:9.

24. Chap. 11, note 16.

CHAPTER 16

1. *Decretales* 13, "Novit ille," 2. 242.

2. Matt. 18:15–17.

3. John Chrysostom, as cited in *Glossa ordinaria in Matthaeum*, 18. 5. 306.

4. The meaning of "church" here—the community of the faithful and not the community of clerics alone—is found in Marsilius of Padua, *Defensor pacis*, 2. 2. 3. Definition of the term *ecclesia* to include all the faithful, however, was common: cf. Hugh of St. Victor, "De sacramentis" 2. 2. 2. (*PL* 176. 917); Thomas Aquinas, *In IV sententiarum* 20. 1. 4. 1; James of Viterbo, *De regimine christiano* 1. 1; Augustinus Triumphus, *Summa de ecclesiastica potestate* 7. 3; Alvarus Pelagius, *De planctu ecclesiae* 1. 36.

5. *Glossa ordinaria in Matthaeum* 18. 5. 305.

6. Theodosius II ordered the compilation of laws known as the Theodosian Code, on December 20, 435; the promulgation of these laws took place in Constantinople on February 15, 438, in what has come to be known as the *Novellae Constitutiones*, of which no complete and authentic copy is extant.

7. This position was commonly accepted among the canonists.

8. *Decretum* 11, "Quicumque litem," 1. 636.

9. *Deut.* 18:8.

10. Though perhaps logically unobjectionable, it is not difficult to imagine that the practical consequences of granting to the pope the ultimate authority to decide whether or not he has jurisdiction over a given matter would be fraught with problems and filled with the seeds of controversy.

11. *Glossa ordinaria in Deuteronomia* 18, p. 1567.

12. This argument is also found in *Quaestio in utramque partem*, p. 107.

CHAPTER 17

1. The assertion that jurisdiction over legacies and restitutions was the province of the papal authority was still another arrow in the quiver of plenitude of papal power. Ecclesiastical interference was claimed on the ground of faith: see above, chap. 13, note 25.

2. Decretales 7, "Ab abolendum," 2. 780.

3. Decretales 7, "Vergentes," 2. 782.

4. "Codex Justiniani" 1. 3. 28, in Corpus iuris civilis 2. 12.

5. "Digesta" 5. 3. 50, in Corpus iuris civilis 2. 137.

6. This is an Aristotelian formulation in frequent use among the papalists: see Walter Ullmann, Medieval Papalism, the Political Theories of the Medieval Canonists (London: Methuen, 1949), pp. 110 ff. John's reply, not surprisingly, invokes the Philosopher in support of his own position.

7. Aristotle, Nicomachean Ethics 2. 1. 1130b3.

8. Aristotle, Politics 1. 3. 1252b2.

9. Thomas Aquinas, Summa theologiae 1. 115. 3.

10. Hugh of St. Victor, "De sacramentis," 2. 2. 4 (PL 176. 418). It is unusual for John to be so critical of an individual opponent, particularly one who is not a contemporary: cf. his attitude toward Henry of Cremona, chap. 19, ad 31. In offering this argument John did not refer to Hugh of St. Victor initially: see chap. 11, arg. 31.

11. Augustine, De civitate dei, 1, 12.

12. See chap. 10.

13. I Cor. 2:15.

14. Glossa ordinaria in I corinthianos 6. 213–14.

15. Ibid.

16. Ibid.

17. The argument from the order of ends was one of the most decisive employed by the papalists, and accordingly one of the most popular: see James of Viterbo, De regimine christiano 2. 7; Aegidius of Rome, De ecclesiastica potestate 1. 9; 2. 6; Augustinus Triumphus, De duplici potestate praelatorum, pp. 498–99; Alvarus Pelagius, De planctu ecclesiae 1. 37; Thomas Aquinas, De regimine principum 1. 14. See also chap. 5, note 2.

18. Aristotle, Nicomachean Ethics 8. 2. 1155b16 ff.

19. Aristotle, Nicomachean Ethics 10. 5. 1175a21 ff.

20. Job 34:30.

21. Prov. 21:1.

22. Ecclus. 10:14.

23. Ezek. 34:10. John's emphasis on the value of the people suffering under the evils of tyranny, and his assertion that the divine purpose behind such circumstances relates to God's wish to "test the evidence" of men's patience and "compel them to take refuge in God," do not square easily with any view that the people can depose tyrannical authority. Nevertheless, John clearly recognized the legitimacy of deposing unjust papal authority, and it can be assumed, even though he does not refer to the issue, that he is prepared to countenance equally the removal of unjust tyrannical temporal rulers. See chap. 23.

24. *Decretum* 10, "De capitulis," 1. 21.

25. *Glossa ordinaria decreti* 10, "De capitulis," p. 34.

26. Aristotle, *Politics* 3. 13. 1284a13–15.

27. Aristotle, *Politics* 1. 1. 1252a15.

28. John is quite clear that the attribution of temporal power to the papacy, even in a derivative sense of its being delegated to the king by and from the pope, effectively destroys the natural integrity of political authority. Of course, the papalists would agree, although they were not concerned to preserve a separate and naturally integral sphere for political authority.

CHAPTER 18

1. I Peter 2:9.

2. The notion that all the faithful are kings and priests through their relationship with Christ as head of the Church is common enough in this period: chap. 8 (esp. note 4); chap. 16, *ad* 4.

3. Tichonius, "Liber de septem regulis" 1 (*PL* 18. 16).

4. The issue of the act of anointing—whether it actually conferred power or whether it simply gave symbolic expression to a fact—was one of the most controversial elements in the medieval examination of relations between church and state. Entangled in it were two quite separate but related points: the essential nature of an ecclesiastical sacrament, such as baptism or orders, and its relationship with the "outward and visible sign" of the transmission of grace and power through the sacrament; and the character of external actions relating to feudal obligations and relationships. Papal anointing of temporal rulers began in western Europe when Stephen II anointed Pippin; and the whole history of ecclesiastical anointing of temporal rulers and of the use of anointing as part of sacerdotal ordination is extremely complex. See Walter Ullmann, *The Growth of Papal Government in the Middle Ages; a Study in the Ideological Relation of Clerical to Lay Power*, 2d ed. (London: Methuen, 1964), pp. 67–68; 72–74; 149–156; 227–228.

5. The etymological identity between "the anointed," "messiah," and "Christos" was clear at this time. John's reply to this argument echoes *Quaestio in utramque partem*, p. 104.

6. Augustine, *Enarratio in psalmis* 44. See also chaps. 4, 8, 9.

7. John probably had in mind the Christian Visigothic kings of Spain of the seventh century.

8. The *lex Julia et Papia* of A.D. 9 was a voluminous matrimonial code which exercised so great an influence for several centuries that it came to be regarded as one of the basic sources for Roman law. Much of it was repealed by Christian emperors as being inconsistent with the New Testament.

9. *Decretum* 7, "Nos si inconpetenter," 1. 496.

10. This is the traditional argument based on the Augustinian concept of true justice necessarily residing only in Christ, and by extension in the virtuous man who must be a Christian: "Remota ita justitia quid sunt regna nisi magna latrocinia," *De civitate dei* 4. 4. The papalist tendency, in concurring with this view, was to accept the Augustinian identification of justice with theological virtue and subjection to God: Augustine, *De civitate dei* 19, 21, 23, 25. See also Aegidius of Rome, *De ecclesiastica potestate* 1. 5; 2. 7; 3. 2, 10; James of Viterbo, *De regimine christiano* 3. 10; Ptolemy of Lucca, *De regimine principum* 2. 5; Alexander of St. Elpidius, *Tractatus de ecclesiastica potestate* 2. 3; Augustine Triumphus, *Summa de ecclesiastica potestate* 46. 2; Alvarus Pelagius, *De planctu ecclesiae* 1. 37; and to go on from there to identify the the latter with subjection to the pope: *cf.* Aegidius of Rome, *De ecclesiastica potestate* 3. 10; James of Viterbo, *De regimine christiano* 2. 10; Alvarus Pelagius, *De planctu ecclesiae* 1. 24.

11. The distinction between the theological and the moral virtues is crucial for John's evasion of the consequences of the papalist position on this point. Another method of evasion, accepting the assertion that true justice is not in the state and going on to contend that Christ has *two* vicars in this world, is to be found in the anonymous *Quaestio de potestate papae*, p. 680. John's distinction between the moral and the theological virtues, but not its application to the integrity of political authority in the state, can be found in Thomas Aquinas, *Summa theologiae* 1. 68. 8.

12. Prosper of Aquitaine, "Sententiae" 7 (*PL* 51. 428).

13. John deals with the issue of order and hierarchy at some length in his reply to Argument 29, below.

14. Rom. 13:1.

15. I Cor. 12. The early portion of this reply can be found in *Quaestio in utramque partem*, p. 103.

16. Eph. 1:22–3.

17. Ambrose, as cited in *Glossa ordinaria in ephesianos* 1. 6. 532.

18. Eph. 5:23.

19. John is categorical on the primacy of Rome.

20. John employs the traditional concept of emperor as "head of the world" (*caput mundi*): *cf.* chap. 13.

21. *Cf.* other references made to the Dionysian doctrine of hierarchy: chap. 3, *ad* 28.

22. Pseudo-Dionysius, "De ecclesiastica hierarchia" 5. 3 (*PG* 3. 503).

23. Thomas Aquinas, *Summa theologiae* 1. 104. 3.

24. Rom. 13:1.

25. Rom. 13:2.

26. Rom. 13:1.

27. Bernard of Clairvaux, *De consideratione* 3. 4. 17, p. 44.

28. Matt. 16:19.

29. Rabanus Maurus, "Commentarium in Matthaeum" 5 (*PL* 107, 992).

30. *Glossa ordinaria in Matthaeum* 16. 5. 28.

31. Matt. 16:19.

32. Matt. 18:18.

33. John 20:23.

34. John Chrysostom, as cited in *Glossa ordinaria in Matthaeum* 16. 5. 282.

35. *Cf.* Aegidius of Rome, *De ecclesiastica potestate*, pp. 12–13.

36. Exod. 25:40. Bernard of Clairvaux, *De consideratione* 3. 4. 17, p. 444.

37. Luke 22:38. Volumes could be written on this text. Dante's position on it is simply that the allegory cannot be interpreted as applying to spiritual and temporal power: Dante, *De monarchia* 3. 9.

38. Chaps. 14, *ad* 4, 19, *ad* 34. Pseudo-Dionysius, "Epistola IX," (*PG* 3. 1106).

39. Augustine, "Epistola XCIII," (*PL* 33. 334).

40. See chap. 10, especially note 10.

41. Eph. 6:17.

42. Luke 2:35.

43. II Sam. 12:10.

44. Matt. 26:52.

45. Matt. 10:34.

46. Ps. 44:4.

47. Rev. 1:13.

48. Rev. 19:15.

49. The last portion of John's reply repeats *Quaestio in utramque partem*, p. 105.

50. Bernard of Clairvaux, *De consideratione* 3. 4. 17, p. 444.

51. John's reference here to the emperor simply follows out Bernard's explanation.

CHAPTER 19

1. Henry of Cremona, a publicist of the contemporary papalist position of Boniface VIII. See chap. 11, *arg.* 11, note 34.

2. James 5:16.

3. Gen. 9:20.

4. Ps. 99:6.

5. *Decretum* 84, "Porro Moysi," 1. 296.

6. *Ibid.*, 196. Quidort is mistaken in this reference.

7. *Cf.* John's reply to *arg.* 33.

8. *Cf.* Thomas Aquinas, *Summa theologiae,* 1–2. 8. 2.

9. I Cor. 4:1.

10. I Cor. 12:4–6.

11. Bernard of Clairvaux, *De consideratione* 4. 3. 6, p. 453.

12. I Peter 5:3.

13. I Cor. 3:22.

14. *Decretum* 23, "Quicumque vos," 1. 950.

15. *Glossa ordinaria in I corinthianos,* 13. 6. 313–14.

16. Augustine, *De civitate dei* 4. 33. It is curious that John did not cite Augustine on this point against the other Augustinian text interpreted in an opposite way by the papalists: *Cf.* chap. 18, *ad* 27.

17. On this concept of popular support for temporal authority *cf.* chap. 15, note 8. John cites a canon to this effect almost immediately.

18. Augustine, *De libero arbitrio* 3. 10.

19. *Decretum* 93, "Legimus," 1. 327.

20. *Decretum* 23, "Quesitum est," 1. 924.

21. Averroes, *Moralium Nicomachorum paraphrasis* 8. 7 (Venice, 1550), fol 57v. It is interesting to note John's use of Averroes as an authority for the position that kings rule by virtue of popular consent.

22. For John, of course, the Church ought not to have any powers not originating from its founding.

23. Augustine, "Epistola XVIII," (*PL* 33. 334).

24. Pseudo-Dionysius, "Epistola IX, 1," (*PG* 3. 998).

25. Luke 14:16–23.

26. Ps. 2:1.

27. Heb. 9:1.

28. Augustine, "Sermo CXII," (*PL* 38. 647).

29. John accepts the necessity and value of coercion against heretics, but not against "Jews and Gentiles." *Cf.* Marsilius of Padua's view that coercion of heretics and infidels belongs to the human legislator. *Defensor pacis* 2. 5. 7; and Gewirth's explanation of the Paduan's views: Alan Gewirth, *Marsilius of Padua, the Defender of Peace,* vol. 1, *Marsilius of Padua and Medieval Political Philosophy* (New York: Columbia University Press, 1951), pp. 155 ff. See also the following chapter, *ad* 42.

30. *Decretum* 23, "Qui peccat," 1. 920; "Scismatici sunt," 1. 947.

31. I Sam. 8:7.

32. Num. 27:16.

33. Judg. 3:9.

34. John's argument that the Israelites did not originally enjoy a "pure rule of kingship" is an interesting one.

35. Deut. 17:15.

36. I Sam. 8:7.

37. Exod. 4:13–14.

38. Deut. 7:6.

39. *Cf.* Aristotle, *Politics* 3. 2. 1281a40 ff.

40. Aristotle, *Politics* 3. 17. 1288a15–19.

41. Aristotle, *Politics,* 2. 9. 1270b20.

42. Deut. 1:15.

43. *Cf.* chaps. 10, 13, 14, 25, *ad* 3. This is John's most explicit comment on the desirability of democratization in church affairs. Though undeveloped, it is a remarkable statement to find in a medieval treatise on political theory, and taken with his other remarks concerning the relations of pope and general councils it shows a clear grasp at least in outline of a constitutional type of approach to church government: see chaps. 20, *ad* 42, 22, 25, *ad* 4. John's argument about the superiority of a mixed governmental structure follows that of Thomas Aquinas, *Summa theologiae,* 1–2. 105. 1, *ad* 1, except that Aquinas does *not* advocate democratizing the ecclesiastical structure.

44. Aristotle, *Politics* 3. 16. 1287a30. In his earlier formulation of theory concerning the best form of political authority, John offered no such reservation on his own advocacy of kingship as the best form of government (chap. 1). Nor did he mention Aristotle's stricture on this point when he invoked Aristotle's authority in support of the position (chap. 1, notes 3–6). Other medieval political theorists also maintained the view that kingship could degenerate into tyranny and aristocracy into oligarchy: see Thomas Aquinas, *Summa theologiae* 1–2. 105. 1, *ad* 2: Aegidius of Rome, *De regimine principum* 3. 2. 4, 7; Dante, *De monarchia* 1. 11; James of Viterbo, *De regimine christiano* 2. 7; Marsilius of Padua, *Defensor pacis* 1. 12. 5; 1. 13, 5.

45. Aristotle, *Nicomachean Ethics* 10. 8. 1179a10–12.

46. Aristotle, *Politics* 3. 15. 1285a34 ff.

47. Hos. 8:4.

48. Bernard of Clairvaux, *De consideratione* 2. 6. 11, p. 418.

49. Gen. 47:20–22.

50. *Decretum* 23, "Tributum," 1. 961.

51. *Decretum* 23, "Secundum canonicam," 1. 962.

CHAPTER 20

1. *Glossa ordinaria decreti* 19, 39, p. 1376.

2. *Glossa ordinaria decreti* 26. 33. 8, p. 1383.

3. Numbers 18:21.

4. Clearly, John saw nothing incompatible between a bishop's accepting temporal jurisdiction of some sort from a "king" (or other temporal lord) and his holding spiritual authority and responsibilities from an ecclesiastical overlord.

5. Hugh of St. Victor, "De sacramentis" 2. 2. 4 (*PL* 176. 420).

6. A monarch's refusal to allow monies to leave his realm for Rome was well recognized by this period. See Leclercq, *Jean de Paris et l'écclesiologie du XIIIè siècle* (Paris, 1942), p. 146. In fact this was the successful tactic Philip employed against Boniface in consequence of the bull *clericos laicos*.

7. *Cf.* John's earlier discussion of the "two swords" argument in his reply to chap. 18, argument 30.

8. A prebend, as used here, was the land or tithe yielding to a cathedral or conventual church a stated income, by way of benefice, for the provision of ecclesiastical services in that church.

9. Aristotle, *Nicomachean Ethics* 8. 14, 1163b13.

10. Plato, *Timaeus*, 68–69.

11. II Cor. 13:10.

12. Rom. 11:29.

13. Job 36:7.

14. This argument is found in Thomas Aquinas, *Summa theologiae* 2–2. 100, *arg.* 3, c. and *ad* 3.

15. Aristotle, *Nicomachean Ethics* 8. 13. 1162b31.

16. *Ibid.*, 8. 14. 1163b13.

17. *Decretum* 54, "Generalis etiam," 1. 210.

18. Godfrey of Trani, *Summa super titulis decretalium,* "De restitutione in integrum" (Venice, 1564), p. 139.

19. *Cf.* James of Viterbo, *De regimine christiano* 1. 2; chap. 11, *arg.* 39, note 56.

20. Alan Gewirth sees in this brief argument and John's reply at least an implicit rejection of the Aristotelian doctrine of natural slavery as based on inferiority of intellect: Alan Gewirth, *Marsilius of Padua, the Defender of Peace*, vol. 1, *Marsilius of Padua and Medieval Political Philosophy* (New York: Columbia University Press, 1951), p. 178. Marsilius of Padua speaks more forcefully against this argument, with the contention that all citizens "are of sound mind and judgment": Marsilius of Padua, *Defensor pacis* 1. 13. 3.

21. Aegidius of Rome, *De ecclesiastica potestate* 1. 5, p. 13.

22. Matt. 19:8.

23. John has already expressed himself on the position of the pope's right to use physical force against heretics (*cf.* chap. 19, *ad* 34). His position is the typically medieval one which accepts coercion against heretics as legitimate, and he develops it at greater length here.

24. *Decretales* 7, "Ab abolendam," 2. 780.

25. *Decretales* 7, "Vergentis," 2. 782.

26. Deut. 4:2.

27. "Acta consilii ephesani," in J. D. Mansi, *Sacrorum conciliorum nova et amplissima collectio*, 31 vols. (Florence, Venice, 1757–98); reprinted and continued by L. Petit and J. B. Martin, 60 vols. (Paris, 1899–1927) 4: 1364; *cf.* Thomas Aquinas, *Summa theologiae* 2–2. 1. 10, *arg.* 2.

28. Cited in Thomas Aquinas, *ibid.*

29. *Decretum* 19, "Anastasius," 1. 64.

30. *Decretales* 6, "Significasti," 2. 49.

31. *Decretum* 35, "Veniam," 1. 1284.

32. *Decretum* 93, "Legimus," 1. 327. John's use of this expression regarding the authority of a general church council will receive greater amplification in the later so-called "conciliar movement," basic traces of which can be seen in John's treatise, this being one example: see chaps. 22, 25, *ad* 4.

CHAPTER 21

1. *Cf.* chap. 11, *arg.* 9; chap. 15, *ad* 9. It is interesting to note that as early as Otto III (980–1002) doubts as to the Donation's lack of authenticity were voiced. Generally speaking, however, it was accepted by thirteenth-century writers as authentic, although some antipapalists like John disputed its validity. For a survey of the donation's influence on medieval literature, particularly that dealing with political theory, see G. Laehr, *Die Konstantinische Schenkung in der abenlandischen Literatur des Mittelalters bis zur Mitte des 14 Jahrhunderts* (Berlin, 1926), and in the review of this work by M. Levison, in *Zeitschrift, kanon Abt.* 16: 447. See Walter Ullmann, *The Growth of Papal*

Government in the Middle Ages, a Study in the Ideological Relation of Clerical to Lay Power, 2d ed. (London: Methuen, 1964), p. 241.

2. See chap. 11, *arg.* 6–10.

3. The problem of guaranteeing the continuity of imperial rule in the de-facto absence of a reigning emperor was easily solved by the papalist advocates of supreme power: the power of the emperor, insofar as it derived from the pope and devolved from him on any individual who reigned as emperor, resided in the pope at any time the imperial throne was vacant. This contention of papal right was contained in the text of Innocent III incorporated into the canonical corpus in 2. 2. 10—a source which made no reference at all to the Donation of Constantine. All canonists and papalist writers were agreed, however, that Innocent's claim in this respect could not have been made without the Donation: see Walter Ullmann, *Medieval Papalism, the Political Theories of the Medieval Canonists* (London: Methuen, 1949), p. 109.

4. Hugh of Florence, as cited in Vincent of Beauvais, *Speculum historiale,* p. 525.

5. *Ibid.*

6. *Ibid.*

7. *Ibid.* See also chap. 14, *ad* 5.

8. John is particularly anxious to exclude France from any political subordination to the empire. Therefore, and he argues this point a little further on, even if the pope were to exercise political authority over the empire—a contention he categorically rejects—papal authority still would not fall directly on France.

9. *Cf.* chap. 11, *arg.* 9; and John's reply, chap. 15, *ad* 9.

10. See chap. 15, *ad* 9.

11. Others in the antipapalist school offered objections to the validity of the Donation of Constantine: see Dante, *De monarchia* 3. 10.

12. John seems slightly more certain here that the empire was divided for Charlemagne than he was in chapter 15, *ad* 9.

13. *Glossa ordinaria authenticorum* 7. 6 (Venice, 1574), p. 34.

14. *Digesta* 27. 7. 12; 1. 343.

15. *Novellae* 6. 1; 3. 36.

16. *Novellae* 6. 3; 3. 40. Dante argues that it would be contrary to the nature of empire that it be diminished, and thus contrary to the office of emperor that anyone occupying that office diminish the empire in the fashion Constantine is alleged to have done: Dante, *De monarchia* 3. 10.

17. *Digesta* 1. 4. 1; 1. 7.

18. *Digesta* 41. 4. 7. 3; 1. 662.

19. *Codex* 4. 8. 4; 1. 67.

20. *Digesta* 4. 8. 4; 1. 67.

21. Dante employs the same argument: Dante, *De monarchia* 3. 10.

22. *Digesta* 1. 18. 20; 1. 45.

23. *Novellae* 8, *prooemium;* 3, 65. The adducing of these four reasons that invalidate the Donation as applied to France can be seen also in *Quaestio in utramque partem*, p. 106.

24. Unedited legend of *vita sancti Sylvestri*, sources for which are found in *MGH, Constitutiones* 2. 536.

25. Jerome, as cited in Vincent of Beauvais, *Speculum historiale*, p. 540.

26. *Ibid.*

27. *Ibid.*

28. *Ibid.*

29. Gregory the Great, "Epistolarum libri quinque, Ep. XXXIX" (*PL* 77. 763).

30. *Cf.* Godfrey of Fontaines, "Pantheon" (*PL* 198. 919).

31. The date of Louis' canonization was 1297, so that John's appeal to this event is very topical.

32. Augustine, "In Joannem tractatus" 6. 25 (*PL* 35. 1457).

33. Vincent of Beauvais, *Speculum historiale*, pp. 958–59.

34. *Ibid.*

35. *Ibid.*

36. I have not found this position as formulated here.

37. For Dante, citing Orosius, Ninus was the first emperor: see chap. 2.

38. Num. 24:24.

39. Peter the Eater, "Historia scholastica" 33 (*PL* 198. 1239).

40. Dan. 7:7.

41. *Glossa ordinaria in Danielem* 7. 4. 1579.

CHAPTER 22

1. John has employed the same form of criticism against his opponents in chaps. 6, 13, 23.

2. This is not John's first mention of a general church council: see chap. 20, *ad* 42. Its function is described here in terms of its judicial capacity in respect of the papacy. In chapter 25, *ad* 4 John speaks of its role as declarative of church doctrine.

3. Vincent of Beauvais, *Speculum historiale*, pp. 1011, 525.

4. *Decretales* 26, "Quia ingredientibus," 2. 538.

5. *Decretum* 21, "In tantum," 2. 72.

6. I have not found this reference to Samson's death.

7. Augustine, *De civitate dei*, 1. 21.

8. Gal. 2:11.

9. John's question may not have been without immediate personal application.

10. Matt. 5:41.

11. *Cf.* chap. 17, *ad* 23. Note the interesting comments by Gewirth concerning the more positivistic and practical provisions urged by Marsilius of Padua for correcting a tyrannical ruler—measures that the people can employ and that are within the positive legal and governmental framework of the state, thus avoiding the only other and extreme alternative of tyrannicide or revolution: Alan Gewirth, *Marsilius of Padua, the Defender of Peace,* vol. 1, *Marsilius of Padua and Medieval Political Philosophy* (New York: Columbia University Press, 1951), pp. 245–46. *Cf.* Thomas Aquinas, *Summa theologiae,* 2–2. 42. 2, *ad* 3; 104. 6, *ad* 3.

12. While John builds his case for papal deposition in terms of this action being a "last resort," there is no doubt that as a last resort he is quite prepared to countenance such an act. *Cf.* Thomas Aquinas, *De regimine principium,* 1. 6; *Summa theologiae* 2–2. 40. 3.

13. Judg. 3:21.

14. Vincent of Beauvais, *Speculum historiale,* pp. 525, 1011.

CHAPTER 23

1. The arguments in this and the following two chapters are all to be found in Aegidius of Rome, *De renuntiatione papae,* and Godfrey of Fontaines, *Quodlibet XIII.*

2. *Decretales* 7, "Inter corporalia," 2. 97.

3. Heb. 7:24.

CHAPTER 24

1. Aegidius of Rome, *De renuntiatione papae.* Earlier John has severely limited the value of arguments based on historical examples: chaps. 14, *ad* 5; 15, *ad* 11.

2. Vincent of Beauvais, *Speculum historiale,* p. 329.

3. *Ibid.*

4. *Glossa ordinaria decreti* 12. 7. 1, p. 621.

5. *Decretum* 21, "Nunc autem," 1. 71.

6. Huguccio, as cited in Aegidius of Rome, *De renuntiatione papae,* p. 60; *cf.* chap. 10.

7. Vincent of Beauvais, *Speculum historiale,* p. 794.

8. *Glossa ordinaria decreti* 12. 7. 1, p. 821.

9. *Glossa ordinaria decreti* 7. 21, p. 97.

10. John's repetition of the role of the people with respect to the holding of papal office reflects his earlier advocacy of democracy in the Church: chaps. 19, *ad* 35, 25, *ad* 3.

11. The cardinals are said here to act on behalf of the whole people as well as the clergy: *cf.* chap. 13.

12. *Decretum,* 19 "Duae sunt," 1. 839.

13. *Decretales* 5, "Quidam cedendi," 2. 113.

14. *Decretum* 21, "Nunc autem," 1. 71.

CHAPTER 25

1. Isa. 26:12.

2. Phil. 2:13.

3. Augustine, *Sermo CLXIX,* 13.

4. *Decretales* 1, "Inter corporalia," 2. 97.

5. See Thomas Aquinas, *Summa theologiae* 1. 98. 1, *arg.* 1.

6. Note the imprecision with which John refers to the function of the people in an ecclesiastical resignation: the bishop can explain himself to the people *or* to his chapter: see chaps. 19, *ad* 35; 24.

7. *Decretales* 1, "Inter corporalia," 2. 97.

8. *Decretum* 7, "Mutaciones," 1. 579.

9. *Decretum* 7, "Pastoralis," 1. 582.

10. *Decretum* 50, "Postquam quemquam," 1. 181.

11. *Decretales* 9, "De renunciatione," 2. 102–15.

12. Matt. 19:6.

13. I Cor. 7:10–11.

14. *Decretum* 21, "Nunc autem," 1. 71.

15. *Ibid.*

16. *Decretum* 7, "Qualiter ordinati," 1. 571; "Quamvis triste," 1. 572.

17. *Glossa ordinaria decreti* 13, 14. 7. 1, pp. 823–24.

18. *Decretales* 9, "Quidam cedendi," 2. 113.

19. *Decretum* 40, "Si papa suae," 1. 146.

20. *Glossa ordinaria decreti* 6. 40, p. 194.

21. Augustine, "In Joannem," 1. 13 (*PL* 35. 1385).

22. Earlier John has said that "the pope in council is greater than the pope

alone" (chap. 20, *ad* 42). Here he says that "Equal or greater power [than the pope's] exists in the college [of cardinals] or in the whole Church." *Cf.* chap. 22.

23. James 5:16.

24. Luke 17:14.

25. Replies to arguments 6 and 8.

Index